Pleasure Dome

Also by Yusef Komunyakaa

Dedications & Other Darkhorses (1977)

Lost in the Bonewheel Factory (1979)

Copacetic (1984)

I Apologize for the Eyes in My Head (1986)

Toys in a Field (1986)

Dien Cai Dau (1988)

February in Sydney (1989)

Magic City (1992)

Neon Vernacular (1993)

Thieves of Paradise (1998)

YUSEF
KOMUNYAKAA

Pleasure Dome

NEW AND
COLLECTED POEMS

Wesleyan University Press

Middletown, Connecticut

Published by Wesleyan University Press, Middletown, CT 06459

CIP data appear at the end of the book.

Acknowledgments

Grateful acknowledgment is made to the following publications, in which the "New Poems" originally appeared: *Amazon.com, The American Poetry Review, The Chicago Review, Crab Orchard Review, Faultline, The Harvard Advocate, Hayden's Ferry Review, The Irish Review,* National Public Radio—*"All Things Considered," Ploughshares, Seneca Review, Shenandoah, 64, Slate.*

Poems in "Early Uncollected" appeared in *Writer's Forum* and *Intro 7/8.*

I am grateful also to the publishers of my previous books: *Dedications & Other Darkhorses,* Rocky Mountain Creative Arts Journal, 1977; *Lost in the Bonewheel Factory,* Lynx House Press, 1979; *Copacetic,* Wesleyan University Press, 1984; *Toys in a Field,* Black River Press, 1986; *I Apologize for the Eyes in My Head,* Wesleyan University Press, 1986; *Dien Cai Dau,* Wesleyan University Press, 1988; *February in Sydney,* Matchbooks, 1989; *Magic City,* Wesleyan University Press, 1992; *Neon Vernacular,* Wesleyan University Press, 1993; *Thieves of Paradise,* Wesleyan University Press, 1998.

For Reetika & Lucky

Contents

New Poems

Early Uncollected

Dedications & Other Darkhorses

Lost in the Bonewheel Factory

Copacetic

Toys in a Field

I Apologize for the Eyes in My Head

Dien Cai Dau

February in Sydney

Magic City

Neon Vernacular

Thieves of Paradise

New Poems

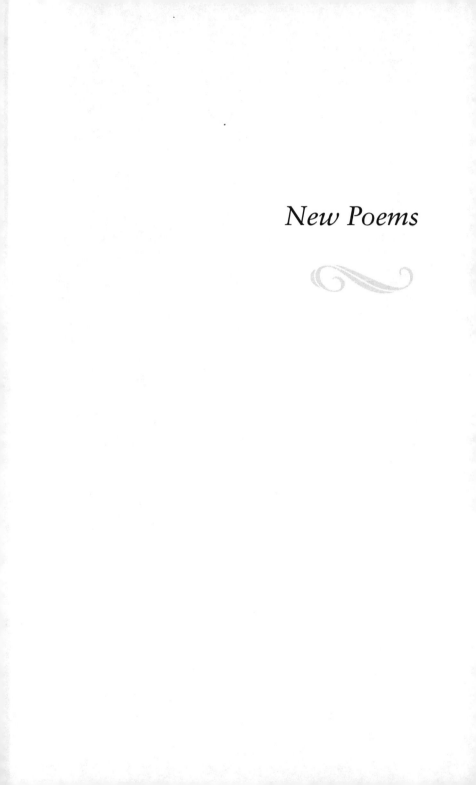

Providence

I walked away with your face
stolen from a crowded room,
& the sting of requited memory
lived beneath my skin. A name
raw on my tongue, in my brain, a glimpse
nestled years later like a red bird
among wet leaves on a dull day.

A face. The tilt of a head. Dark
lipstick. *Aletheia.* The unknown
marked on a shoulder, night
weather in our heads.
I pushed out of this half-stunned
yes, begging light, beyond the caul's
shadow, dangling the lifeline of Oh.

I took seven roads to get here
& almost died three times.
How many near misses before
new days slouched into the left corner
pocket, before the hanging fruit
made me kneel? I crossed
five times in the blood to see

the plots against the future—
descendent of a house that knows
all my strong & weak points.
No bounty of love apples glistened
with sweat, a pear-shaped lute
plucked in the valley of the tuber rose
& Madonna lily. Your name untied

every knot in my body, a honey-eating
animal reflected in shop windows
& twinned against this underworld.

Out of tide-lull & upwash
a perfect hunger slipped in
tooled by an eye, & this morning
makes us the oldest song in any god's throat.

We had gone back walking
on our hands. Opened by a kiss,
by fingertips on the Abyssinian
stem & nape, we bloomed
from underneath stone. Moon-pulled
fish skirted the gangplank,
a dung-scented ark of gopherwood.

Now, you are on my skin, in my mouth
& hair as if you were always
woven in my walk, a rib
unearthed like a necklace of sand dollars
out of black hush. You are a call
& response going back to the first
praise-lament, the old wish

made flesh. The two of us
a third voice, an incantation
sweet-talked & grunted out of The Hawk's
midnight horn. I have you inside
a hard question, & it won't let go,
hooked through the gills & strung up
to the western horizon. We are one,

burning with belief till the thing
inside the cage whimpers
& everything crazes out to a flash
of silver. Begged into the fat juice
of promises, our embrace is a naked
wing lifting us into premonition
worked down to a sigh & plea.

Water

If only I could cleave myself from the water table
below this two-step, from this opaque moan
& tremble that urge each bright shoot up,
this pull of the sea on fish under a pregnant
moon. I sweat to buy water. It breaks
into a dirge polishing stone. The oathtaker
who isn't in hock to salt merchants & trinket kings,
says, Drink more water, Mister Bones.
The taste of azure. To rinse bile from the bony cup
of regret, to trouble rivers till the touch of gold
Columbus & his men killed the Arawak for
floats up to ravenous light, to flush out every tinge
of pity & gall—each of us a compass star
& taproot down to what we are made of.

Jasmine

I sit beside two women, kitty-corner
to the stage, as Elvin's sticks blur
the club into a blue fantasia.
I thought my body had forgotten the Deep
South, how I'd cross the street
if a woman likes these two walked
towards me, as if a cat traversed
my path beneath the evening star.
Which one is wearing jasmine?
If my grandmothers saw me now
they'd say, Boy, the devil never sleeps.
My mind is lost among November
cotton flowers, a soft rain on my face
as Richard Davis plucks the fat notes
of chance on his upright

leaning into the future.
The blonde, the brunette—
which one is scented with jasmine?
I can hear Duke in the right hand
& Basie in the left
as the young piano player
nudges us into the past.
The trumpet's almost kissed
by enough pain. Give him a few more years,
a few more ghosts to embrace—Clifford's
shadow on the edge of the stage.
The sign says, *No Talking.*
Elvin's guardian angel lingers
at the top of the stairs,
counting each drop of sweat
paid in tribute. The blonde
has her eyes closed, & the brunette
is looking at me. Our bodies
sway to each riff, the jasmine
rising from a valley somewhere
in Egypt, a white moon
opening countless false mouths
of laughter. The midnight
gatherers are boys & girls
with the headlights of trucks
aimed at their backs, because
their small hands refuse to wound
the knowing scent hidden in each bloom.

The Whispering Gallery

She's turning away, about to step
out of the concave cuddle of Italian tiles
before walking through the grand
doorway to cross 42nd Street

to glance up at The Glory of Commerce
as she hails a yellow taxicab
when he whispers, I love you, Harriet.
Did he say something to himself,
something he swore he'd never think
again? Or, was she now limestone
like Minerva, a half-revealed secret,
her breasts insinuating the same
domed wisdom? Maybe his mind
was already heading home to Hoboken—
his body facing hers—his unsure feet
rushing to make a connection
with Sinatra's ghost
among a trainload of love cries
from the Rustic Cabin to Caesar's Palace.
Hugged there under the curved grandeur,
she says, I love you, too, Johnny.

Tuesday Night at the Savoy Ballroom

Entangled in one motion
    of hues stolen from innuendo,
    their exulted limbs couple

& uncouple till the bluish
    yellow fuses with three
    other ways of looking at this.

With a touch of blood
    & congealed tempera,
    black & white faces surge

through a nightlife
    sweating perfumed air.
    Their moves caught

by brush strokes
   force us to now feel
   the band on an unseen

stage. Bedazzlement
   & body chemistry . . .
   eyes on each other break

the law. They work
   hard for fun, twirling
   through sighing loops

of fray & splendor,
   watering down pain till naked
   hope glimmers in a shot glass.

Doppelgängers

I wait outside the Beacon Hotel
   for a taxicab to La Guardia,
   & dead ringers from Memnon

slink past. Here's another.
   Wasn't Aurora's son
   killed fighting in Troy

for the Trojans?
   His look-alikes stroll
   through glass towers

& waylay each other's shadows.
   How many southern roads
   brought their grandparents

here? Why so many chalk-lined
    bodies mapping departure
routes? The Daylight Boys

haunt these footsteps tuned
    to rap & butterfly
knives that grow into

Saturday-night specials
    tucked inside jackets
ensigned with *Suns, Bulls* . . .

Ice. Ecstasy. Crack.
    Here's another young,
bad, good-looking one

walking on air solid
    as the Memnon Colossi,
& may not be here at dawn.

Somewhere

I was on the corner
    when she paused
at the crosswalk.

If a cobra's in a coil, it can't
    take back its strike. Her
purse was already in my hands

when the first punch landed.
    She kept saying, "You won't
take nobody else's money no

more." Her voice was like
    Mama's. I couldn't
break free. Women & kids

multiplied before me.
    At least thirty or forty.
Everywhere. Kicking & biting.

I kept saying, "I give
    up." But they wouldn't
stop aiming at my balls.

The sky tumbled. I was a
    star in a late-night movie
where all these swallows—no,

a throng of boys swooped
    like a cloud of birds
& devoured a man

on a lonely beach
    in Mexico, & somewhere
outside Acapulco that damn

squad of sunflowers
    blazed up around me.
What I heard the stupid

paramedics say scared me
    to death, as the bastards
worked on my fucking heart.

Never Land

I don't wish you were one
   of The Jackson Five
   tonight, only you were

still inside yourself
   unchanged by the vampire
   moonlight. So eager to

play The Other,
   did you forget
   Dracula was singled out

because of his dark hair
   & olive skin? After
   you became your cover,

tabloid headlines
   grafted your name
   to a blond boy's.

The personals bled
   through newsprint,
   across your face. Victor

Frankenstein knew we must
   love our inventions. Now,
   maybe skin will start to grow

over the lies & subtract
   everything that under-
   mines nose & cheekbone.

You could tell us if
   loneliness is what
   makes the sparrow sing.

Michael, don't care
     what the makeup
  artist says, you know

your sperm will never
     reproduce that face
  in the oval mirror.

Pepper

If you were alive, Art
     Pepper, I'd collar you
  as you stepped off the

bandstand. Last notes
  of "Softly as a Morning
  Sunrise" fall between us,

a hint of Africa
     still inside your alto.
  Someone wants to blame

your tongue on drugs: "If I
     found out some white broad
  was married to a black guy

I'd rave at her in games
     & call her tramp, slut,
  whore." Did you steal

the Phoenix's ashes
     listening to Bird?
  I'm angry for loving

your horn these years,
   wooed by the monkey
riding you in L.A.

as if changes in "Mambo
   De La Pinta" could be
rounded off to less

than zero. Words
   you tried to take back
left blood on the reed.

South Carolina Morning

Her red dress & hat
   tease the sky's level-
headed blue. Outside

a country depot,
   she could be a harlot
or saint on Sunday

morning. We know
   Hopper could slant
light till it falls

on our faces. She waits
   for a tall blues singer
whose twelve-string is

hours out of hock,
   for a pullman porter
with a pigskin wallet

of steamed rice. "At Mount Zhiju
   is an inscription about black
hair. Oh, well, I don't know

what I'm talking about
   these days." She pops
a prawn into her mouth.

The hot curry tingles
   his tongue. A cube of onion
tastes like something sinful.

"Have you ever heard of Ah
   Coy & Ha Gin?" He shakes
his head, knitting his brows.

"I'm just fooling, being
   awful silly tonight."
He notices the poster of *Monkey*

Creates Havoc in Heaven
   tacked beside the kitchen door
where the scent of ginger & garlic

stream up from hot sesame oil
   like ghosts. "I used to come
here last year. Every Friday.

The place hasn't changed.
   We used to sit right here
in this same booth. Paul

& me." He wishes she'd stop
   talking. Those flowers
beside the cash register

are too damn red to be
   real. "That was before he
started dating a Chinese girl.

I think her family has money."
   The waitress refills their
 glasses. "Are you sure you

want to talk about this?"
   he says. She picks at
 the snow peas with her fork.

"They come here all the time,
   & I bet he'd just die
 if he saw us together."

Once the Dream Begins

I wish the bell saved you.
   "Float like a butterfly
 & sting like a bee."

Too bad you didn't
   learn to disappear
 before a left jab.

Fighting your way out of a clench,
   you counter-punched & bicycled
 but it was already too late—

gray weather had started
   shoving the sun into a corner.
 "He didn't mess up my face."

But he was an iron hammer
   against stone, as you
 bobbed & weaved through hooks.

Now we strain to hear you.
   Once the dream begins
 to erase itself, can the

dissolve be stopped?
     No more card tricks
   for the TV cameras,

Ali. Please come back to us
     sharp-tongued & quick-footed,
   spinning out of the blurred

dance. Whoever said men
     hit harder when women
   are around, is right.

Word for word,
     we beat the love
   out of each other.

Ogoni

Neighbors, please don't
     mind me this morning
   at windows balling my fists

at the sun. Lowdown
     bastards, imbeciles
   & infidels, a tribunal

of jackasses behind
     mirrored sunglasses
   with satchels of loot—wait,

calm down, count to twenty
     & take a few deep breaths.
   You don't want to disgrace

his heroic tongue. Go
     to the kitchen window
   & sit in that easy chair

striped like a zebra,
    & imagine how a herd runs
  with an oscillating rhythm,

like a string bass & drums
    trading riffs. The big cats
  can only see a striped hill

moving beneath a sunset,
    a grid of grass & trees
  in motion, a pattern to fear

& instinct, because they run
    as one, as sky & earth. Look
  at the scrappy robin & bluejay

squabble over earthworms
    underneath the ginkgo,
  as a boy on the edge

of memory raises a Daisy
    air rifle. Look at the robin
  puff out its bright chest

like a bull's eye. Only
    a boy could conjure
  a ricochet in his cocky head

that hits a horseshoe
    looped around an iron peg,
  a little of God's geometry

to get things perfect.
    A single red leaf
  spirals to the ground.

Where did the birds
    go, & why am I
  weeping at this window?

That's not my face
    strung to the hands
  holding the gun, unmasked

by the Shell trademark
    on his gold moneyclip,
  worms throbbing behind

the scab grown over
    his eyes. Those damn
  bastards murdered a good man

when they hanged Ken
    Saro-Wiwa. Why was he
  so cool, did the faces of his

wife & children steady
    his voice? "I predict
  the denouement of the riddle

of the Niger delta
    will soon come." Did
  you feel dead grass quiver

& birds stop singing?
    To cut the acid rage
  & put some sugar back

on the lying tongue,
    I'll say my wife's name
  forever—the only song

I'm willing to beat
    myself up a hill for,
  to die with in my mouth.

Keeper of the Vigil

When the last song
　　was about to leave
　dust in the mouth,

where termite-eaten
　　masks gazed down
　in a broken repose, you

unearthed a language
　　ignited by horror
　& joy. A cassava

seed trembled in a pellet
　　of fossilized goat dung.
　The lifelines on my palms

mapped buried footprints
　　along forgotten paths
　into Lagos. The past

& present balanced till
　　the future formed a
　wishbone: Achebe,

you helped me steal
　　back myself. Although
　sometimes the right hand

wrestles the left, you
　　showed me there's a time
　for plaintive reed flutes

& another for machetes.
　　I couldn't help but see
　the church & guardtower

on the same picturesque
hill. *Umuada* & *chi*
reclaimed my tongue

quick as palm wine
& kola nut, praisesongs
made of scar tissue.

—*for Chinua Achebe*

Nightbird

If she didn't sing the day
here, a votive sky
wouldn't be at the foot
of the trees. We're in
Rome at Teatro Sistina
on Ella's 40th birthday,
& she's in a cutting contest
with all the one-night stands.
"St. Louis Blues" pushes through
flesh till Chick Webb's here
beside her. A shadow
edges away from an eye,
& the clear bell of each note
echoes breath blown across
some mouth-hole of wood
& pumice. So many fingers
on the keys. She knows
not to ride the drums
too close, following the bass
down all the black alleys
of a subterranean heart.
The bird outside my window
mimics her, working songbooks
of Porter & Berlin into confetti

& gracenotes. Some tangled laugh
& cry, human & sparrow,
scat through honey locust
leaves, wounded by thorns.

Tenebrae

"May your spirit sleep in peace
One grain of corn can fill the silo."
—the Samba of Tanzania

You try to beat loneliness
out of a drum,
but cries only spring
from your mouth.
Synapse & memory—
the day quivers like dancers
with bells on their feet,
weaving a path of songs
to bring you back,
to heal our future
with the old voices
we breathe. Sometimes
our hands hang like weights
anchoring us inside
ourselves. You can go
to Africa on a note
transfigured into a tribe
of silhouettes in a field
of reeds, & circling the Cape
of Good Hope you find
yourself in Paris
backing The Hot Five.

You try to beat loneliness
out of a drum.

As you ascend
the crescendo,
please help us touch what remains
most human. Your absence
brings us one step closer
to the whole cloth
& full measure.
We're under the orange trees again, as you work life
back into the double-headed
drumskin with a spasm
of fingertips
till a chant leaps
into the dreamer's mouth.

You try to beat loneliness
out of a drum, always
coming back to opera & baseball.
A constellation of blood-tuned
notes shake against the night
forest bowed to the ground
by snow & ice. Yes,
this kind of solitude
can lift you up
between two thieves.

You can do a drumroll
that rattles slavechains
on the sea floor.
What wrong makes you
loop that silent knot
& step up on the gallows-
chair? What reminds you of the wounded paradise
we stumbled out of?

You try to beat loneliness
out of a drum,
searching for a note
of kindness here at the edge
of this grab-wheel,

with little or no dragline
beyond the flowering trees
where only ghosts live—
no grip to clutch the truth
under a facade of skylarks.

—in memory of Richard Johnson

Double Limbo

A sun dog hurries a lover
home from a desk job
or a factory of noise.
Car horns & solstitial candlepower.
Another long day runs
with a pack of house-broken mutts
around the neighborhood, treeing
cats on fenceposts. The runt
which sprung into Cerberus
slinks beneath the moon's mad
dogma, tamed when bloody feet
touch springy St. Augustine
grass where Ra & Shamash
linger at the timberline.

The winter sun is now Bessie's
"Yellow Dog Blues"
given to you by a lover
who drove off with a friend
years ago. The shadows long,
& kisses too. A celestial claw
bluffs the last sprigs of wolfbane
into hush as "Yellow Submarine"
submerges in the hue of machines
where a good feeling goes before
it's known. But there's a dog-eared

season that never fails to be reborn
as Sirius beside the back door,
hungry for the sound of your VW.

NJ Transit

Penn Station
Images of the homeless
& pigeons on a third rail
roost in my bowed head.

Newark
An apartheid of snow
crowns itinerant ghosts inside
abandoned blue machines.

Elizabeth
"Careless Love": She is
Athena's re-flowering,
a rebirth of awe.

Linden
Couples kiss under
B-movie ads, the motion
nudging them on—on. . . .

Rahway
The Taj Mahal glows
through the out-of-season silk
of her composure.

Metropark
I daydream Ezra Pound
as faces cluster on night's bough—
where did she come from?

Metuchen
Winter flowers droop
to her nods, suspended there
inside pain's headshop.

Edison
Here, gods extinguish
a light whenever a lineman
drops dead on the job.

New Brunswick
The voice of Black Horse
a logbook of old sorrows
lives beside the river.

Jersey Avenue
White ice in the trees
mute cathedral. Her dark skin,
her dark eyes, bright mouth.

Princeton Junction
I glimpse happiness
heading the other direction
sometimes, not quite here.

Trenton
I missed my stop
looking at heartbreak, the sky
almost criminal.

Early Uncollected

Mississippi John Hurt

Now the disorder of your words
makes some lavender sense
a knife-edge of seeing.
Birds meditate on powerlines
over Red Rocks, quills
ravel into a drift of muscle,
& your fingers swear
they'd die if they couldn't
touch a guitar. Some surprise
bursts under your breath
boils of honey.

Langston Hughes

Those days when Jesse B.
Semple was quick to say,
"You can take the boy
outta the country . . ."
Joplin, Lawrence, Lincoln,
all left watermarks: an eye
of habit from turning up hems
& talking at the bottom of blue.
Agate polished itself
as this word weaver
groped for a foothold
in the boneyard,
watching hypnotic bird
voices condense in spoons.
A greenhorn among zoot-suited
swingers who danced with skirts
lost in a glare of horns
as long chains flowed out of empty pockets.

Blue Tonality

No, not Sprung Rhythm.
That guy with Thunder
Smith on Gold Star
who said, "I was born with the blues."
After mile-long cotton rows
& Blind Lemon Jefferson
at The Rainbow,
he'd touch the strings
& know every note in the groin.
Catgut & a diamond needle
cut grooves in race records—
the flatted thirds, twelve
bars of flesh idiom.

De Síntoma Profundo

We inherited more than body language.
Pantomimic ghost flowers & *sones*:
our hands tied through gray weather
refuse to salute treadmill foremen.
Some waltz backwards off bridges,
& others sleepwalk to Solzhenitsyn's
State Department communiqué.
My mind's on Americus,
Georgia. Caught up in paperwork
of murder & audio surveillance,
weapons experts tread air
in oxblood Bostonians.

       —for Nicolas Guillen

Lover

A turning away from flowers.
A cutting out of
stone understands, naked
before the sculptor.

I watch you down Telegraph Avenue
till you sprout into a quivering
song color.

But I hope you fall
from your high horse
& break your damn neck.

Reminiscence

I had brainphotos
of riding you down into music.
I tried to kiss you back then,
but didn't know the sweet punishment
of a tongue inside another voice.
You were a tree breaking with mangoes,
bent toward deeper earth,
& ran out into the world
before me. Songs floated ahead
like comic-strip balloons
where they could breathe hard
& blow dreams apart.

The green light kept going
beyond Blueberry Hill.
Bandages of silence
didn't conceal unsolved crimes,

& I deserted my voice crawling
over cobblestone.
My ribcage a harp
for many fingers.
I've seen overturned deathcarts
with their wheels churning
Guadalajara mornings,
but your face will always be
a private country.

Waiting for a Tree Through a Window

The coffeepot percolates,
a dying man's last breath.
Alone at this onyx window
I've seen Balanced Rock
perched on the brink of midnight.
Hard times wrestle water up hills,
mineshafts worked down to daybreak.
At this window, I've witnessed
knowledge of hyacinth & burdock,
how night snow cascades & out of nowhere
praise flashes like bobwhites
out of dead grass.
I want to tell them, when it comes,
not to question my death,
the moon will have its say.

The Lamp Carrier

He swings his lamp into a hovel,
a circle of vermillion.
Hunger rushes forward.

He steps back, but the raw odor
reaches out & hugs him.
Someone whispers,
"Our lives fallen angels.
Songs stolen from the mouths
of our children, worrybeads
snatched from dead fingers."
Another voice from a year
of darkness says, "Ask Captain Nobones—
the one with hemlock in his lapel,
who always has the flamenco dancer,
Maria, on his arm." The lamp
shimmies up, out of the hole
in the floor of the summer night,
& disappears in eucalyptus scent.

The Life & Times of Billy Boy

His mother would sigh,
"God giveth & He taketh.
My dear child of a dog's luck.
A precious thorn works
deeper into my side."

When Billy Boy was seven
he didn't know the sound of his name,
like talking to an oak.
He'd fall in constant love
with ravens & bluejays,

then urge their perch
on the crowns of scarecrows,
thinking of himself
as a conclusion
of their wings.

A House of Snow

A woman stepped out of no-
where, humpbacked, struggling
with the moon. She asked me if
I was lonely, if I was happy.
Before I could lie, she said,
"In many ways, you remind me
of what's-his-name, who sees poetry
in the leaf. In the ugliest,
smallest thing. He says katydids
influence tongues. His hands are
roots, his song a wolf's lost
in a cloud of migratory birds."

Recital of Water Over Stones

We wait to see you nail
your voice to the floor.
You stand in a doorway
talking clothes off dreams.
The groupie in the front row
wears lavender stockings,
& knows Blue Nun & Panama Red.
She stares at the glass ceiling
of crimson birds,
as if you hide among rafters.
You step up to the podium,
drag on a cigarette, touch
the half-dead microphone,
& jazz leaps into your mouth.
It sounds like you've lived
dog days & slept in a hollowed log,
as you lead us through orange

groves, exposing white bones
& drums buried under dirt.

—for Robert Creeley

The Dog's Theology

He walks ahead
of the man. His
chain drags on the ground,
clanking a song of dark colors
in the acid air. He
knows where he's going;
echoing blood cells
in the man's head,
his imagination a quail
among dirty words.

They Say in Yellow Jacket

The mind's anchored to a stone.
Dandelion wine grows bittersweet
in the musty cellars. The old
beat-up Buick's a buffalo,
drinking cries of coyotes

as it stumbles toward a beginning.
The land eats itself, a half-mile
into the heart. Sage blooms in the heads
of Billy the Kid & Jesse James.
I hope the road hurries to Denver.

Here, even the gully-brown jackrabbit
gets a dirty deal. Buntings lay low
among the rocks where tumbleweed
stakes claim. Any moment the sky
could leap open as the body

settles into itself like a stone
tossed into a lake. You're safe
with knives & Front Range daybreak.
I'm spellbound by the mountains,
a woman dropping her last veil.

When Men Can't Trust Hands with Wood

You can pull off back roads
astonished with honeysuckle
& Virginia rails in marsh grass.
In Oven Fork, they know how to witch
for water deep as stars underground.
Here, rough men know how
to handle iron & die hard
in blue vaults of racial memory.
Under villanelles of pleated dresses
women forget flesh. In Black Mountain
Coleman headlanterns tunnel through
the mole's tombed season.

Birthday Song

The sharecropper's wife
stands in unharvested
stillness. Her womb

turned inside out by God's
grief. She kneels beside
a newly-dug bodyhole,
& her man hands her
the black handkerchief.

Legacy

Suck dove meat from the bones,
tallyho around the electric fence
of this guardhouse.

Pin medals to chests. Our shadows
sleep in the ground, old combat boots
laced on the feet of the dead.

For as long as I can remember
men have sewn their tongues
to the roofs of their mouths.

Eye Witness

I want to forget everything.
I want to pull the venetian blinds
& extinguish the lights. Sometimes
six high-stepping boots
emerge from the sumac thicket
toward this unlit house. Six
black boots kick at my front door
till a vase of periwinkles overturns
& rolls under the bed.
A spray of glass covers

the middle of next year.
A hunting knife arcs the air.
I'm a smashed violin covered with dust,
& rise to drip red leaves down streets.

Unnatural Deaths

Foster child of ragweed,
can you hear grain
silos opening in the night?
Where the sun's a dirt farmer's
good-luck timepiece,
yucca drips white
& the afternoon forecasts
irony. Dust-bowl
people disappear walking
toward rain, in August
thickets of magenta thistle.
When you enter the town
voices of children will stone you
till your clothes are rags.
Mr. Ditch Commissioner
of La Acequia Del Llano,
did you know a gopher hole
can swallow a man?

A Different Story

Teenyboppers crowd No Exit.
Lep Zeppelin & illegal
shadows. I hate words
burning twist lemon menthol 100s.

No, nothing I say can stop them
from splitting themselves open
like those honeydew melons
I saw last summer
driving the midwest.
They clap hands & laugh
like Sam River's sax,
dancing the rose's perfect vernacular
as they push their lives into streets
on the tongues of men.

One-Breath Song

you are the third term
carried to the fourth power of numbers
two steps overlooked inbetween
colors of night-burning sky
a priori light blue of your dress
our faces everything except
against odds of self-discovery
we find our bodies locked
together in a room of breath
threefold at the rotting threshold
divided into ontogenetic questions
a fluke of radio waves in the storm
the song that uses up our lives.

Frontal Lobe Postscript

God's love is busy with the trees.
Arch-mechanic of electrical sky,
blood-red tree of knowledge, ichnology,

witch hazel, mid-May. I think of Bob,
with his "little piece of string & sharp
stone," over at Minnie's Can-Do Club,
as if the go-go dancer in her cage cares
who knows injustice's oblique cape.

Sagittarius Approaching Thirty-Five

Yes, you're still a little eccentric
around the velvet edges of your voice.
Your martini eyes say you wish you could
stop Cherokee Creek behind the unpainted house
you were born in. Boards drop off like slabs
of digital ice. The mortar of the doorsteps
cracks with green flames. You're crouched
in a corner, crying because your face plays
the girl who returns summers to watch the yard
swell with wildflowers. The iron signpost,
an arm holding the nameplate
almost corroded away.

Cubism

Deep-eyed painter through black windows
Across night
                 Mountain rain
Drips blue
Cezanne thinking   Six triangles of sun

Insinuations

Around from Kentucky Fried Chicken
at Liberty Belle, I met someone
who looked like somebody's dream.
We talked about the obsequy
behind John Berryman's eyes,

about how we loved
reading *The Voice* in bed
while sipping Southern Comfort.
She showed me where some bastard
kicked his baby out of her.

We said we didn't know why
we loved walking in the rain
till everything disappeared,
but knew why Eric Dolphy
pried the lids off skulls.

Loneliness

New Mexico peels off
plum skin.
A night-blooming cereus
leans against an adjacent building
like the town's drunk.
Morning swells in my brain
till my fingers retrace a woman
on the air. We all use our hands
for something, against something.
The Orange Pekoe taste of her
stays, even after a brown bottle
wraps my voice in cerecloth.

Again, I find myself
watching the old silversmith
work plains of buffalo
from his head. I return
to my rented room,
put a bullet into the chamber
& snap the trigger four times.
The sun's now on the shoulder
of an Indian woman walking into
distance filled with dirt trees.
I go to the pay phone again
outside El Triumpho Tamales,
& Ray Charles cries from a car radio
speeding past.

Dedications & Other Darkhorses

Returning the Borrowed Road

The hard white land
calls you back across
iron months to Missoula,
overtaken in Colorado's slow mountains
among gray cloud horses.
Lines, muscles, the heart's
great naked timbers, swing
music. You said, *Get away*
from the poem. You're too close.
Now, I let each stone
seek its new mouth.
In Boulder, your first word
homage, a lifetime of birds
gone wild with brightness,
like bundled hayfields.
That day when you entered
the room, we mistook you
for a man who works
a mile down in the ground.

—*for Richard Hugo*

Chair Gallows

Beating wind with a stick
Riding herd on the human spirit.

It's how a man slips his head into a noose
& watches the easy weight of gods pull down

on his legs. I hope this is just another lie,
just another typo in a newspaper headline.

But I know war criminals
live longer than men lost between railroad tracks

& crossroad blues, with twelve strings
two days out of hock.

I've seen in women's eyes
men who swallow themselves in mirrors.

—*memory of Phil Ochs*

Allegorical Seduction

I am piled up so high
in your walk, I
slide down a chute of years.
Touch me, mountains
rise, & the pleasure
tears us into a song.
Quicksilver skies, these birds
over The Four Corners
down through Gallup & Window Rock
catch fire in clouds.
No god tells them
different. No hand
disclaims our closing
distance, as doors open
under the sea.

—*for Linda G.*

Under House Arrest

I won't crawl into
your cathedral of ashes
& gopherwood to buy an hour
digging my grave. Nightsticks
have bashed every drumhead,
but in the Anlo of my bones
I'll fight till the grave-
digger throws dirt in my face.
Listen, big man around town,
hear my silence. Tom-toms
rattle across indigo hills,
& my tongue's heavy as a gold piece.
One grunt of wisdom
remains. But Yemanja
knows how to heal
this song, dancing naked
in my brain. I gaze all night
at the moon through a crack
in the wall, till nothing
rises & sinks back on its haunches
into damp secret earth.

—for Kofi Awoonor

Translating Footsteps

She says Go fuck yourself
when I say Good-bye & good luck
with potted plants
under a granite moon.

A hand reaches from behind
to slash my throat.
Some things refuse translation:
the way I place my hands under
red silk to hear
a thin-skinned drum;
language of growing grass;
tombed treaties forgotten like lamps
left to burn out in a ghost town.

Each pause a clock inside stone . . .
digital, monumental as a grain
of wheat. Translate this
mojo song, footsteps
in a midnight hallway.

My doors enter from the sidestreet,
my windows painted basement black,
my mouth kisses the blues harp,
my heart hides like notes
locked in a cedar chest.

Urban Renewal

The sun slides down behind brick dust,
today's angle of life. Everything

melts, even when backbones
are I-beams braced for impact.

Sequential sledgehammers fall, stone
shaped into dry air

white soundsystem of loose metal
under every footstep. Wrecking crews,

men unable to catch sparrows without breaking
wings into splinters. Blues-horn

mercy. Bloodlines. Nothing
but the white odor of absence.

The big iron ball
swings, keeping time

to pigeons cooing in eaves
as black feathers

float on to blueprint
parking lots.

Magpies

In Magpie Hollow thorns
scratch a cow's hide
in a snowfield. But
what's a nick where iron
hissed a circle around an X?

This inky swarm
tries to peck its way
into a cage through snowy air,
into open wounds.

They dive for the eyes
of the uninfected, spreading
affliction, rise

& circle back
like a blaze of locust,
the sky falling to the ground.

The Tongue Is

xeroxed on brainmatter.
Grid-squares of words spread
like dirty oil over a lake.
The tongue even lies to itself,
gathering wildfire for songs of gibe.
Malcontented clamor, swish of reeds.
Slow, erratic, memory's loose
grain goes deep as water
in the savage green of oleander.
The tongue skips a beat, link of truth . . .
a chain running off a blue bicycle.
It starts like the slow knocking
in a radiator's rusty belly.
I enter my guilty plea
dry as the tongue of a beggar's
unlaced shoe. The tongue labors,
a victrola in the mad mouth-hole
of 3 A.M. sorrow.

Ten Speeds

A deer in the body
bends into a kaleidoscopic hurrah
of bellbirds let go.
Imported ten speeds
zoom past like a shoal
of women struggling
against the aluminum day
to get out of their clothes.
The same wind that seeds
the valley with nasturtium
rattles every door & window,

& tangles in calico.
She jabs thigh-flashes
into the heart, riding away
with the sun on her shoulder.

(E)Motion

The oldest wheel, the setting sun
carries this world
seaward on its back.

Piece by piece. Star
by star, & stone
by stone it goes.

The wheel grunts
& labors under
night's black shoulders.

I cannot stand for another letdown
to crawl into my life
thin as a half-cracked egg.

Hey! wherever you've been
I've been there with my tongue
in your red mouth.

Observatory

Three fat flies copulate
on the lip of my coffee cup.
Too many damn worlds
of possibilities. Everything
isn't to be known
or divided into itself
by enigma's big eyes,
their heads glassy-black
space helmets.

Lost in the
Bonewheel Factory

Looking a Mad Dog Dead in the Eyes

Perception can force you to crawl
On God's great damn stone floor
& scrape your knees to the bone,
in love with the smooth round ass
of death. You've come to admire
that never-miss sniper on the rooftops.
The man who dances in circles
has fistbeaten a dog to the ground.
All the newsreel faces turn away
from the woman hanging naked
by her hair in a picture window,
as a scarecrow drags across a yellow field.
The young man with a nail in his foot
is your son, who believes
he's Christ, telling his father
what he wants to hear,
using a thorn for a toothpick.

Floor Plans

Secret walls swing open when a dream loses focus & lights click
on inside the head. The road here isn't a flatbed of light, isn't a
soft ride, this bridge over our backs, & we won't remember how
we came here even if we stand naked in the Garden of Eden like
fools with bright axes. Our intent philosophic as a black hand
that steers the brain behind a liquid motor, pulled by every voice
we've heard like a rumor of faded coins in our pockets. In the
wild purple night we leave prints of extinct animals in white
sand where footsteps echo a hoodoo drum. All the cruel rooms
are identical behind different-colored doors: a black cellophane
window to the outside, a woman sprawled nude on a red velvet
loveseat, a copy of *Premonitions of the Bread Line* on a white

shag rug, as the shadow of a dagger slides along the walls. Cicadas hum fire in a valley. This is where a god gets his heart cut out, someone underneath the blueprint wrestles with roots. Where a woman crawls on cobblestones & a man chops off three fingers to beg bread. In a country without moon, sun, or solitary star, lies rot in the mouth. Kit Carson caresses Magda Goebbels. Death sits in a skull pale as a dove, & Nero's fiddle whines like a sick animal in the night. A rook dips its beak in gold powder & flies backwards toward the sea's roar, into what the blind man translates in each voice he looks at.

Tour Guide

It eats into the brain
between daylight & coma
like some small animal.
You're propelled onward,
cackling like the old woman
at the end of the night hall,
her face smeared with rouge.
She's every pretty face you've known.
This is where you begin
in yourself, in the room
alone with terror.
This is really when
the mannequin moves
its head in a camera flash.
In the chest a trembling starts
the soul rocking off-balance—
the last grin whittled
from the pain in you
where the shattered millstone
takes shape again.

Sitting in a Rocking Chair,
Going Blind

the exact
                    second
              the lights come on
          like the aurora borealis
i'm sitting at the window of summer
              for two weeks   waiting for
          a pomegranate tree
      to fall outside, scattering
its fruit over the ground
          on the corner
          a black buick
              special
                  runs down a child
              like 40 brass cymbals
              & 40 tambourines
              the air coagulates
          in the background
          a bright bird
      falls from the sky
      its scream is black
   a dog drops dead
pissing on a fire hydrant
      a woman's dance   burns off
      with a green flame
          anemones
      spray the air white
      in a world of dark
i can only remember to put my hands all over you

Pushing in All the Buttons

With armloads of lignum vitae, hands frightened over mouths,
kinfolk gape at the paradox. Rods knock in the braincase as
syndactyl hands plead like a Gypsy guitar. Not a daughter, but
an angel whose legs Zeus tied together.

How many times, in how many head-hung rooms I've taken my
life with a look you can read things into? Leg irons wouldn't let
me go into woods spilt with light. Like a seaward dream, the day
grayed with gulls. When was the last time I wanted to drag death
home, foxy in all her masquerade?

When the last beaten woman awakes no longer with the sun in
her eyes, when no more poets are hanged effigies in the Library
of Congress, when all the bagmen have fallen dead & fingers
leap into pockets of love, a song will bloom under glass weather.

Confessing My Ignorance

Perhaps the cello meant
to be broken the moment
you wanted music.
Perhaps hog-back hills
meant to obscure
some incredible vision.
I can't say what tree
drives us mad in the distance
when we strain to see the heart at work.
Something moves, worms
of ghost meat under the moon—
can we learn from what we
see? Did those crows
teach Van Gogh anything?

I don't know
just what this is
that begs
to heal the earth
under each footstep
or what pulls me back
to innocence like the tongue cut out.
Mistress of Commonsense,
perhaps it's meant for me
to swing open night's door
& catch you naked
at the mirror
trying to shake hands
with yourself.

1938

The granite-colored gulls unlocked
their wings & the door to a wall
swung open. Ghosts ducked through,
disappeared, so much spinal cord
looped & curved into spider darkness
hacked out of a calcium tomb,
where water screams back into you.
Each night became a red machine.

You were cornered in Paris, in the granary
where the raw brain snorted
like a blue horse & a moneysack
of hunger growled. Where shadows
of trees pulled your face down to kiss
stones. Each day murdered the black clock
of your voice, each day, each depravity
a pretty woman might throw her arms around,
knifed your shadow, Vallejo.
Death wore out your boot heels.

S & M

"Tie my hands, hang me up
by my gorgeous feet,
braid a rope-ladder
with my hair—a corsage,"
you say. For a moment I am
a many-headed beast
embracing a pretty woman
in her sleek black get-up.
Spike-heeled habanera.
Take me away from myself
& don't make me look.
The blue mouth
begs for what it needs.
Lover woman of the cat-o'-nine tails
there's a man wounded
in your bedroom
no medicine can cure.
You whimper, you
come like a buttercup
opening darkness.

Stepfather: A Girl's Song

Again heavy rain drives him home
from the cornfield, washing away
footsteps & covering tracks.
For years his eyes undressed me.
There's a river in his stance
sweeping me away.

He comes into my bedroom
around corners of moonlight;
unexpected, he catches me

in his big arms. An ancient music
at the edge of my mouth.
He looks at me slantwise, warns:
"These hands whipped a mule crazy
& killed a man in '63."

My hands are like sparrows, stars
caught in tangled dance of branches.
He raises my clothes.
An undertow drags me down.
His mouth on mine, kissing my mother.

Stepmother: A Boy's Song

Twenty years step between
you two, only five between us.
Unbroken woman who walks nude
out of shambled wheat, my heart
a pocketful of thin mirrors
throwing your names about.
You cross the threshold
& beg me to flex my biceps.
Remember, you can't wash down suburbia
with black coffee & tantalizers,
neighbors goose-stepping jackals
on leashes. See, look at me
tear out handfuls of hair.
Papa's always quoting that brutal
book, trying to get hills to march
home. Your tongue lights
the air. Tonight, I can't help
but hold your breasts till
my mouth fills with honey.
You're dragging the dark
waters in me with hooks,
& I talk from under your clothes.

No Love in This House

Tonight I touch your breasts.
September's fruit.
Nipples, eyes of fire.
I kiss you deep
As a knife could go.

I pull you out of your jeans.
Black panties, red rose,
my fingers find
the center of you
where the blues begin.

I'm in a room of you
where a white horse
shockwaves. It's hard to break
away: flesh, wine, language.
We curve into dance.

When I drive myself into you
you're singing the name
of a man in Rifle Gap
with his cowboy boots propped
on another woman's kitchen table.

High on Sadness

I think about you
till you're naked
at a window waving goodbye.
Till the bones come out,
bright airplane
on an assembly line.

Violin bows, ribs.
I think about you
till a great beetle
beams on six legs
of unreason. I take you
baroque ballerina
into my arms for the last time,
& your metallic feelers
search intellectual air.
It's always out
in the next city
of rooms filled with California
Spiritual Sunshine incense
I go, a sleepwalker
on a cliff.

Sunbather

She lies under July, a blue towel
across her buttocks, her bare back
new metal arched in a dark room.
A sycamore guards her. Three crows
in symmetrical branches
watch their feathers fall,
black leaves. Today is
an 8" × 10" platinum photograph
in an old man's dresser drawer.
The sky's a slow fire,
car lights over night ice.
I close my eyes, concentrate,
& try to remove the blue towel
till the sun goes out.

Apprenticeship

His fingernails are black
& torn from blows,
as if the hammer
declares its own angle of reference.
The young carpenter curses:
"Awww, fuck! Sonovabitch! Dumb shit!"

His girlfriend lowers her white dress,
then moves away.
She reappears nude,
props one foot upon a red chair,
looks him square in the eyes.
Her skin glistens like a woman
who's made love all afternoon.
Twenty-two stories up, he steps out
over the beams like a man with wings.

Light on the Subject

Hello, Mister Jack,
make yourself at home.
Here in Deadwood City
our eyes flash back to
knives on silver whetstones.
Can I get you anything,
perhaps a shot of Four Roses?
In this gray station of wood
our hearts are wet rags
& we turn to ourselves,
holding our own hands
as the scaffolds sway.
I can tell you this much

Brother Justice, our faith's
unshakable, even if we rock stones
asleep in broken arms.
Because we have a thing
about law & order,
we've all seen moonlight on lakes
& crows whittled from a block
of air. In this animal-night, no
siree, we won't disappoint you
when we rise out of hawkweed.

Punchdrunk

So what if he walks into red
North Carolina traffic at night
like Jarrell, dreaming hollyhock,
blowing some horn of bone?

Hellbent for green dark
because a man's mind runs
away from him like a wild horse.
The second thought of a wood thrush,

wings waxed to August sky. Deep relic
truths & strange tales. Once he
went ringing doorbells, singing
Sticks & stones may break my bones, but....

If he knows nothing else, he knows
how to take a solid, left, black jab,
how to force a big man to kiss the canvas,
a life stronger than fossil & boxwood.

Vigilante

Each hired hand places
a dusty boot in a stirrup,
swings himself into a sweat-burnt
saddle, hoping to handle
a noose. The boss's moneysack
& Willie D. Jones gone.
Far as the eye can see
a sparrow, conifers jut toward
enamel sky. Snagged cloth
leads a trail into hackberry.
Near the northridge
he crossed the river into
another country of nights.
A human form scuffles knee-deep
in this year's first snow,
bobbing on the sights of five guns.

Nothing to Do with Janice Drake

Mister Humbug
returns. She runs
to him, wailing his name
as if her clothes were on fire.

Then she sweeps
this killer's tracks
clean, removing fingerprints
from the murder weapon.

He looks at her
& says, "Let that dress fall, Sweetie.
Don't tell me

dogwoods grow crooked
because of Jesus."

He grins
like a new case-knife.
Then stands at the bedroom
window, & says:

"Don't you know
one of these days
you gonna make me
blow your brains out?"

Reconstructing a Crime

The back door opened
quiet as a coffin lid.
From the yard a Douglas fir
stared over his shoulder
like some god.
He was shoeless,
a man tiptoeing upon a dream.
From the right angle, the way
the moon now falls through damask curtains,
if anything, you'd only seen
the gun.

Outside their bedroom door
he could hear blossoms
of flesh. He slammed it open
& then huge white spaces
fell.

Come over here & lie down
within these chalked contours.

Okay. From this position,
the point of entry
was a gate . . .
the two lovers,
the way their legs were tangled,
he was still inside her.

Two

The dumb aura
deserts its guts
inside the queen
bee. The drone's genitals
tear out like a blind eye
extricated in each honeyegg.

Sexual cadenza
of the praying mantis—
after her acrimonious mate
has been forced to eat
the song of his presence
his head is gnawed off
like a half-green
rosebud in the dirt.

Beg Song

*. . where geometry borders on dream, and where the
duende wears a muse's mask for the eternal punishment
of the great king.*
—Federico Garcia Lorca

Foolhearted mindreader,
help us see how
the heart begs,
how fangs of opprobrium
possess our eyes. Truth
serum: how the index finger works
up into love, how the greased hand
slides up the wombholler of madness
& rebirth, whispering:
Look, back of the eyes. Each
gazes into its fish heart, final mirror
of beauty & monkeyshine.
Run your tongue along
fear in the frontal lobe.
Introduce us to that crazy man
with his face buried
in your hands.
In the slack bed, meat
falls through the door
of itself. Soul of a lamp.
Slipshod genius, show us
the cutworm's silly heart,
how the telescopic love-eye
probes back to its genesis.

Death Threat Note

Dear Poetry Editor,
why did it have to
come to this?
Walk out any door
& you will never know.
Turn any doorknob
& open a butcher shop.
The chair rocks by itself.
A cat paces the windowsill;
the moon's followed you home.
Another set of footprints
surfaces in new snow.
At any moment
a steel door slams
& locks a man in an icehouse.
I see Weldon Kees' car
parked on the Golden Gate Bridge.
I've fallen in love
with a woman's hands
on deathrow. Listen, a knife
can heal your mouth.
It's no good to fall
pointing to the North Star,
moaning foxfire.
The meat wagon
runs off the road.
I don't give warnings.

Child Stealer

You grin like a grape
peels open. One more step

& you will find yourself
lost in a room—
ten colors from floor
to ceiling in the old house
near the boxwood grove.

Let me kiss a tattoo
on your forehead.
You will come to love
this place where sunsets
hang red lanterns
in the windows.

For them to take you now,
will take nothing
short of death.
They say something's wrong
with me upstairs,
& their eyes stare me down.
Torches in trees creep forward.

A Poet Whose Photo Never Grows Old

Snow is a white horse
around the bends of oaks
again. Someone you loved
now rocks herself
asleep in the ground.

The young coed curled
against you like a rainbow,
blood of a new season
connected to a distant land.

Your eyes were once lethal
in a way you've seen nightbirds

erase shadows & burn
a slow flame of songs,
the way you've seen a goddess
stooped over an old machine
whining like a violin—
what you call "these small miracles,"
the way you've seen roses released
from manure in a field.

Poetics

Beauty, I've seen you
pressed hard against the windowpane.
But the ugliness was unsolved
in the heart & mouth.
I've seen the quick-draw artist
crouch among the chrysanthemums.
Do I need to say more?

Everything isn't ha-ha
in this valley. The striptease
on stage at the Blue Movie
is your sweet little Sara Lee.
An argument of eyes
cut through the metaphor,
& I hear someone crying
among crystal trees & confetti.

The sack of bones in the magnolia,
what's more true than that?
Before you can see
her long pretty legs,
look into her unlit eyes.
A song of B-flat breath
staggers on death row. Real

men, voices that limp
behind the one-way glass wall.
I've seen the legless beggar
chopped down to his four wheels.

Imagination

There's a deer no gun
can bring down like a big
woman in the grass sinks
to her knees to pray
in a white slouch.

He stands at the sunlit edge
of a snowy woods. Can you make him out?
An owl from its hiding place
spies on the buck.
Quails settle like a quiet

disturbance. The deer
stands more perfect
than man, like a slab
of half-gray granite
strong as midnight.

Precious as lust.
Eyes sharp & wild.
A wolf's scent makes him stagger
As a hawk sails, powered by a hint
of day. One morning this deer will fall

when nothing or no one can nudge this man
awake. Where eyes cannot meet,
silence is a song, old bones
stashed in a decayed nest
in the ground.

Ghost Chant, et alii

Daydream the old Indian medicine man
who boards the Greyhound
at midnight outside Jackson Hole
& sits next to you,
the fat belly of life,
a lilacbush in May,
the smoke that curls
back up to eat itself.
Daydream a mongrel dog
who yelps at the footsteps of your sister.
The coyote-goddess' lonely hill
to climb with the moon,
a stone vase
with a copperhead inside.
Daydream a mountain lion
riding air—to dismiss
the half song
of this machine's forgetfulness.
A white ceramic Ferris wheel
surrendering sacks of grain,
the eccentric black book
that gnaws off your hands.
Daydream the viper & Easter lily.
A fifth of Ronrico
on the poet's night table,
morning's empty bottle,
a grunt-song that spins
itself from flesh
at the top of a spiral staircase,
the talking drum
the center of water.
Daydream a mermaid
peering into the four windows
of a lighthouse, the fandango
like a rooster struggles out of golden grass

with its head cut off.
Faust's old greed & sick hair,
a gas leak
with twenty padlocks on your one door.
Daydream lies rot in the mouth,
a black Mercedes-Benz
& brass knuckles,
an old man who has seen too much
in a dark alley, the killer's face
in seven mirrors on each wall,
hemlock in a silver chalice,
the shadow of a grave
beneath your slow feet.

Passions

Coitus
Ah, pink tip of sixth sense,
oyster fat of lovepearl,
dew-seed & singing leaf-tongue,
lizard's head of pure thought.

Body Painting
To step into the golden lute
& paint one's soul
on the body. Bird
goddess & slow snake
in the flowered tree. Circle,
lineage, womb, mouth, leaf-footed
godanimal on a man's chest
who leaps into the moon
on a woman's belly.

Blue-green Iridescent Flies
Meat, excrement, a source
of life attracts this
message & definition
of the ultimate us.
They fly off
with the weight of the world.

Peepshow
A new moon rises
on an elevator over the mountain.

String Bass
The moon's at the window,
as she rocks in the arms
of this lonely player
like a tall Yoruba woman.

Pinball Machines
Encased in glass, a woman
opens her eyes. The room floods
with a century of bells.
Magnetic balls & sound of metal
seem enough to build a locomotive
moving through the room's wooden bones.

Butterflies
Incandescent anthologies
semi-zoological alphabets of fire,
these short lives transmigrate, topaz
memories cling to air, release wordflesh
from the cocoon of silk fear.

Psilocybe
One hundred purple rooms
in a mirror of black water.
I must enter each,
interrogated by a different demon.
In the distance I can hear

the sea coming. A woman at Laguna Beach.
Her eyes now seashells.
Her arms two far-off sails.
Like a tree drags the ground on a windy day
with yellow & red fruit too soft to eat,
she comes toward me. Stars cluster
her laughter like a nest of moth eyes—
her focus on the world.
The closer she comes, the deeper
I work myself away into music
that I hope can save us both.
A man steps from a junkyard of chrome
fenders & hubcaps,
pulling off masks.
At least a hundred scattered about.
The last one: I'm him.

The Dog Act

I'm the warm-up act.
I punch myself in the face
across the makeshift stage.
Fall through imaginary trapdoors.
Like the devil, I turn cartwheels
& set my hair afire.
Contradiction, the old barker
drunk again on these lights
& camaraderie. The white poodles,
Leo, Camellia, St. John, & Anna,
leap through fiery hoops
to shake my hand.
I make a face
that wants to die
inside me.
"Step right up ladies & gentlemen,

see the Greatest Show on Earth,
two-headed lions, seraphim,
unicorns, satyrs, a woman
who saws herself in half."
I can buckdance till I am
in love with the trapeze artist.
Can I have your attention now?
I'm crawling across the stagefloor
like a dog with four broken legs.
You're supposed to jump up
& down now, laugh & applaud.

For You, Sweetheart, I'll Sell Plutonium Reactors

For you, sweetheart, I'll ride back down
into black smoke early Sunday morning
cutting fog, grab the moneysack
of gold teeth. Diamond mines
soil creep groan ancient cities, archaeological
diggings, & yellow bulldozers turn around all night
in blood-lit villages. Inhabitants here once gathered seashells
that glimmered like pearls. When the smoke clears, you'll see
an erected throne like a mountain to scale,
institutions built with bones, guns hidden in walls
that swing open like big-mouthed B-52s.
Your face in the mirror is my face. You tapdance
on tabletops for me, while corporate bosses
arm wrestle in back rooms for your essential downfall.
I entice homosexuals into my basement butcher shop.
I put my hands around another sharecropper's throat
for that mink coat you want from Saks Fifth,
short-change another beggarwoman,
steal another hit song from Sleepy
John Estes, salt another gold mine in Cripple Creek,
drive another motorcycle up a circular ice wall,

face another public gunslinger like a bad chest wound,
just to slide hands under black silk.
Like the Ancient Mariner steering a skeleton ship
against the moon, I'm their hired gunman
if the price is right, take a contract on myself.
They'll name mountains & rivers in my honor.
I'm a drawbridge over manholes for you, sweetheart.
I'm paid two hundred grand
to pick up a red telephone anytime & call up God.
I'm making tobacco pouches out of the breasts of Indian maidens
so we can stand in a valley & watch grass grow.

Feet Nailed to the Floor

The Gypsy gazes into her crystal ball
to see a rooster drop in the dust.
One note of samba still burns
in the skull. The white-haired orator
has fallen asleep in his fireside chair,
& it's now out of my hands.
Even your dear mama has taken the gold
crucifix from around her neck
& dropped it into a beggar's tincup.
The seal is affixed. What can I say?
That informer, I bet his hands
are now on your sister's legs.
I want to wash mine. Seven times
today the guards have chased children
who shout your name. You are a saint
to them, but blood isn't yet dripping
in the courtyard from mango leaves.
The hole has been dug & a blindfold
cut from a lover's nightgown.

The Nazi Doll

It sits lopsided
in a cage. Membrane.

Vertebra. This precious, white
ceramic doll's brain

twisted out of a knob of tungsten.
It bleeds a crooked smile

& arsenic sizzles in the air.
Its eyes an old lie.

Its bogus tongue, Le Diable.
Its lampshade of memory.

Guilt yahoos, benedictions
in its Cro-Magnon skull

blossom, a flurry of fireflies,
vowels of rattlesnake beads.

Its heart hums the song of dust
like a sweet beehive.

Breaking Camp

Crops fall apart
in our hands, the whole year
stripped down to a penny's
seed grain, huddled under
last night's dogstar.

Places like Portales & Amarillo,
the only road out of town coughs
blood & dust. Tied to the ground
with songs, we sit along roadsides
like grass waiting for blades.

We clutch beads & pray our children grow
blind, stitching closed black pockets
while the stone-gatherers close in.
Property lines & night-blooming cereus
rush up to us, corrugated roofs

remembering the sky in rearview mirrors.
We leave voices buried under a sycamore,
ashes in a vase feeding its roots.
Following crops & shooting stars,
birds whirl south before a rainstorm

scrubs the stone floor
of the Panhandle. Each day is now
a yellow tractor rusting under a tin shed
where we feel our clothes grow thinner.

Corrigenda

I take it back.
The crow doesn't have red wings.
They're pages of dust.
The woman in the dark room
takes the barrel of a .357 magnum
out of her mouth, reclines
on your bed, a Helena Rubinstein smile.
I'm sorry, you won't know your father
by his darksome old clothes.
He won't be standing by that tree.

I haven't salted the tail
of the sparrow.
Erase its song from this page.
I haven't seen the moon
fall open at the golden edge of our sleep.
I haven't been there
like the tumor in each of us.
There's no death that can
hold us together like twin brothers
coming home to bury their mother.
I never said there's a book inside
every tree. I never said I know how
the legless beggar feels when
the memory of his toes itch.
If I did, drunkenness
was then my god & naked dancer.
I take it back.
I'm not a suicidal mooncalf;
you don't have to take my shoelaces.
If you must quote me, remember
I said that love heals from inside.

Copacetic

False Leads

Hey! Mister Bloodhound Boss,
I hear you're looking for Slick Sam
the Freight Train Hopper.
They tell me he's a crack shot.
He can shoot a cigarette out of a man's mouth
thirty paces of an owl's call.
This morning I glimpsed red
against that treeline.
Aïe, aïe, mo gagnin toi.
Wise not to let night catch you out there.
You can get so close to a man
you can taste his breath.
They say Slick Sam's a mind reader:
he knows what you gonna do
before you think it.
He can lead you into quicksand
under a veil of swamp gas.
Now you know me, Uncle T,
I wouldn't tell you no lie.
Slick Sam knows these piney woods
& he's at home here in cottonmouth country.
Mister, your life could be worth
less than a hole in a plug nickel.
I bet old Slick Sam knows
about bloodhounds & black pepper,
how to put a bobcat into a crocus sack.

Soliloquy: Man Talking to a Mirror

Working night shift
    panhandling Larimer Square
  ain't been easy.

A pair of black brogans
can make a man
limp badly.
　　Lawd, this flophouse
　　has a hangover—
　　you just can't
love hard knowledge
　this way, Buddy Boy.
　　Big shouldered,
　　　you're still a born pushover,
　　a tree climber
　　in the devil's skull.
You hide behind panes
of unwashed light,
　grazing with stubborn goats.
　　Mister Big Shot,
　　　once you dredged down
　　years towards China
but didn't find
a pot of gold—
　chopped down a forest of doors
& told deadly machines
where to go.
　　Now you're counting taverns,
　　dumbfounded
by a hunk of oily keys
　to foul weather.
　Tangled in the bell ropes
　　of each new day,
scribbling on the bottom line
　　of someone else's dream,
　　loitering
　　in public courtyards
telling statues where to fall.

The Way the Cards Fall

Why did you stay away
so long? I've buried another
husband, since I last saw you
holding to the horizon.
I hear where you now live
it snows year-round.
The pear & apple trees
have even missed you—
dead branches scattered
about like war. Come closer,
my eyes have grown night-dim.
Across the field white boxes
of honeybees silent as dirt,
silent as your missent
postcards. Evening
sunlight's faded my hair,
the old stable's slouched
to the ground. I dug a hole
for that calico, Cyclops,
two years ago. Now
milkweed & blackberries
are keepers of the cornfield.
That's how the cards fall;
& Anna, that beautiful girl
you once loved enough
to die over & over again for,
now lives in New Orleans
on both sides
of Bourbon Street.

Reflections

In the day's mirror
you see a tall black man.
Fingers of gold cattail
tremble, then you witness
the rope dangling from
a limb of white oak.
It's come to this.
You yell his direction,
the wind taking
your voice away.
You holler his mama's name
& he glances up at the red sky.
You can almost
touch what he's thinking,
reaching for his hand
across the river.
The noose pendulous
over his head,
you can feel him
grow inside you,
straining to hoist himself,
climbing a ladder
of air, your feet
in his shoes.

Annabelle

My head hangs.

It's all to do with
a woman back in Alabama.
All to do with Annabelle

hugging every road sign
between here & Austin, Texas.
All to do with rope & blood.

He's all to do with America.
All to do with all the No-Dick
Joneses. Mornings shattered.
Crickets mourn—
sign out of genetic code.

All to do with shadows
kneeling in the woods.
All to do with inherited iron maidens.
Beg for death in the womb.
Beg for it inside skulls—flower,
dust, lilac perfume, cold fire.

Gonna get lowdown tonight.

Faith Healer

Come singing in your chains,
Sweet Daughter. Dance, yes.
All the light-fingered artisans
of sacrilege, of wishful thinking
who failed, all the goat-footed heretics
crying for a High John the Conqueror
root, now here you are,
dear child, naked facing God.

A laying on of hands. Yes,
walk out of the grave whole.
Blood on the thorns. *Vox*
& *ossa*. You're here, girl,
to obey His design in the flesh.

I plant a kiss where it hurts.
Trees walk forth. Throw away
your sticks & lean on Jesus.

Touch my hand, touch my hand!

More Girl Than Boy

You'll always be my friend.
Is that clear, Robert Lee?
We go beyond the weighing
of each other's words,
hand on a shoulder,
go beyond the color of hair.
Playing Down the Man on the Field
we embraced each other before
I discovered girls.
You taught me a heavy love
for jazz, how words can hurt
more than a quick jab.
Something there's no word for
saved us from the streets.

Night's pale horse
rode you past common sense,
but you made it home from Chicago.
So many dreams dead.
All the man-sweet gigs
meant absolutely nothing.
Welcome back to earth, Robert.
You always could make that piano
talk like somebody's mama.

April Fools' Day

They had me laid out in a white
satin casket. What the hell
went wrong, I wanted to ask.
Whose midnight-blue sedan
mowed me down, what unnameable fever
bloomed amber & colchicum
in my brain, which doctor's scalpel
slipped? Did it happen
on a rainy Saturday, blue
Monday, Vallejo's Thursday?
I think I was on a balcony
overlooking the whole thing.
My soul sat in a black chair
near the door, sullen
& no-mouthed. I was fifteen
in a star-riddled box,
in heaven up to my eyelids.
My skin shone like damp light,
my face was the gray of something
gone. They were all there.
My mother behind an opaque veil,
so young. My brothers huddled like stones,
my sister rocked her Shirley Temple
doll to sleep. Three fat ushers fanned
my grandmamas, used smelling salts.
All my best friends—Cowlick,
Sneaky Pete, Happy Jack, Pie Joe,
& Comedown Jones.
I could smell lavender,
a tinge of dust. Their mouths,
palms of their hands
stained with mulberries.
Daddy posed in his navy-blue suit
as doubting Thomas: some twisted
soft need in his eyes, wondering if

I was just another loss
he divided his days into.

Untitled Blues

after a photography by Yevgeni Yevtushenko

I catch myself trying
to look into the eyes
of the photo, at a black boy
behind a laughing white mask
he's painted on. I
could've been that boy
years ago.
Sure, I could say
everything's copacetic,
listen to a Buddy Bolden cornet
cry from one of those coffin-
shaped houses called
shotgun. We could
meet in Storyville,
famous for quadroons,
with drunks discussing God
around a honky-tonk piano.
We could pretend we can't
see the kitchen help
under a cloud of steam.
Other lurid snow jobs:
night & day, the city
clothed in her see-through
French lace, as pigeons
coo like a beggar chorus
among makeshift studios
on wheels—Vieux Carré
belles having portraits painted

twenty years younger.
We could hand jive
down on Bourbon & Conti
where tap dancers hold
to their last steps,
mammy dolls frozen
in glass cages. The boy
locked inside your camera,
perhaps he's lucky—
he knows how to steal
laughs in a place
where your skin
is your passport.

Jumping Bad Blues

I've played cool,
hung out with the hardest
bargains, but never copped a plea.
I've shot dice heads-up
with Poppa Stoppa
& helped him nail
his phenomenal luck
to the felt floor with snake eyes.
I've fondled my life in back rooms,
called Jim Crow out of his mansion
in Waycross, Georgia, & taught
him a lesson he'll never forget.

Initials on Aspens

The scar tissue says
t. c. from dallas
loves gertrude logan,
etc. Flesh & metaphor.
Sizzling iron, initials,
whole families branded
as private property.
I am taken back
to where torture chambers
crank up at midnight
like gothic gristmills
in the big house
& black tarantulas
of blood cling to faces
where industrial
revolution repeatedly
groans in the brain.

Family Tree

I know better
than a whip
across my back,
eyes swearing
all the pain. Her father
cut down so young
in this stone garden.
She knows how easy death
takes root in a love song.
That long chain
in the red dust.
Geechee

bloodholler—
my mother
married at 15,
with my ear pressed
against the drum.
When my father speaks
of childhood, sunlight
strikes a plowshare.
Across the cotton field
Muddy Waters' bone-song
rings true when my father speaks
of Depression winters
& a wheel within a wheel.
My great-grandmama's name
always turns up
like a twenty-dollar
gold piece.
Born a slave,
how old her hands were.
When my father speaks
of hanging trees
I know
all the old prophets
tied down in the electric chair.
My grandmamas—
Sunday night
Genesis to Revelations
testimonial hard line
neo-auction block
women. Kerosene
lamps & cherry-red
potbellied wood stoves
& chopping cotton
sunup to sundown
mule-plowing black-metal
blues women grow closer
each year like bent oaks
to the ground. Both still
look you in the eyes

& say, "You gotta eat
a pound of dirt
'fore you can get
to heaven."
Uncle Jesse
would show up
after a rainstorm
some tin-roof night
after two years
working turpentine camps,
pine scent in his clothes—
shove a wad of greenbacks
into Grandmama's apron pocket.
A Prince Albert
cigarette between two fingers,
Old Crow on his breath,
that .38 Smith & Wesson
under his overalls jumper,
& the click-click of dice
& bright shuffle of cards.
Just a few things he learned at 17
in World War I.
Family tree,
taproot,
genealogy of blues.
We've seen shadows
like workhorses
limp across ghost fields
& heard the rifle crack.
Blackbirds
blood flowered
in the heart
of the southern sun.
Brass tambourines,
octave of pain
clear as blood on a silent mirror.
Someone close to us
dragged away in dawnlight
here in these iron years.

Instructions for Building Straw Huts

First you must have
unbelievable faith in water,
in women dancing like hands playing harps
for straw to grow stalks of fire.
You must understand the year
that begins with your hands tied
behind your back,
worship of dark totems
weighed down with night birds that shift their weight
& leave holes in the sky. You must know
what's behind the shadow of a treadmill—
its window the moon's reflection
& silent season reaching
into red sunlight hills.
You must know the hard science
of building walls that sway with summer storms.
Locking arms to a frame of air, frame of oak
rooted to ancient ground
where the door's constructed last,
just wide enough for two lovers
to enter on hands & knees.
You must dance
the weaverbird's song
for mending water & light
with straw, earth, mind, bright loom of grain
untortured by bushels of thorns.

An Exchange Student Awaits
the Arrival of an African Princess

Waiting behind the cyclone fence
Of the International Airport

Where live histories memories
Dreams disconnect change
                    Categorically

His big clumsy hands
Allegorical
Trembling like two
Black butterflies
                To touch her

Already
He feels soft weight
Coming down the ramp
From Air Afrique
Sky drapes over her
                    African print

Slow-motion drum dance
Within her walk
Shadows of birds
Float up & down
                The Mono

He pities what he knows
Tears away blood knowledge
Flesh voice & her old songs
Left here to dry rot
Where Nazi swastikas
Adorn walls of public
                    Places

Back Then

I've eaten handfuls of fire
back to the bright sea

of my first breath
riding the hipbone of memory
& saw a wheel of birds
a bridge into the morning
but that was when gold
didn't burn out a man's eyes
before auction blocks
groaned in courtyards
& nearly got the best of me
that was when the spine
of every ebony tree wasn't
a pale woman's easy chair
black earth-mother of us all
crack in the bones & sombre
eyes embedded like beetles
in stoic heartwood
seldom have I needed
to shake a hornet's nest
from the beastplate
fire over the ground
pain tears me to pieces
at the pottery wheel
of each dawn
an antelope leaps
in the heartbeat
of the talking drum

Blasphemy"

You named those lies clustered
in each rib cage. Attached
to some circular truth, you
glimpsed soldiers of fortune
sweeping their footprints
with branches of mistletoe.

You showed them the corpse garden
couldn't keep blooming,
not forever—black bags
of songs split open at sunrise.
You coped down the earthworm's
calligraphy, broke illusion's hymen,
uncovered the scars smiling
under Dutch silk, translated
the hyena's soliloquy.
You carbon-dated the skull
paperweight on the commissioner's desk
& filled in with charcoal
those mental lapses—
when all the gone ones
resurfaced as dancing rags
in the wind, you named
the beast upon the gallows tree,
its sag-belly dragging
the ground. You appraised
the medieval rot taking hold
of dirt floors, crawling up
the cathedral's high rafters.
Madness, you brought it home.

*Harold Rubin was tried for blasphemy on the basis
of his artwork and exiled from South Africa.*

Lost Wax

I can't help but think
of bodies spoon-fashion
in the belly of a ship.

Gods pour us into the molds
they dream; Legba mends
hope, the breath-cup, footsteps

in plaster of Paris. A bird
so perfect, the wind
steals it from my hand.

Inscription on a vase—
I am whatever it holds,
songs that fit into my mouth.

I am without mercy
because I am what
night poured her lament into,

here on the edge of Kilimanjaro.
All the raw work gone
into each carved ghost

of an antelope, loved
no less than the gods
who spring from our loins.

Woman-mold, man-mold:
whatever shape we think
will save us, what's left

in us preserved by joy.
We won't trade our gods
for money. The hot wax

bubbles up like tar,
& the dream's scaled down
to a gazelle, a figure

with *Benin* printed
on the forehead.
How about a lamp to see by?

Two hands folded together
as a drinking cup,
something that simple.

Safe Subjects

How can love heal
the mouth shut this way?
Say something worth breath.
Let it surface, recapitulate
how fat leeches press down
gently on a sex goddess's eyelids.
Let truth have its way with us
like a fishhook holds
to life, holds dearly to nothing
worth saying—pull it out,
bringing with it hard facts,
knowledge that the fine underbone
of hope is also attached
to inner self, underneath it all.
Undress. No, don't be afraid
even to get Satan mixed up in this
acknowledgement of thorns:
meaning there's madness
in the sperm, in the egg,
fear breathing in its blood sac,
true accounts not so easily
written off the sad book.

Say something about pomegranates.
Say something about real love.
Yes, true love—more than
parted lips, than parted legs
in sorrow's darkroom of potash
& blues. Let the brain stumble
from its hiding place, from its cell block,
to the edge of oblivion
to come to itself, sharp-tongued
as a boar's grin in summer moss
where a vision rides the back
of God, at this masquerade.

Redemptive as a straight razor
against a jugular vein—
unacknowledged & unforgiven.
It's truth we're after here,
hurting for, out in the streets
where my brothers kill each other,
each other's daughters & guardian angels
in the opera of dead on arrival.

Say something that resuscitates
us, behind the masks,
as we stumble off into neon nights
to loveless beds & a second skin
of loneliness. Something political as dust
& earthworms at work in the temple
of greed & mildew, where bowed lamps
cast down shadows like blueprints of graves.
Say something for us who can't believe
in the creed of nightshade.
Yes, say something to us dreamers
who decode the message of dirt
between ancient floorboards
as black widow spiders
lay translucent eggs
in the skull of a dead mole
under a dogwood in full bloom.

Black String of Days

Tonight I feel the stars are out
to use me for target practice.
I don't know why
they zero in like old
business, each a moment of blood
unraveling forgotten names.

This world of dog-eat-dog
& anything goes.
On the black string of days
there's an unlucky number
undeniably ours.
As the Milky Way
spreads out its map
of wounds, I feel
like a snail on a salt lick.
What can I say? Morning's crow
poses on a few sticks, a cross
dressed in Daddy's work shirt—
how its yellow eyes shine.
It knows I believe
in small things.
I dig my fingers into wet dirt
where each parachute seed pod
matters. Some insect
a fleck of fool's gold.
I touch it,
a man asking for help
as only he knows how.

Eleemosynary

Friend, Ego's a bastard.
I owe this nasty scar
to a drunk merchant marine
one night outside Cato's.
But this is nothing.
Now you take Lothario,
that lotus-eater, once
I was the butt of his gambado.
Let me say this—this
isn't a beauty mark,

mister. These two sad coins
in my cup tonight, copper
for a dead man's stare.
Oh, boy, how their eyes work
into you. Shucks, man,
I know I'm nothing to look at
but I tell you this—broken
as I am, you should've seen me
back in '38. Friend, you want to
talk about death, I have a song
for you. Before the devil's deal
with the Lord, they called me
Cut & Sugar Man. Because
I never fell for their act,
those good ladies of charity,
I don't even owe a smile.
Yeah, I've fought with dogs
for bread in moonlit alleys.
But, I tell you, friend,
bring the whores & pimps
to my rescue any night.

Speaking of Luck

They drift to her
like lost years & she doesn't
know how to say
No. More than forty
begging for a chunk of blame.
All those strays in her dog jail,
a constant whimpering in the air
almost sinful. They
encircle her like a prayer meeting
under the chinaberry tree
as she cleans fish

her mind on the trillium
in bloom along the fence,
humming "Precious Lord, Take My Hand."
Sunlight toying with her
cleaning knife, she can
already taste the catfish
on the sky-blue plate.

Villon/Leadbelly

Two bad actors canonized by ballads
flowering into dusk, crowned with hoarfrost.
But the final blows weren't dealt in Meung-
sur-Loire or the Angola pen. "Irene,
Irene, I'll see you in my dreams."

Unmoved by the hangman's leer,
these two roughhouse bards ignored
his finger traveling down the list.
They followed every season's penniless
last will & testament. Their songs

bleed together years. A bridge,
more than a ledger of bones.
Ghosts under the skin in bedlam,
Princes of Fools, they prowled
syncopated nights of wolfbane

& gin mills of starlight
at The Golden Mortar & The Bucket
of Blood, double-daring men across
thresholds, living down the list,
strung out on immortality's rag.

Borinken Blues

Down by La Perla
the sea rattles the moon
till silver litters the shore.

What comes natural,
las obras de arte,
black-haired girls mambo to conga &

Victor's words grow in the meat-air
into an African aubade
& Spanish capriccio.

In the mind's eye
he must sometimes stand
with his hands in his pockets,

watching the Caribbean's
big blue mouth wolf
down red sunsets.

for Victor Hernandez Cruz

Let's Say

He leans over—well,
let's say his name's Nilo
& he's black in Argentina.
He bends to look into his eyes
staring back *nada*
from a starry limbo,
balancing his world
on an eyelash.

Down there chance
distills into booze
& he sees himself walking
on the sea floor.
The small miserable boat
bobs over his head.

By midday someone
has already taken over
his stall in the marketplace
where the village opens
into a tango every red-sash day.

The new man, Vázquez,
who has a lover & a wife
five miles down the road,
drags in his display
of sea bass, squid,
black eel, blood trail,
singing "*Para Nosotros*"
under his white breath.

Elegy for Thelonious

Damn the snow.
Its senseless beauty
pours a hard light
through the hemlock.
Thelonious is dead. Winter
drifts in the hourglass;
notes pour from the brain cup.
Damn the alley cat
wailing a muted dirge
off Lenox Ave.
Thelonious is dead.

Tonight's a lazy rhapsody of shadows
swaying to blue vertigo
& metaphysical funk.
Black trees in the wind.
Crepuscule with Nelly
plays inside the bowed head.
"Dig the Man Ray of piano!"
O Satisfaction,
hot fingers blur
on those white rib keys.
Coming on the Hudson.
Monk's Dream.
The ghost of bebop
from 52nd Street,
footprints in the snow.
Damn February.
Let's go to Minton's
& play "modern malice"
till daybreak. Lord,
there's Thelonious
wearing that old funky hat
pulled down over his eyes.

Copacetic Mingus

> "'Mingus One, Two and Three.
> Which is the image you want the world to see?'"
> —Charles Mingus, *Beneath the Underdog*

Heartstring. Blessed wood
& every moment the thing's made of:
ball of fatback
licked by fingers of fire.
Hard love, it's hard love.
Running big hands down
the upright's wide hips,

rocking his moon-eyed mistress
with gold in her teeth.
Art & life bleed
into each other
as he works the bow.
But tonight we're both a long ways
from the Mile High City,
1973. Here in New Orleans
years below sea level,
I listen to *Pithecanthropus*
Erectus: Up & down, under
& over, every which way—
thump, thump, dada—ah, yes.
Wood heavy with tenderness,
Mingus fingers the loom
gone on Segovia,
dogging the raw strings
unwaxed with rosin.
Hyperbolic bass line. Oh, no!
Hard love, it's hard love.

Letter to Bob Kaufman

The gold dust of your voice
& twenty-five cents
can buy a cup of coffee.
We sell pain for next to nothing! Nope,
you don't know me but your flesh-
&-blood language lingers in my head
like treason & raw honey.
I read GOLDEN SARDINE
& dance the Calinda
to come to myself.
Needles, booze, high-steppers
with dangerous eyes.
Believe this, brother,

we're dice in a hard time hustle.
No more than handfuls of meat.
C'mon, play the dozens,
you root worker & neo-hoodooist,
you earth lover & hole-card peeper.
We know roads dusty with old griefs
& hot kiss joys.
Bloodhounds await ambush.
Something, perhaps the scent
of love, draws them closer.

Woman, I Got the Blues

I'm sporting a floppy existential sky-blue hat
when we meet in the Museum of Modern Art.

Later, we hold each other
with a gentleness that would break open
ripe fruit. Then we slow drag
to Little Willie John, we bebop
to Bird LPs, bloodfunk, lungs paraphrased
till we break each other's fall.
For us there's no reason the scorpion
has to become our faith healer.

Sweet Mercy, I worship
the curvature of your ass.
I build an altar in my head.
I kiss your breasts & forget my name.

Woman, I got the blues.
Our shadows on floral wallpaper
struggle with cold-blooded mythologies.
But there's a stillness in us
like the tip of a magenta mountain.

Half-naked on the living-room floor;
the moon falling through the window
on you like a rapist.

Your breath's a dewy flower stalk
leaning into sweaty air.

Street Cool Clara

Clara, there's a hole
behind your voice.
If the dead talked
I'd rather believe
those warped shadows
& go for their false leads—
lichen on grey planks
of speech. You sit here
wringing your hands
like the hired washwoman
who reaches into an old
wooden tub for a scarlet
shawl, as if our reunion
tonight is an undertaker's trade.
You were the girl
every local boy tried hard
to get his hands on
in his dad's Coupe
de Ville. There was a time
you'd skinny-dip
with the wolf-circled
moon in Parker's Pond.
Now all night
you pour Wild Turkey
on the rocks, searching
Moorish streets

for your blue-eyed
back-door man.

Newport Beach, 1979

To them I'm just a crazy nigger
out watching the ocean
drag in silvery nets of sunfish,
dancing against God's spine—
if He's earth, if He's a hunk of celestial bone,
if He's real as Superman
holding up the San Andreas Fault.

Now look, Miss Baby Blue Bikini,
don't get me wrong.
I'm not the Redlight Bandit,
not Mack the Knife, or Legs Diamond
risen from the dead
in a speak-easy of magenta sunsets perpetually
overshadowing nervous breakdowns.

I'm just here where first-degree eyes
look at me like loaded dice,
as each day hangs open
in hurting light like my sex
cut away & tied to stalks
of lilies, with nothing else
left to do for fun.

Gloria's Clues

Whenever we're left alone in the room she performs. Sucking on
a lemon-yellow lollipop, she goes for the heart. When she pulls

her panties down I turn my eyes to the blond Jesus glowing on the wall. Some dance propels her across the floor. When Gabe & Annabelle return from the kitchen, she's back playing with her ABC blocks, all twelve colors stacked into a pyramid. We shuffle the bones, we slap 'em down: blank to blank, five to five. We get the right rhythm going & it sounds like a punch press at the mill, minutes fly like metal shards from a lathe. Gloria plays with her life-size doll that closes its eyes. With peripheral vision I see her sneak a cigarette from the clamshell ashtray—a slow kiss of burns bubbles around the doll's belly-button. I wonder if it's all in my head. The bones rain down like blows against the oak tabletop. Tequila Sunrises & San Miguels work us over, while outside snowflakes accumulate on Dutch elms. Finally the game winds down to Gabe's smile as he tallies points—"the damage" we've done to each other tonight. I tell them it's a nice walk six blocks through the snow. No, no, I'm not drunk. Annabelle stands where the doorway's heavy light falls through her white muslin dress like sad wisdom. An induced schizophrenia—we look at each other without looking. Gloria's green eyes follow me out the door into the street. I don't know where my feet are headed.

Charmed

I jump between the cat
& a bird. The cat cries
as though I had struck her with a stick.
If animals possess souls
her cry's close to sin.
She moves toward the bird.
Women have moved gently
toward me—& me toward them—
this way. Some dance
concealed under the skin.

The bird sits perfectly lost
like a flower. So red.
Lost behind the five colors
of the cat's eyes brighter
than truest memory of water.
The cat has pierced him
deeper than bad luck,
moving like a hand buried
in the dark. Years ago
I stepped between a woman & man
at each other's throat,
both turning against me.
I try to shoo the bird away.
I pick him up & his small heart
flutters through me.
The bird has no song left.
I close my eyes,
I place him on the ground,
I back away.

Captain Diable's Receptionist

The way light
falls on her face
has already made one man
commit push-button suicide.
Eye trick. Skirt
trick. Even the bombastic
dogwood isn't responsible
as it falls into crosses.
Knowing in the blood how
her archetypal eyes say,
It's written in the script;
now grind to the number,
Daddy-O.

The Cage Walker

He shoves the .38
into his coat pocket
& walks back into
the dark. Night
takes him like a conveyer belt.

For a split second
he's been there
in the ditch,
hood pulled from over a death's-head.

He sits on a park bench.
Blue uniform behind every elm,
night sticks. He thinks how a man
enters the deeper, darker machine.

His fingers touch gun metal.
He stands & walks down
toward the wharf; ships rock
in white foghorn silence.
Water slams, steel doors
closing in a tunnel.

The quarter-moon goes blank
behind a cloud. He frames a picture
in his head, retraces footsteps
to Shorty's Liquor Store.
He will go in this time.

He stands under a street lamp.
Moths float by
& he counts cars:
1, 2, 3, 4, 5, aw shit.

A woman walks past & smiles.
Her red dress turns the corner
like blood in a man's eyes.
He stares at his hands.
They say August is a good time
for a man to go crazy.

Addendum

I'm a bone roller,
a high roller,
listening to Lester Young
& Big Mama Thornton,
Peacock 1612.

I'm a street nigger
from way back when: I am
multilateral
extended metaphors
for cellblock blues
& Cat-Eye balling the jack

I'm a womb-scratcher.
I'm a double-dealer.
I'm the chance you take
with the past tonight.

Epilogue to the Opera
of Dead on Arrival

I can still sing
"Ain't Goin' Down to the Well

No Mo'" Like Leadbelly.
Blow out the candles
& start all anew.
Where's Sweet Luck?—
a kiss from that woman.
It's the way starlight
struck the blade. If only
I could push down on her chest
& blow a little breath
into her mouth, maybe.
Handcuff me, slam my head
against bars of the jailhouse,
use your blackjacks,
zero in on my weaknesses,
let enough melancholy
to kill a mule
settle into my lungs.

By Proxy

No, I'm not ashamed
to hug an old wish
lost. Her name
clings to the roof of my mouth,
but the goose flesh
of desire can't bring back
her voice. I remember
some part of me
educated by disbelief,
hiding in a sunless corner
reading Poe. Another part
learned the taste of muscatel
& Lucky Strikes glowing
in the dark like fat lightning bugs.
They say we always love most

what we can't have.
Already a rainbow
under six feet of earth,
that cockeyed summer
fiery as first love
& first blood,
she caught everyone off guard
marrying a jailbird.
Goldie Rae's high yellow man,
what was his name?
Faces come & go
but I remember
their broken dance
on the front porch,
how they swayed
to light striking metal,
how our pleas swarmed him,
how even God couldn't
get to them fast enough
to stop his knife.

1931

Hard times loom in Texas
adobe & money trees. The man
with a slender white hand
resting on the meat scale,
the price of cut-rate soup bones.
He's standing right here, one jab away,
talking to me about cobalt in Angola,
perhaps daydreaming a bloodbath
among crimson weeping willows.
Half-paralyzed, he drags his left leg,
little or no feeling. There's an angel
in his left side, hinged to the pelvis,
slowly closing noncommittal eyes.

The Leper's Bell

It pleads through dogwood
with all I know,
follows me around
the sad blue periphery
of other lives. I laugh
at my shadow, peaceful
in ditch water
with a lily, my dreams nourished
by the sorrow worm's
hunger, my love
healed like a stone.
Each step I take
I plant an old pain,
not even a dog's mercy
for company. What I sing
these blood-red mornings
belongs to the black cricket.
This shack where stars
fall through the roof,
with a bell for a tongue,
just my libido intact
like the mute wood
of some moth-infested bough.
No balls & so goddamn civil
as I ride its downward
wheel, I have nothing
the earth wants to steal.

Blues Chant Hoodoo Rival

my story is
how deep the heart runs

to hide & laugh
with your hands
over your blank mouth
face behind the mask
talking in tongues
something tearing
feathers from a crow
that screams
from the furnace
the black candle
in a skull
sweet pain of meat

    let's pour the river's rainbow
    into our stone water jars
    bad luck isn't red flowers
    crushed under jackboots

your story is
a crippled animal
dragging a steel trap
across desert sand
a bee's sting inside your heart
& its song of honey
in my groin
a factory of blue jays
in honey locust leaves
wet pages of smoke
like a man
deserting his shadow
in dark woods
the dog that limps away
& rotten fruit on the trees

this story is
the speaking skull
on the mantelpiece
the wingspan of a hawk
at the edge of a coyote's cry

the seventh son's mojo hand
holding his life together
with a black cat bone
the six grandfathers
& spider woman
the dust wings
of ghost dance vision
deer that can't
stand for falling
wunmonije witch doctor
backwater blues
juju man
a silk gown on the floor
a black bowl
on a red lacquered table
x-rated
because it's true

    let's pour starlight
    from our stone water jars
    pain isn't just red flowers
    crushed under jackboots

my story is
inside a wino's bottle
the cup blood leaps into
eight-to-the-bar
a man on his knees
facing the golden calf
the silverfish of old lust
mama hoodoo
a gullah basket
woven from your hair
love note from the madhouse
thornbushes
naming the shape
of things to come
old murder weapons
strings of piano wire

let's pour the night
into our stone water jars
this song isn't red flowers
crushed under silence

our story is
a rifle butt
across our heads
arpeggio of bowed grass
among glass trees
where they kick down doors
& we swan-dive from
the brooklyn bridge
a post-hypnotic suggestion
a mosaic membrane
skin of words
mirrors shattered
in roadhouses
in the gun-barrel night
how a machine moves
deeper into piles
of bones
the way we
crowd at the foot
of the gallows

Toys in a Field

Nothing Big

The hummingbird's rainbow
        lands among red
                geraniums.
God's little hell-rising
  helicopter flies away,

& I'm back in Danang.
  Was the rich boy's cocaine
                this good
or have I been trying years
to return to this hard night

of mahogany trees shadowing men
back from a firefight? The sun
strikes broken glass on the ground
& triggers dancing lights in my head—
the sky's flesh wounds.
          I'm back at the Blue Dahlia
         lying beside someone I can't
forget.

Inside me a flurry of wings
stirs up trouble,
& I'm lifting off.

Ambush

So quiet birds
start singing again.
Lizards bring a touch of light.
The squad leader counts bullets

a third time. Stars
glint off gunbarrels.
We can almost hear a leaf
falling. "For chrissake. Please."
Raw opium intoxicates
a blaze of insects.
Buddhist monks on a hill
burn twelve red lanterns.
"Put out your stupid cigarette,
PFC," the Recon corporal whispers.
The trees play games.
A tiger circles us, in his broken cage
between sky & what's human.
"We'll wait out the bastards.
They have to come this way,
& when they do, not
even God can help 'em."
Headless shadows skirt the hedgerow.
A crossroad for lost birds
singing their hearts out
calling to the dead,
& then a sound that makes you jump
in your sleep years later,
the cough of a mortar tube.

Water Buffalo

God, this mud. Fear's habit.
This red-caped dusk.
The iron bird rattles
overhead again, with stars
falling, the green man
strapped in its smoky doorhole.
I drop my head & charge
a vulture's shadow gliding

over a rice paddy dike.
Hung belly, hooves, & asshole,
everything pushes against my eyes.
I bellow at the sunset
like a brass foghorn.
Shooting up, away from my holler,
sparrows eclipse. Sunday's
whole weight rests on my back.
The whirlwind machine
returns, hammering its gong.
I'm nothing but a target.
It nose-dives.
I plant my feet, big as myth,
& hear silent applause.
The earth pulls at me
& the day caves in.
Silver lances ignite the air.
Bullheaded dynamo—I am
no match for that fire,
for what's in a heart.

Monsoon Season

A river shines in the jungle's
wet leaves. The rain's finally
let up but whenever wind shakes
the foliage it starts to fall.
The monsoon uncovers troubled
seasons we tried to forget.
Dead men slip through bad weather,
stamping their muddy boots to wake us,
their curses coming easier.
There's a bend in everything,
in elephant grass & flame trees,
raindrops pelting the sand-bagged

bunker like a muted gong.
White phosphorus washed from the air,
wind sways with violet myrtle,
beating it naked. Soaked to the bone,
jungle rot brings us down to earth.
We sit in our hooches
with too much time,
where grounded choppers
can't fly out the wounded.
Somewhere nearby a frog
begs a snake.
I try counting droplets,
stars that aren't in the sky.
My poncho feels like a body bag.
I lose count. Red leaves
whirl by, the monsoon
unburying the dead.

Le Xuan, Beautiful Spring

I run my fingers over a photo
torn from a magazine & folded
inside *Sons and Lovers*.
She's got one hand on her hip
& the other aiming a revolver
at some target hiding
from the camera. Flanked by a cadre
of women in fatigues, she's daring
the sun to penetrate her *ao dai*.
High-ranking officers let their eyes
travel over silk as they push pins
into maps under a dead-looking sky.

Shadows crawl from under her feet.
Does she know soldiers undress her

behind dark aviation glasses?
She's delicate as a reed
against a river, just weighing the gun
in her hand, a blood-tipped lotus
rooted in the torn air.
Another kind of lust blooms
in flesh, ominous as a photo
on a coffin waiting to be
lost among papers & notes,
but it still hurts when a pistol
plays with the heart this way.

Toys in a Field

Using the gun mounts
for monkey bars,
children skin the cat,
pulling themselves through,
suspended in doorways
of abandoned helicopters
in graveyards. With arms
spread-eagled they imitate
vultures landing in fields.
Their play is silent
as distant rain,
the volume turned down
on the 6 o'clock news,
except for the boy
with American eyes
who keeps singing
rat-a-tat-tat, hugging
a broken machine gun.

Please

Forgive me, soldier.
Forgive my right hand
for pointing you
to the flawless
tree line now
outlined in my brain.
There was so much
bloodsky at daybreak
in Pleiku, but I won't say
those infernal guns
blinded me on that hill.

Mistakes piled up men like clouds
pushed to the dark side.
Sometimes I try to retrace
them, running
fingers down the map
telling less than a woman's body—
we followed the grid coordinates
in some battalion commander's mind.
If I could make my mouth
unsay those orders,
I'd holler: Don't
move a muscle. Stay put,
keep your fucking head
down, soldier.

Ambush. Gutsmoke.
Last night while making love
I cried out, Hit the dirt!
I've tried to swallow my tongue.
You were a greenhorn, so fearless,
even foolish, & when I said go,
Henry, you went dancing on a red string
of bullets from that tree line
as it moved from a low cloud.

Returning (1975)

He comes toward me
                    out of white
porcelain hallways
in his remote control
                    contraption.
He begins to talk
about running feet,
                    nowhere to go,
batter symphony
of grown men
                    crying for their mothers,
broken strongholds—
how nightlong
                    he held his dead
buddy's hand,
praying for yellow smoke
                            & gunships.
A young nurse's image
from down the hall
                    glides past him
& he begins to sing:
"Gonna git me,
                    yeah, gonna git me
a mojo hand."

I Apologize for the Eyes in My Head

Unnatural State of the Unicorn

Introduce me first as a man.
Don't mention superficial laurels
the dead heap up on the living.
I am a man. Cut me & I bleed.
Before embossed limited editions,
before fat artichoke hearts marinated
in rich sauce & served with imported wines,
before antics & Agnus Dei,
before the stars in your eyes
mean birth sign or Impression,
I am a man. I've scuffled
in mudholes, broken teeth in a grinning skull
like the moon behind bars. I've done it all
to be known as myself. No titles.
I have principles. I won't speak
on the natural state of the unicorn
in literature or self-analysis.
I have no birthright to prove,
no insignia, no secret
password, no fleur-de-lis.
My initials aren't on a branding iron.
I'm standing here in unpolished
shoes & faded jeans, sweating
my manly sweat. Inside my skin,
loving you, I am this space
my body believes in.

Lightshow

Lightning dances down a naked
wire, while I sit at a window
reading my cards. The High Priestess
says I'm wrong about losses.

What would change this story,
an overnight ice age,
a telephone call to say
love's over?
Watching August's lightshow
shimmy up & down barred windows,
butterflies grow in my belly.
Some fear close to the bone ignites
the brain stem like a black wick.
Each day I badger myself with harder questions,
knowing how paper draws lightning.
Hologrammed gods pop neon whips,
cries leap out of the wood,
& the cards go momentarily indigo
in my hands. Answers elude,
fire runs under the skin,
thunder rolls out to a blue precipice
like artillery rounds—
pieces of afternoon torn off,
as if the brain's collapsed.
I feel like a devil's decoy
at this window, but I can't move
till The Hanged Man says *yes*.

Sorrow

She's on Main Street
lifting her yellow skirt.
Her perfume's a strange lucidity
or, more exactly, a pestilence.
She calls me her sweetheart,
her unlucky boy, her favorite ghost
in the looking glass.
                    Suddenly
she has her tongue in my mouth.

I brace myself against her;
already bigger than life,
she puts her head together with God's
until her call sign breaks in
& sends fighters into the sky.

Gazing through grey wood slats
of the poorhouse, I see her in a valley
ablaze with hyacinth & atropine.
In a Paris café, self-exiled,
I glimpse her sipping espresso,
eyeing the front door,
leafing through a copy of *The Tale
of the Devil's Fart*.
                        I spot her again
in Rio playing a concertina
in a roadhouse. Just as I step off
a curb in Mission Viejo
I notice her in a red sports car,
gunning the engine. At midnight
she climbs into bed, smiling,
her weight no more than a clue.
The bedsprings begin a low moan.

Touch-up Man

I playact the three monkeys
carved over the lintel of a Japanese shrine,
mouthing my mantra: *I do
what I'm told*. I work
from Mr. Pain's notecards;
he plants the germ of each idea,
& I'm careful not to look
at his private secretary's legs,
as I turn the harvest through the dumb-mill

of my hands. Half-drunk
with my tray of bright tools,
I lean over the enlarger,
in the light table's chromatic glare
where I'm king, doctoring photographs,
airbrushing away the corpses.

How I See Things

I hear you were
sprawled on the cover of *Newsweek*
with freedom marchers, those years
when blood tinted the photographs,
when fire leaped into the trees.

Negatives of nightriders
develop in the brain.
The Strawberry Festival Queen
waves her silk handkerchief,
executing a fancy high kick

flashback through the heart.
Pickups with plastic Jesuses
on dashboards head for hoedowns.
Men run twelve miles into wet cypress
swinging bellropes. Ignis fatuus can't be blamed

for the charred Johnson grass.
Have we earned the right
to forget, forgive
ropes for holding
to moonstruck branches?

Every last stolen whisper
the hoot owl echoes
turns leaves scarlet.

Hush shakes the monkeypod
till pink petal-tongues fall.

You're home in New York.
I'm back here in Bogalusa
with one foot in pinewoods.
The mockingbird's blue note
sounds to me like *please*,

please. A beaten song
threaded through the skull
by cross hairs.
Black hands still turn blood red
working the strawberry fields.

Insufficient Blue

At St. Marks Bookshop I buy
Berrigan's *So Going Around Cities*,
saying, "I have to meet him
someday." July 4th's
fireworks boom away dusk.

Out on the street starclusters
rainbow & bottle rockets
arc across New York.
Summer hangs up a scarlet cape,
what's left unsaid between lovers.

Something happened in another city
& we're here to patch things up.
Forget. Forgive. Stop
reading between lines, thumbing
snowy pages from a woeful season.

Lately love's shown us
such ugly scars,
such criminal sweetness.
Strings of firecrackers pop
& spook dogs down the street.

At the Centre Pub I'm hungry
for a hamburger & you want onion soup.
The wine's magical. A woman at the table
across from us sits careless as a lie.
Her dress is dreamy blue
& she's wearing no underwear.

How could we have known
Ted Berrigan was somewhere
baffling the Angel of Death?
Even though night's crimson stars
kept raining down on us.

The Thorn Merchant

There are teeth marks
on everything he loves.
When he enters the long room
more solemn than a threadbare Joseph coat,
the Minister of Hard Knocks & Golden Keys
begins to shuffle his feet.
The ink on contracts disappears.
Another stool pigeon leans
over a wrought-iron balcony.
Blood money's at work.
While men in black wetsuits
drag Blue Lake, his hands dally
at the hem of his daughter's skirt.

In the brain's shooting gallery
he goes down real slow.
His heart suspended in a mirror,
shadow of a crow over a lake.
With his fingers around his throat
he moans like a statue
of straw on a hillside.
Ready to auction off his hands
to the highest bidder,
he knows how death waits
in us like a light switch.

The Thorn Merchant's Right-Hand Man

Well, that's Pretty Boy Emeritus
alias Leo the Machine, great-grandson
of Eddie the Immune, a real ladies' man
in his handmade elevated Spanish shoes.
It's funny how he walks into town
with just a bouquet or violin
& lost faces reappear, eclipsed
by fedoras in bulletproof
limousines. A looted brain case
succumbs & a cage of prayers
sways in night air. Pretty Boy throws a kiss
to death, a paradoxical star in each eye. Naturally
he's surprised when he stumbles
& snags his suit coat on an ice pick.
It had to happen. He's caught
in a Texaco john humming the Mass in D.
The fight moves out to the corner
of Midsummer Avenue & Galante Blvd.
like two men tussling with red lanterns.
Pretty Boy's shoelaces tied together,
the full moon behind flowering manzanita

deserts him with his tongue in pawn
clear down to where a plea forms
the root word for flesh.

After the Heart's Interrogation

In December's slaughterhouse
I'm still standing my ground.
The wall clock picks itself apart.
What's left of my life stumbles forward
in heavy boots. The trouble is,
I know what it all means.

There's more to come. A white goat
is staring into windows again.
Bats clog the chimney like rags.
An angel in the attic
mends a torn wing. Dog-eared luck.
The gun cocking outside
my front door is another question
I'm here to answer.

Happy-Go-Lucky's Wolf Skull Dream Mask

OK, lift this mask
up to your eyes, over your face,
a perfect fit.

Well, Mr. Magnifico,
what do you see? How's your world?

Now you must live on silence.
I know you can only see gold

glistening with another's sweat,
hear only a strand of barbed wire
a half-mile in the heart, music

of poison sumac.
In your well-earned lunacy
you can smell death coming.
There's something you just can't
shake; you bite into it—
laced up through eyeholes of self-pity.

I know there's a blank space
big enough for a man to shove his fist into,
where your heart used to be
playing its black keys.

The Heart's Graveyard Shift

I lose faith in my left hand
not because my dog Echo's eloped
with ignis fatuus into pinewoods
or that my limp's unhealed
after 13 years. What can go wrong
goes wrong, & between loves an empty
space defines itself like a stone's weight
helps it to sink into earth.
My devil-may-care attitude
returns overnight, the bagwoman
outside the 42nd Street Automat
is now my muse. I should know
by heart the schema, routes
A & B, points where we
flip coins, heads or tails,
to stay alive. Between loves
I crave danger; the assassin's cross hairs
underline my point of view.

                    Between loves,
with a pinch of madness tucked under
the tongue, a man might fly off the handle
& kill his best friend over a penny.
His voice can break into butterflies
just as the eight ball cracks
across deep-green felt,
growing silent with something unsaid
like a mouth stuffed with nails.
He can go off his rocker, sell the family
business for a dollar, next morning
pull a Brink's job & hijack a 747.
He can hook up with a woman in silver
spike heels who carries a metallic blue guitar
or he can get right with Jesus
through phenobarbital.

                    Between loves
I sing all night with the jukebox:
"Every man's gotta cry for himself."
I play chicken with the Midnight Special
rounding Dead Man's Curve, enthralled
by the northern lights & machinery
of falling stars. Internal solstice,
my body, a poorly rigged by-pass
along Desperado Ave., taking me away
from myself. Equilibrium's whorehouses.
Arcades scattered along the eastern seaboard.
I search dead-colored shells for clues,
visions, for a thread of meat,
untelling interior landscapes.
A scarecrow dances away with my shadow.
Between loves I could stand all day
at a window watching honeysuckle open
as I make love to the ghosts
smuggled inside my head.

Hard Up

The quiet way the sun hangs dead center
of everything, I'm looking through a woman's dress.
Her name might be Beatrice.
Noon trees, appendages of light, nothing to do
   with love.
Yes, we're falling over our two shoes
to escape each other.
My soul comes toward her, a shaking calabash sonata.
Today's naked. She runs under a pink umbrella.
I run under a locust tree. She runs behind a billboard
proclaiming: BETTER BUY STOCK IN BOMB SHELTERS.
I run into a telephone booth.
I dial my mother's number.
I come at her two directions at once,
skirting the edge of nowhere to run now.
She smiles, gives in, hopelessly
trying to hide under her light blue dress.

Boy Wearing a Dead Man's Clothes

1
I must say I never liked
garbardine's wornout shine.

Cold weather fills this coat,
& the shoulders have drooped anyhow!

Jesus, his yellow silk handkerchief;
I'm keeping this next to my heart.

The police chief's daughter's smile
has started to peel off

the curled photo I found
here in his breast pocket.

2

Blue denim cap, no other
crown for a poor man's head.

I wear it the same angle
he did, hipper than thou.

If I tilt it over my eyes
a bit to the left this way,

cut the sky in half,
can I see the world

through his eyes? Cloud-cap
washed till there's hardly any blue left.

3

Uncle Jimmy's flowered shirt
keeps its shape. Body's character—

enamored of sweat, touch
gone out of the cloth,

no dark red map widening
across my chest to recall

that night.
Sleeves filled with silence.

The lipstick won't
come off.

4

I don't belong here. I
can't help but say

to Uncle's cordovan boots,
Get me outta East Texas, back to L.A.,

but please don't take me
by their place: Four weeks ago, that time

I saw him & Mrs. Overstreet
kissing in the doorway,

& Mr. Overstreet drunk
with his head on the table.

Gift Horse

Your wife's forty-five
today & you've promised her
someone like me, did I
hear you right? You
wave a hundred-dollar bill
under my nose & a diamond
of snowlight falls through
the bar's isinglass walls
as Dylan comes up on the jukebox.

You saw me hustling pool tables
for nickels & dimes, now my refusal
rocks you like a rabbit punch
in the solar plexus. You pull
snapshots from your wallet.
Yeah, she does look like
Shirley Jones in *Elmer Gantry*.
You say you're a man
who loves the truth,
& maybe my mistake is
I believe you.

I know the dark oath
flesh makes with earth.
You drive a hard bargain
for a stone to rest your head on.
On the jukebox, Otis Redding's "Dock of the Bay."
Days fall around us
bigger than the snowstorm
that drove you in here
to dodge wind driving pine needles
through the hearts of birds.

You up the ante another fifty.
My bottle of beer sweats
a cool skin for us both.
You blow smoke-ring halos
for dust-colored angels among tinsel,
reindeer & year-round Christmas lights,
where sexual hunger's like ripe apples,
but by now you must know I can't
sleep in your bed while you drive
around the countryside till

sunrise, taking the blind
curves on two wheels.

The Music That Hurts

Put away those insipid spoons.
The frontal lobe horn section went home hours ago.
The trap drum has been kicked
down the fire escape,
& the tenor's ballad amputated.
Inspiration packed her bags.
Her caftan recurs in the foggy doorway
like brain damage; the soft piano solo of her walk

evaporates; memory loses her exquisite tongue,
looking for "green silk stockings with gold seams"
on a nail over the bathroom mirror.
Tonight I sleep with Silence,
my impossible white wife.

When in Rome—Apologia

Please forgive me, sir
for getting involved

in the music—
it's my innate weakness

for the cello: so human.
Please forgive me
for the attention

I've given your wife
tonight, sir.

I was taken in by her
strands of pearls,
enchanted by a piano
riff in the cortex,
by a secret

anticipation. I don't know
what came over me, sir.

After three Jack Daniel's
you must overlook
my candor, my lack of
sequitur.

I could talk
about Odysseus

& Athena, sexual
flowers, autogamy
or Nothingness.

I got carried away
by the swing of her hips.

But take no offense
if I return to the matter

as if hormonal.
I must confess
my love for black silk, sir.
I apologize for
the eyes in my head.

The Thorn Merchant's Wife

She mediates on how rocks rise
in Bluebird Canyon, how hills
tremble as she makes love
to herself, how memories drift
& nod like belladonna
kissing the ground.

She remembers the first time, there
in his flashy two-tone Buick.
That night she was a big smile
in the moon's broken-down alley.
When she became the Madonna of Closed Eyes
nightmares bandaged each other
with old alibis & surgical gauze,

that red dress he fell for
turned to ghost cloth
in some bagwoman's wardrobe.

She thinks about the gardener's son.
But those black-haired hours only lasted
till the shake dancer's daughter
got into his blood & he grew sober—
before solitaire began to steal
her nights, stringing an opus
of worry beads, before Morphine
leaned into the gold frame.

The Thorn Merchant's Mistress

I was on my high
horse then. I
wore red with ease

& I knew how
to walk. There
were men undressing me

everywhere I went,
& women wishing
themselves in my place,

a swan unfractured
by August. I was still
a girl. If they

wanted culture,
I said Vivaldi
& Plato's Cave.

If they wanted
the streets, I said
Fuck you.

I knew how
to plead, Wait, Wait,
till I caught the eye

of some *deus ex
machina*. I was in
a deep dance

pulling the hidden
strings of nude
shadows. But when

his car drove by
my heart caught
like a fat moth

in spider web. Goddamn!
I didn't know
how to say No.

Somewhere Else

Making angels in the snow.
We aren't ourselves, hardly
trusting what we've become.
The years now weigh
as much as the bad king's crown.
I find it harder to dance,
shy father of my own
downfall, no more than water
singing through the drainpipe

at a black speed.
A man in another season
laughs beside a woman
& they're the only song
in Manitou Springs' night air.
Loss, what's that? Those two
hands which once held mine
now holding up a blanket
of snow—does this qualify?
Frankly, all I can say is
I've been to a funny place
inside myself, where simple
answers fall like ashes
through an iron grate.

After Summer Fell Apart

I can't touch you.
His face always returns;
we exchange long looks
in each bad dream
& what I see, my God.
Honey, sweetheart,
I hold you against me
but nothing works.
Two boats moored,
rocking between nowhere
& nowhere.
A bone inside me whispers
maybe tonight,
but I keep thinking
about the two men wrestling nude
in Lawrence's *Women in Love.*
I can't get past
reels of breath unwinding.

He has you. Now
he doesn't. He has you
again. Now he doesn't.

You're at the edge of azaleas
shaken loose by a word.
I see your rose-colored
skirt unfurl.
He has a knife
to your throat,
night birds come back
to their branches.
A hard wind raps at the door,
the new year prowling
in a black overcoat.
It's been six months
since we made love.
Tonight I look at you
hugging the pillow,
half smiling in your sleep.
I want to shake you & ask
who. Again I touch myself,
unashamed, until
his face comes into focus.
He's stolen something
from me & I don't know
if it has a name or not—
like counting your ribs
with one foolish hand
& mine with the other.

Uncertainty in Blue

I'd feel lost as Lorca
here in the Big Apple

if we weren't holding hands.
Years run together, days drop
off the blue edge. Faces
dissolve into a blameless mist.

In Washington Square
I notice body language,
who's leaning towards whom.
Black hands on a weary clock.
Across morning two crooked
trees grow out of each other,

married to a blue background.
We watch skaters daredevil,
weave silver circumferences
& play loop-the-loop,
barely escaping head-on collisions
with totems in bloom.

Plugged into their boogie boxes,
they don't see July.
New Wave & Punk Rock
jolt the Modern Jazz Quartet
in our heads from the night before
at Carnegie Hall. We know a hard light

forces the pale bud to red,
but we're surprised to learn
what's unsaid. We bend rules & sidestep.
When we find ourselves arguing about Picasso's
African masks I laugh, knowing
we sometimes give so we can take.

    for Carolyne

The Brain to the Heart

Stars tied to breath
don't have to be there
when you look.
No more than drops
of blood on ginkgo
leaves & inconsequential

eggs & frog spittle
clinging to damp grass.
Sure, I've seen doubts
clustered like peacock
eyes flash green fire.
So what?

When days are strung together,
the hourglass fills
with worm's dirt.
What do you take
the brain for? I know
how hard you work

in that dark place, but
I can't be tied down
to shadows of men
in trenches you won't
forget. You look at
a mulberry leaf

like a silkworm does, with all your insides,
but please don't ask me to be responsible.

Audacity of the Lower Gods

I know salt marshes that move along like one big
trembling wing. I've noticed insects
shiny as gold in a blues singer's teeth
& more keenly calibrated than a railroad watch,
but at heart I'm another breed.

The audacity of the lower gods—
whatever we name we own.
Diversiloba, we say, unfolding poison oak.
Lovers go untouched as we lean from bay windows
with telescopes trained on a yellow sky.

I'd rather let the flowers
keep doing what they do best.
Unblessing each petal,
letting go a year's worth of white
death notes, busily unnaming themselves.

The Falling-Down Song

       Here I am
with one foot on a floating platform
    breaking myself into small defeats—
  I'm the ghost of a moneychanger
     & halo of flies, half-moon of false teeth
  unable to bite bread. Please
  go, & tell no one you've seen me under the cypress,
    a fool-hearted footstool,
      termites in my two
       sad wooden
        legs,
sawdust in my black leather shoes.

Syzygy

Darling, I understand
this is the Year of the Dog,
so please be careful.
Walk only those well-lit streets
& know who your friends are.
We can all take the Fifth.
Or, better yet, play crazy.
Can move into the Rockies & make love
to mountain sheep in springtime,
listening to white rivers sing
through our broken hearts.
We can fool ourselves
with a touch of lust
under our tongues. Indifference
would be a better word.
We can always kill
some integral part of ourselves,
let the right hand hold
down the left,
crying in our sleep
OK, you bastards
come & get me, if you're bad.
Manifestoes to green frogs
on lily pads. Across
the estuary where dogbane
blooms under the Dog Star,
birds have a song called Death
in their throats. We
put our eyeteeth in hock,
& swear we didn't
hear a thing.

The Thorn Merchant's Son

Using an old water-stained
Seven Year Itch movie poster
as his dartboard, he places
all six into the bull's-eye.
The phonograph clicks silently,
playing "Teen Angel" the tenth time.
Sipping a Pepsi-Cola,
he moves over to *Pretty Baby*
unrolled on his daddy's desk.
He runs his tongue around
the edge of her smile,
then picks up a paperweight
& shakes it till the black horse
disappears inside the glass.
Grey-eyed opacity, low cloud
coming over the room, he throws
a wooden puzzle against a wall
& the first-shaped piece
flies apart like a clay pigeon.
He stares fifteen minutes
at a tintype face
so blue it's hardly there.
With a little dance step
he eases over & props an elbow
on the window sill, aiming
his high-powered binoculars
at a woman's bedroom window.

I Apologize

My mind wasn't even there.
Mirage, sir. I didn't see

what I thought I saw.
Que será, será. That's that.
I was in my woman's bedroom
removing her red shoes & dress.
I'm just like the rest of the world:
No comment; no way, Jose;
I want spring always
dancing with the pepper trees.
I was miles away, I saw nothing!
Did I say their diamond rings
blinded me & I nearly lost my head?
I think it was how the North
Star fell through plate glass.
I don't remember what they wore.
What if I said they were
only shadows of overcoats
stooped in the doorway
where the light's bad?
No, no one roughed me up last night.
Sir, there's no story to change.
I heard no names. There were no
distinguishing marks or other clues.
No slip of the tongue. This morning
I can't even remember who I am.

1984

The year burns an icon
into the blood. Birdlime
discolors the glass domes
& roof beams grow shaky as old men
in the lobby of Heartbreak Hotel.
Purple oxide gas lamps light
the way out of this paradise.
We laugh behind masks & lip-sync Cobol.

We're transmitters for pigeons
with microphones in their heads.
Yellow sky over stockyards,
& by the grace of God
rockets hum in white silos
buried in Kansas wheat fields
or nailed to some ragged hill
zoned as a perfect fearscape.

We say, "I've seen it all."
Bombardment & psychic flux,
not just art nouveau tabula rasa
or double helix. We're ancient mariners
counting wishbones, in supersonic hulls
humming the falconer's ditty
over a banged-up job.
Three Mile Island blooms
her dreamworld as we wait
on the edge of our chairs
for the drunk radiologist.
Such a lovely view—
Big Brother to shadows
slipping under the door
where the millstones are stored.

We sing the ghost-catcher's madrigal.
The end of what? To count dismembered years
we say Gandhi, JFK, King,
leafing through names & faces. Waves
of locusts fall like black snow
in our sleep. Grackles
foresee ruins & battlements
where the Bone Breakers & God Squad
have had a good old time—
destined to sleep under
swaying trestles, as yes-men
crowded into a bad season,
listening all night to a calliope
hoot the equinox.

Since our hair's standing up
on the backs of our necks,
we must be on to something good,
Oppenheimer, right? Killjoy's
perched like Khan of the Golden Horde
on the back of a prisoner,
& we sit eating crow,
picking teeth with gold toothpicks.
Angels playing with trick mirrors,
sweet on a Minotaur in the dark
muscular air of a penny arcade.
We can transplant broken hearts
but can we put goodness back into them?

Brass knuckles flash
& this year is like flesh
torn under a lover's eye.
The end of what?
Going after posthumous love letters
dumped in black holes
light-years away, we line up
for practice runs with portable
neutron bombs strapped
to our backs—lopsided fun houses
where everyone wants to be
king of the stacked deck.

Streamlined androids construct
replicas three thousand miles away.
We guardians of uglier things to come
with our camera obscuras,
light vigil candles
& work the White Angel
bread line. Following the lunar crab
& loving the skyline, we discover
there's nothing to hold down tombstones,
lovers wishing upon astronauts
flashier than rock stars.

Alloyed against common sense,
somehow we're all King Lears
calling forth kingdom come—
scherzo for brimstone.
Fireworks bring in the New Year
& Zeus the confused robot
punches a fist through a skylight
as he dances across the floor
with his mechanical bride
doing a bionic two-step.

Hammered silver,
those badges we wear:
U-235 UTOPIA.
Made in America.
"Give us enough time,
we'll make the damn thing.
Let's look at the manual.
OK, here's *human breath*
on page 319."

Weather wars hang in skies
over the Third World. The dead
keep walking toward the sea
with everything they own
on their backs. Caught off guard
our falsehoods break into parts
of speech, like mayflies
on windshields of white Corvettes.

We're stargazers, weirdos,
prestidigitators in bluesy
bedrooms, on private trips
to the moon. The end of what?
We lock our hearts
into idle, not sure
of this world or the next.

Let's come down to earth.
Let's forget those video wrist watches
& "E.T." dolls triggered
by interstellar sundials
where electric eyes
hum on 18-carat key chains

& Dr. Strangelove tracks
the titanium gods. Let's go
beyond Devil's Triangle,
back to where the heart knows.
All the machines are on.
We sleepwalk among black roses
like characters in a dime novel,
& psychotherapy
can't erase the sign of the beast.

Dreambook Bestiary

Fear's Understudy
Like some lost part of a model kit
for Sir Dogma's cracked armor
an armadillo merges with night.
It rests against a mossy stone.
A steel-gray safe-deposit box,
ground level, two quicksilver eyes
peer out from under a coral helmet
color of fossil. It lives
encased in an asbestos hull
at the edge of a kingdom
of blackberries in quagmire,
in a grassy daydream,
sucked into its shield
by logic of flesh.

The Art of Atrophy
The possum plays dead
as Spanish moss, a seasoned actor
giving us his dumb show.
He dreams of ripe persimmons,
watching a dried stick
beside a white thunderstone,
with one eye half-open, a grin
slipping from the crooked corners
of his mouth, that old silver moon
playing tricks again. How long
can he play this waiting game,
till the season collapses,
till blowflies, worms, & ants
crawl into his dull coat
& sneak him away under
the evening star? Now
he's a master escape artist
like Lazarus, the gray
lining from a workman's glove
lost in frost-colored leaves.

Heart of the Rose Garden
A cluster of microscopic mouths
all working at once—

ants improve the soil, sift dust
through a millennium of wings.

They subsist on fear, drawn
to the lovebone,

to the base of the skull
where a slow undermining takes shape.

Under moonlight they begin their
instinctual autopsy, sensing

when grief tracks
someone down in her red patent-leather shoes,

when a man's soul
slips behind a headstone.

Glimpse

Near a spidery cage of grass
this cripple inches sideways up a sandy trail
with its little confiscated burden.
Just bigger than a man's thumbnail,
light as the shadow of a bone.

The sea falls short again. Claws unfold.
Its body almost creeps out. Morning
ticks away. Playing yes, no,
maybe so, it places its dome-shack
down on the sand & backs off,
surveying for the first tremor of loss.

Underside of Light

Centipede. Tubular, bright egg sac
trailing like a lodestone (unable to say
which is dragging which) out of damp compost:
biological soil, miasma, where lightning
starts like a sharp pain in god's spine.

In its armor, this sentinel rises
from a vault of double blackness.
This vegetal love forecasting April
crawls toward murdering light,
first thing tied to last.

Two Cranial Murals

She's at the mouth of a river
singing tongueless mantras
among reeds. A green parrot
picks up a birth cry
from cattails & broken grass.
No word yet for flesh.
If the gods have mouths now,
they say *raven, raven.*
Darkness wound in camphor
trees, the first smile
unconscious as a mooncalf's
under the sky's white belly—
the first eclipse of mind & body.
She winds the blood's clock.

Happy?
Who knows?
The tree gods
test a flowering branch over the river:
Sway-jig, sway-jig, sway-jig.
They ease out to its white verge:
half in this world, half in another,
ugly & beautiful. Caressing sky,
he reaches for a black-
orange butterfly on her head.
They linger there, caught up
in the slow blue song.
Then they invent a game
called Push & Shove.

Jonestown: More Eyes for *Jadwiga's Dream*

After Rousseau

Brighter than crisp new money.
Birds unfold wings into nervous fans,
adrift like breath-drawn kites, among
tremulous fronds with flowers crimson
as muzzle flash. Tropic silk, root color,
ocean green, they float to tree limbs
like weary scarves.

Hidden eyes deepen the memory
between sunrise & nightmare. Pine-box builders
grin with the pale soothsayer presiding over
this end of songs. The day's a thick hive
of foliage, not the moss grief deposits
on damp stones—we're unable to tell where
fiction bleeds into the real.

Some unspoken voice, small as a lizard's,
is trying to obey the trees.
Green birds flare up behind church bells
against the heartscape: if only
they'd fold their crepe-paper wings
over bruised eyes & see nothing
but night in their brains.

Landscape for the Disappeared

Lo & behold. Yes, peat bogs
in Louisiana. The dead
stumble home like swamp fog,
our lost uncles & granddaddies

come back to us almost healed.
Knob-fingered & splayfooted,
all the has-been men
& women rise through nighttime
into our slow useless days.

Live oak & cypress
counting these shapes in a dance
human forms aren't made for. Faces
waterlogged into their own
pure expression, unanswerable
questions on their lips.

Dumbstruck premonitions rise
from the heckle-grass
to search us out.
Guilty, sings the screech owl.
I hear the hair keeps growing
in the grave. Here
moss lets down a damp light.

We call back the ones
we've never known, with stories
more ours than theirs.
The wind's low cry
their language, a lunar rainbow
lost among Venus's-flytraps
yellowing in frog spittle & downward mire,
boatloads of contraband
guns & slot machines dumped
through the years.

Here's this lovely face so black
with marsh salt. Her smile,
a place where minnows swim.
All the full presence
shiny as a skull under the skin.
Say it again—we are
spared nothing.

Articulation
& Class

The hangman points out
   to the condemned man
      a purple martin

swooping up a jade-green dragonfly,
  then drops the black hood
     over his head.

In the Labor Camp of Good Intentions

There's an angel
snapping his fingers.
He stands nonchalantly outside his low
guardshack made from astral dogwood
braced by a Judas tree,
lifting his arms like torn
signal flags dissecting
the night, the shadow of a Doberman
rearing against its chock chain.
Like a man fanning flies, he just waves
the tooth-&-nail brigade through.
Possibly he does it to soothe
the blind itch under his tongue.

Good Joe

We prop him up
in his easy chair.
We give him a crew cut.

We dust off his blue serge.
We sing his favorite
golden oldies: "Dixie"
& "Ta-ra-ra-boom-de-ay!"
We clamp on his false
finger bones. We lead him
across the floor
saying, "Walk, walk."
We move in circles
dancing the McCarthy—
someone leans over & clicks in
his glass eye. All his ideas
come into focus:
we hear rats in the walls
multiplying.

Professors, photojournalists,
scholars of ashes in urns
buried a thousand years
off the Gulf of Mexico
sign loyalty oaths; actors
forget their meaty lines.
We shine his wing-tip Bostonians.
We bring him oyster stew,
bottles of Chivas Regal
on a jade serving tray.
We show him snapshots of lovers.
We give him a book of names,
turning the pages for him.
Some of us volunteer
to enter a room
where machines take each other apart
& put themselves back
together. We form
a line which spills out
the door, around the corner
for a whole city block,
& pay protection
with bowed heats.

Making Out with the Dream-Shredding Machine

He throws his arms around
a wheel, hunches closer,
resting his head against
the bullheaded millstone
shiny as a shark's back.
Quasimodo taken in by
unmerciful smoothness,
while boldface roman letters
fall into his mouth like grain.
He poses in the broken angle
at which all angels come into
this world, gazing sideways
for a skylight,
pinned down in a full nelson
like Houdini on the floor
kissing his shadow good-bye.

In the Background of Silence

First, worms begin with a man's mind.
Then they eat away his left shoe
to answer his final question.
His heart turns into a gold thimble of ashes,
his bones remind bees of honeycomb,
he falls back into himself like dirt into a hole,
his soul fits into a matchbox
in the shirt pocket
of his brother's well-tailored uniform.

Not even a stray dog dares to stir in the plaza,
after the muzzle flash,
after black coffee & Benzedrine,

after the sign of the cross a hundred times,
after sorrow's skirt drops to the floor,
after the soldier pulls off his spit-shined boots
& crawls into bed with the prettiest woman in town.

Cinderella at Big Sur

His kisses airbrush over her
in shadow play. She lies there
clothed only with his naked
thoughts, feeling night's thistle-star
etch salt into her. "Good girl,"
says Midas, her benefactor.

There must be something she can believe in.
The Invisible Angel
wearing a gold silk dress.
The falsebottom of her nights
means she's in her own world;

not exactly under the influence,
whole in her habit of pure seeing—
tender root holding on to earth
or the hand that uproots.
He hands her three masks
of a young Howard Hughes.

How did she get here, & who's this man?
She's watched the hammer
strike the nail but doesn't
know why each nail holds
his cruel funhouse together.

Days come & go like water
over stones. Cocaine's

lost its kick. She sleeps under Midas's
shiny dome, but the kingdom
of worms eats through to where
passionflowers bleed open.

Loving the odor of gone,
she feels like a cutout
looking up at the sky,
hearing a red tide mumble to itself
songs buried underground.

Born Pretty in a Poor Country

Musical instrument tuned
for the big spenders,
there's hardly an unbroken bone
in your body. Now you know
why your mama wanted
to give you just one kind scar
in the right place.
You're in these snapshots
dancing the cha-cha,
doing the dog with a sailor
from Chattanooga. The good life
poured from a green bottle,
a cigar smoker named Roberto
leaning in the doorway
said your name.
He cocked his hat
& you were twirling
under the corpse-maker's spotlight.
Before you learned his tune,
before the first bone
settled into its meaning,
flesh & dream fell away.

Was it only a face in your head
you nursed those long nights,
doubled over to let life
go at you?

Olympia

Someone in this room
would rather see a swan
fucking Leda. A monocle sways
on a gold chain; someone
in this place would rather
see Jacob with an angel
in a compromising position.
Her awkward left hand says
Iago's outside a hidden door
eavesdropping at a keyhole
Manet painted over; not stammel—
black healed the mistake.
She wears coquettish high heels
in bed, a flower in her hair
seductive as a magnolia,
& he's a stand-in Othello
in his androgynous robe,
with a night-colored cat
beside him named Cliché.

"Everybody's Reading Li Po"
Silkscreened on a Purple T-Shirt

Li Po who?
Says the shoeless

woman moving toward me with
her faded aura, angry
at no one in this world.

Li Po who?
Murmurs December,
speaking in tongues
like the girl in Jackson Square.
Sweet stench of onion
eats at me as the wind
discovers an old man
asleep under newspapers.
His dream a slow leaf
on black water.

Li Po who?
Says the boy junkie, Ricardo.
Tied to night's string,
he sways under neon
like a black girl with red hair
in the doorway of Lucky's.

Li Po who?
Says the prostitute
on Avenue Z.
Smelling loud as a bag
of lavender sachet
spilled on the sidewalk.
Blue-veined pallor,
she lifts her skirt to show
what a diamond-studded
garter looks like.

For the Walking Dead

Veronica passes her cape between breath
& death, rehearsing
the body's old rhyme.
With boyish soldiers on their way
to the front, she dances
the slowdrag in a bar called
Pylos. White phosphorus blooms
five miles away, burning sky
for a long moment, mortars
rock in iron shoes cradled
by earth, within earshot
of carbines stuttering through
elephant grass. Canisters lobbed
over night hills whine
like moonstruck dogs. After-
silence falls into the valley.

Tunes on the outdated jukebox
take her back to St. Louis,
back to where the color of her eyes
served as no one's balsam.
"Please," they whisper in her ear
as she counts the unreturned
faces, pale beads on an abacus.
Skin-colored dawn unravels
& a gun turret pivots on a hill.
Amputated ghosts on the walls—
she pulls them to her,
knowing the bruise beforehand.
She lets them work her into
the bar's darkest corner.
They hold her, a shield
against everything they know.

Too Pretty for Serious Business

Moonlight on antebellum skin
is how he has her
laid out in his mind,
wanting her to say snapdragon
& belladonna. Not to use words like blood,
shit, tiger cages,
that she doesn't know the score
written on the forehead.
Wearing his Billy the Kid grin,
he feels like a pair of boots
with iron spurs. He says, "Honey,
I'm the curator of parchment
skullcaps & broken promises."
He wants her on her back
studying a butterfly's weight
on a tree & singing "Old Black Joe."
He blows on a camellia
to break it open,
gives her a bloodstone,
saying, "Here.
See how hard it is;
now aren't you lucky?"
She says, "Hell no!"
He leans on his rosewood desk,
mumbling something about snow
& amber on Goat Mountain.

Child's Play

Hair slicked back as if
he just eased up out of
womb-water, the young man

wears a fatigue jacket.
The shoulder patch says
Seven Steps to Hell.
Dancing with the machine,
he tries to coax Thundarr
up from the black box
deep in the belly of metal.
The Cosmic Death's-Head
wars with Captain Sky.
A woman in punk-rocker black
plays Asteroids, leaning
her shadow against his
on the bus-terminal wall.
His hands work with chrome,
rockets zoom across the screen
silent as a sperm count.
His knuckles grow white
gripping the knobs,
with his collar turned up
like John Travolta's.
He gazes down in the glass
aiming for a clean kill,
not nearly as dangerous
as he wants you to think.

Raw Data for an Unfinished Questionnaire

Did they expect to find
good horse sense, God
shrunken in a Mason jar
stashed in a cardboard box
at their feet? With
Einstein's brain in Witchita,
did questions grow
like a Saturday night
rainstorm, shadow of wrens

darkening office windows?
Did they really hope for
invisible tripwires tied
to doubt as they unrolled
Dead Sea Scrolls on a stainless-
steel table under a galaxy
of hot lamps, a whole day
of stars in a white room?
Far from his birthplace,
was it easier to tear away
his last song, end the violin
sonata soft as beeswax
held together by remorse,
& forget those high-school girls
at the pier holding red roses
to their breasts? Forgotten
among rumpled gray newspapers
23 years, how long did he dream
Hiroshima's black rain,
& did they recognize love
hiding in the frontal lobe?

The Beast & Burden: Seven Improvisations

I   The Vicious
Fear threads its song
through the bones.
Syringe, stylus,
or pearl-handled stiletto?
He's fallen in love
with the Spanish garrote;
trailing a blue feather over the beast's belly
on down between his toes.
Night-long laughter
leaks from under the sheet-metal door.

Blackout.

———

He sits under a floodlight
mumbling that a theory of ants
will finally deal with us,

& reading My Lord Rochester
to a golden sky over Johannesburg,
a stray dog beside him, Sirius
licking his combat boots.

    2   *The Decadent*
Herr Scalawag, Esq.
dances the come-on
in Miss Misery's
spike heels.
He does a hellcat
high step stolen
from Josephine Baker,
holding a fake flower
like a flimsy excuse.
A paper rose, poppy
odor of luck
& lust. Look,
he's placed himself
upon the night's maddening wheel,
reduced from flesh
into the stuff
dreams are made of.
                    Hum-job,
his smile working
like a time-released
Mickey Finn.

3 *The Esoteric*

Unable to move the muse with narcotic
sweet talk, he muscles in on someone's grief.

He's on the glassy edge
of his stepping stone, a ghost
puppet stealing light from the real
world. With a wild guess
for spine, a face half-finished
on the blind lithographer's desk.

Canticle, cleftstong & heartriff
stolen out of another's mouth,
effigy's prologue & bravado.
He fingers his heirloom
Bible with rows of exed out names
& dried roses between yellow pages,

searching for an idiom
based on the color of his eyes.

4 *The Sanctimonious*

She wakes to find herself washing
the beast's wounds.
The Woman at the Well
with bare feet in compost,
emissary to the broken. She leans

her body against this born loser,
her hip into his ungodly mercy,
her hair sways with his breathing,
her mind intent on an hourglass
on a stone shelf. Bronze green.

By now, as they rock
in each other's embrace
in the cold half-light,
she knows every doubtful wish
inside his housebroken head.

5 The Vindictive

Smiley, the jailer
hums the bowstring's litany.
His pale voice breaks
into a bittersweetness,
his face no more
than a half-page
profile from a wanted poster.
The iron door eases open.
Blameful mask, memory's
notorious white glove
unstitches the heartstring.
His leaden stare tabulates
the spinal column like a throw
of the dice. Satisfied
defeat has taken root,
he smiles down at the prisoner
on the cell floor, his touch
burning like candlelight & crab lice
through black hair. Wagner's
Ring of the Nibelung
plays on radio across the corridor
& the smell of mignonette
comes through the bars. He
tightens his mystical sleephold—
a carbuncle of joy
underneath his kiss.

6 Exorcism

The beast's charisma
unravels the way a smoke flower
turns into dust. Hugging
the shadow of a broken wing
beauty & ugliness conspire.
Forced to use his weight perfectly
against himself, the beast is
transmogrified into the burden
& locked in wooden stocks
braced by a cross to bear.

O how geranium-scented melancholia
works on the body—
smell of ether, gut string
trailing lost memories.
Detached from whatever remains,
one note of bliss still burns his tongue.

7   *Epilogue: Communion*

The beast & the burden lock-step waltz. Tiger lily & screwworm,
it all adds up to this: bloodstar & molecular burning kiss. Con-
ception. The grooved sockets slip into each other, sinking into
pain, a little deeper into earth's habit. Tongue in juice meat, un-
certain conversion, cock & heart entangled, ragweed in bloom.
A single sigh of glory, the two put an armlock on each other—
matched for strength, leg over leg. Double bind & slow dance on
ball-bearing feet. Arm in arm & slipknot. Birth, death, back to
back—silent mouth against the other's ear. They sing a duet: e
pluribus unum. The spirit hinged to a single tree. No deeper
color stolen from midnight sky—they're in the same shape, as
meat collects around a bone, almost immortal, like a centaur's
future perfect dream.

Dien Cai Dau

Camouflaging the Chimera

We tied branches to our helmets.
We painted our faces & rifles
with mud from a riverbank,

blades of grass hung from the pockets
of our tiger suits. We wove
ourselves into the terrain,
content to be a hummingbird's target.

We hugged bamboo & leaned
against a breeze off the river,
slow-dragging with ghosts

from Saigon to Bangkok,
with women left in doorways
reaching in from America.
We aimed at dark-hearted songbirds.

In our way station of shadows
rock apes tried to blow our cover,
throwing stones at the sunset. Chameleons

crawled our spines, changing from day
to night: green to gold,
gold to black. But we waited
till the moon touched metal,

till something almost broke
inside us. VC struggled
with the hillside, like black silk

wrestling iron through grass.
We weren't there. The river ran
through our bones. Small animals took refuge
against our bodies; we held our breath,

ready to spring the L-shaped
ambush, as a world revolved
under each man's eyelid.

Tunnels

Crawling down headfirst into the hole,
he kicks the air & disappears.
I feel like I'm down there
with him, moving ahead, pushed
by a river of darkness, feeling
blessed for each inch of the unknown.
Our tunnel rat is the smallest man
in the platoon, in an echo chamber
that makes his ears bleed
when he pulls the trigger.
He moves as if trying to outdo
blind fish easing toward imagined blue,
pulled by something greater than life's
ambitions. He can't think about
spiders & scorpions mending the air,
or care about bats upside down
like gods in the mole's blackness.
The damp smell goes deeper
than the stench of honey buckets.
A web of booby traps waits, ready
to spring into broken stars.
Forced onward by some need,
some urge, he knows the pulse
of mysteries & diversions
like thoughts trapped in the ground.
He questions each root.
Every cornered shadow has a life
to bargain with. Like an angel
pushed against what hurts,

his globe-shaped helmet
follows the gold ring his flashlight
casts into the void. Through silver
lice, shit, maggots, & vapor of pestilence,
he goes, the good soldier,
on hands & knees, tunneling past
death sacked into a blind corner,
loving the weight of the shotgun
that will someday dig his grave.

Somewhere Near Phu Bai

The moon cuts through
night trees like a circular saw
white hot. In the guard shack
I lean on the sandbags,
taking aim at whatever.
Hundreds of blue-steel stars
cut a path, fanning out
silver for a second. If anyone's
there, don't blame me.

I count the shapes ten meters
out front, over & over, making sure
they're always there.
I don't dare blink an eye.
The white-painted backs
of the Claymore mines
like quarter-moons.
They say Victor Charlie will
paint the other sides & turn
the blast toward you.

If I hear a noise
will I push the button
& blow myself away?

The moon grazes treetops.
I count the Claymores again.
Thinking about buckshot
kneaded in the plastic C-4
of the brain, counting
sheep before I know it.

Starlight Scope Myopia

Gray-blue shadows lift
shadows onto an oxcart.

Making night work for us,
the starlight scope brings
men into killing range.

The river under Vi Bridge
takes the heart away

like the Water God
riding his dragon.
Smoke-colored

Viet Cong
move under our eyelids,

lords over loneliness
winding like coral vine through
sandalwood & lotus,

inside our lowered heads
years after this scene

ends. The brain closes
down. What looks like
one step into the trees,

they're lifting crates of ammo
& sacks of rice, swaying

under their shared weight.
Caught in the infrared,
what are they saying?

Are they talking about women
or calling the Americans

beaucoup dien cai dau?
One of them is laughing.
You want to place a finger

to his lips & say "shhhh."
You try reading ghost talk

on their lips. They say
"up-up we go," lifting as one.
This one, old, bowlegged,

you feel you could reach out
& take him into your arms. You

peer down the sights of your M-16,
seeing the full moon
loaded on an oxcart.

Red Pagoda

Our eyes on the hill,
we have to get there
somehow. Three snipers
sing out like hornets.
The red pawn's our last move—

green & yellow squares
backdropped with mangrove
swamps, something to hold to.
Hand over hand, we follow
invisible rope to nowhere,
duck-walking through grass
& nosing across the line
of no return. Remnants
of two thatch huts tremble
to heavy, running feet.
We make it to the hill,
fall down & slide rounds
into the mortar tube,
& smithereens of leaf debris
cover the snipers. Unscathed,
with arms hooked through each other's
like men on some wild
midnight-bound carousal,
in our joy, we kick
& smash the pagoda
till it's dried blood
covering the ground.

A Greenness Taller Than Gods

When we stop,
a green snake starts again
through deep branches.
Spiders mend webs we marched into.
Monkeys jabber in flame trees,
dancing on the limbs to make
fire-colored petals fall. Torch birds
burn through the dark-green day.
The lieutenant puts on sunglasses
& points to an X circled

on his map. When will we learn
to move like trees move?
The point man raises his hand *Wait!*
We've just crossed paths with VC,
branches left quivering.
The lieutenant's right hand says what to do.
We walk into a clearing that blinds.
We move like a platoon of silhouettes
balancing sledge hammers on our heads,
unaware our shadows have untied
from us, wandered off
& gotten lost.

The Dead at Quang Tri

This is harder than counting stones
along paths going nowhere, the way
a tiger circles & backtracks by
smelling his blood on the ground.
The one kneeling beside the pagoda,
remember him? Captain, we won't
talk about that. The Buddhist boy
at the gate with the shaven head
we rubbed for luck
glides by like a white moon.
He won't stay dead, dammit!
Blades aim for the family jewels;
the grass we walk on
won't stay down.

Hanoi Hannah

Ray Charles! His voice
calls from waist-high grass,
& we duck behind gray sandbags.
"Hello, Soul Brothers. Yeah,
Georgia's also on my mind."
Flares bloom over the trees.
"Here's Hannah again.
Let's see if we can't
light her goddamn fuse
this time." Artillery
shells carve a white arc
against dusk. Her voice rises
from a hedgerow on our left.
"It's Saturday night in the States.
Guess what your woman's doing tonight.
I think I'll let Tina Turner
tell you, you homesick GIs."
Howitzers buck like a herd
of horses behind concertina.
"You know you're dead men,
don't you? You're dead
as King today in Memphis.
Boys, you're surrounded by
General Tran Do's division."
Her knife-edge song cuts
deep as a sniper's bullet.
"Soul Brothers, what you dying for?"
We lay down a white-klieg
trail of tracers. Phantom jets
fan out over the trees.
Artillery fire zeros in.
Her voice grows flesh
& we can see her falling
into words, a bleeding flower.

Roll Call

Through rifle sights
we must've looked like crows
perched on a fire-eaten branch,
lined up for reveille, ready
to roll-call each M-16
propped upright
between a pair of jungle boots,
a helmet on its barrel
as if it were a man.
The perfect row aligned
with the chaplain's cross
while a metallic-gray squadron
of sea gulls circled. Only
a few lovers have blurred
the edges of this picture.
Sometimes I can hear them
marching through the house,
closing the distance. All
the lonely beds take me back
to where we saluted those
five pairs of boots
as the sun rose against our faces.

Fragging

Five men pull straws
under a tree on a hillside.
Damp smoke & mist halo them
as they single out each other,
pretending they're not there.
"We won't be wasting a real man.
That lieutenant's too gung ho.

Think, man, 'bout how Turk
got blown away; next time
it's you or me. Hell,
the truth is the truth."
Something small as a clinch pin
can hold men together,
humming their one-word
song. Yes, just a flick
of a wrist & the whole night
comes apart. "Didn't we warn him?
That bastard." "Remember, Joe,
remember how he pushed Perez?"
The five men breathe like a wave
of cicadas, their bowed heads
filled with splintered starlight.
They uncoil fast as a fist.
Looking at the ground, four
walk north, then disappear. One
comes this way, moving through
a bad dream. Slipping a finger
into the metal ring, he's married
to his devil—the spoon-shaped
handle flies off. Everything
breaks for green cover,
like a hundred red birds
released from a wooden box.

"You and I Are Disappearing"

—Björn Håkansson

The cry I bring down from the hills
belongs to a girl still burning
inside my head. At daybreak
        she burns like a piece of paper.

She burns like foxfire
in a thigh-shaped valley.
A skirt of flames
dances around her
at dusk.
        We stand with our hands
hanging at our sides,
while she burns
        like a sack of dry ice.
She burns like oil on water.
She burns like a cattail torch
dipped in gasoline.
She glows like the fat tip
of a banker's cigar,
        silent as quicksilver.
A tiger under a rainbow
   at nightfall.
She burns like a shot glass of vodka.
She burns like a field of poppies
at the edge of a rain forest.
She rises like dragonsmoke
   to my nostrils.
She burns like a burning bush
driven by a godawful wind.

2527th Birthday of the Buddha

When the motorcade rolled to a halt, Quang Duc
climbed out & sat down in the street.
He crossed his legs,
& the other monks & nuns grew around him like petals.
He challenged the morning sun,
debating with the air
he leafed through—visions brought down to earth.
Could his eyes burn the devil out of men?

A breath of peppermint oil
soothed someone's cry. Beyond terror made flesh—
he burned like a bundle of black joss sticks.
A high wind that started in California
fanned flames, turned each blue page,
leaving only his heart intact.
Waves of saffron robes bowed to the gasoline can.

Re-creating the Scene

The metal door groans
& folds shut like an ancient turtle
that won't let go
of a finger till it thunders.
The Confederate flag
flaps from a radio antenna,
& the woman's clothes
come apart in their hands.
Their mouths find hers
in the titanic darkness
of the steel grotto,
as she counts the names of dead
ancestors, shielding a baby
in her arms. The three men
ride her breath, grunting
over lovers back in Mississippi.
She floats on their rage
like a torn water flower,
defining night inside a machine
where men are gods.
The season quietly sweats.
They hold her down
with their eyes,
taking turns, piling stones
on her father's grave.

The APC rolls with curves of the land,
up hills & down into gullies,
crushing trees & grass,
droning like a constellation
of locusts eating through bamboo,
creating the motion for their bodies.

She rises from the dust
& pulls the torn garment
around her, staring after the APC
till it's small enough
to fit like a toy tank in her hands.
She turns in a circle,
pounding the samarium dust
with her feet where the steel
tracks have plowed. The sun
fizzes like a pill in a glass
of water, & for a moment
the world's future tense:
She approaches the MPs
at the gate; a captain from G-5
accosts her with candy kisses;
I inform *The Overseas Weekly*,
flashbulbs refract her face
in a room of polished brass
& spit-shined boots;
on the trial's second day
she turns into mist—
someone says money
changed hands,
& someone else swears
she's buried at LZ Gator.
But for now, the baby
makes a fist & grabs at the air,
searching for a breast.

Night Muse & Mortar Round

She shows up in every war.
Basically the same, maybe
her flowing white gown's a little less
erotic & she's more desperate.
She's always near a bridge.
This time the Perfume River.
You trace the curve in the road
& there she is

trying to flag down your jeep,
but you're a quarter-mile away
when you slam on the brakes.
Sgt. Jackson says, "What the hell
you think you're doing, Jim?"
& Lt. Adonis riding shotgun
yells, "Court-martial."

When you finally drive back
she's gone, just a feeling
left in the night air.
Then you hear the blast
rock the trees & stars
where you would've been that moment.

One More Loss to Count

"Me, I'm Chinese,"
Be Hai says.
She's the sergeant major's woman,
switching from French to English.
We talk with our eyes,
sipping Cokes in my hooch.

Days pass before she shows up again
with a shy look, not herself,
that bowed dance with her head
the Vietnamese do.
Sometimes I look up to find
her standing in the doorway,
not knowing how long
she's been there, watching me
with my earphones plugged in
to James Brown or Aretha,
her man somewhere sleeping off
another all-night drunk.
Once I asked her about family.
"Not important, GI," she said.

We all have our ghosts.
Mine are Anna's letters from L.A.
This morning Be Hai shows up
with a photograph of the sergeant major
& his blond children
back in Alabama.
For months we've dodged
each other in this room,
dancers with bamboo torches.
She clutches the snapshot like a pass
to enter an iron-spiked gate.
There's nothing else to say.
The room's caught up in our movement,
& the novel Anna sent me days ago
slides from the crowded shelf.
Like the cassette rewinding
we roll back the words in our throats.
She closes her eyes, the photograph
falls from her hand
like the ace of spades
shadowing a pale leaf.

Sappers

Opium, horse, nothing
sends anybody through concertina
this way. What is it in the brain
that so totally propels a man?
Caught with women in our heads
three hours before daybreak,
we fire full automatic
but they keep coming,
slinging satchel charges
at our bunkers. They fall
& rise again like torchbearers,
with their naked bodies
greased so moonlight dances
off their skin. They run
with explosives strapped
around their waists,
& try to fling themselves
into our arms.

Nude Pictures

I slapped him a third time.
The song caught in his throat
for a second, & the morning
came back together like after
a stone has been dropped
through a man's reflection
hiding in a river. I slapped him
again, but he wouldn't stop

laughing. As we searched
for the squad, he drew us

to him like a marsh loon
tied to its half-gone song
echoing over rice fields
& through wet elephant grass
smelling of gunpowder & fear.
I slapped him once more.

Booby-trapped pages floated
through dust. His laughter
broke off into a silence
early insects touched
with a tinge of lost music.
He grabbed my hand & wouldn't
let go. Lifted by a breeze,
a face danced in the treetops.

We Never Know

He danced with tall grass
for a moment, like he was swaying
with a woman. Our gun barrels
glowed white-hot.
When I got to him,
a blue halo
of flies had already claimed him.
I pulled the crumbled photograph
from his fingers.
There's no other way
to say this: I fell in love.
The morning cleared again,
except for a distant mortar
& somewhere choppers taking off.
I slid the wallet into his pocket
& turned him over, so he wouldn't be
kissing the ground.

A Break from the Bush

The South China Sea
drives in another herd.
The volleyball's a punching bag:
Clem's already lost a tooth
& Johnny's left eye is swollen shut.
Frozen airlifted steaks burn
on a wire grill, & miles away
machine guns can be heard.
Pretending we're somewhere else,
we play harder.
Lee Otis, the point man,
high on Buddha grass,
buries himself up to his neck
in sand. "Can you see me now?
In this spot they gonna build
a Hilton. Invest in Paradise.
Bang, bozos! You're dead."
Frenchie's cassette player
unravels Hendrix's "Purple Haze."
Snake, 17, from Daytona,
sits at the water's edge,
the ash on his cigarette
pointing to the ground
like a crooked finger. CJ,
who in three days will trip
a fragmentation mine,
runs after the ball
into the whitecaps,
laughing.

Seeing in the Dark

The scratchy sound of skin
flicks works deeper & deeper,
as mortar fire colors the night
flesh tone. The corporal at the door
grins; his teeth shiny as raw pearl,
he stands with a fist of money,
happy to see infantrymen
from the boonies—men who know
more about dodging trip wires &
seeing in the dark than they do
about women. They're in Shangri-la
gaping at washed-out images
thrown against a bedsheet.

We're men ready to be fused
with ghost pictures, trying
to keep the faces we love
from getting shuffled
with those on the wall.
Is that Hawk's tenor
coloring-in the next frame?
Three women on a round bed
coax in a German shepherd—
everything turns white as alabaster.
The picture flickers; the projector
goes dead, & we cuss the dark
& the cicadas' heavy breath.

Tu Do Street

Music divides the evening.
I close my eyes & can see

men drawing lines in the dust.
America pushes through the membrane
of mist & smoke, & I'm a small boy
again in Bogalusa. *White Only*
signs & Hank Snow. But tonight
I walk into a place where bar girls
fade like tropical birds. When
I order a beer, the mama-san
behind the counter acts as if she
can't understand, while her eyes
skirt each white face, as Hank Williams
calls from the psychedelic jukebox.
We have played Judas where
only machine-gun fire brings us
together. Down the street
black GIs hold to their turf also.
An off-limits sign pulls me
deeper into alleys, as I look
for a softness behind these voices
wounded by their beauty & war.
Back in the bush at Dak To
& Khe Sanh, we fought
the brothers of these women
we now run to hold in our arms.
There's more than a nation
inside us, as black & white
soldiers touch the same lovers
minutes apart, tasting
each other's breath,
without knowing these rooms
run into each other like tunnels
leading to the underworld.

Communiqué

Bob Hope's on stage, but we want the Gold Diggers,
want a flash of legs

through the hemorrhage of vermilion, giving us
something to kill for.

We want our hearts wrung out like rags & ground down
to Georgia dust

while Cobras drag the perimeter, gliding along the sea,
swinging searchlights

through the trees. The assault & battery of hot pink
glitter erupts

as the rock 'n' roll band tears down the night—caught
in a safety net

of brightness, The Gold Diggers convulse. White legs
shimmer like strobes.

The lead guitarist's right foot's welded to his wah wah.
"I thought you said

Aretha was gonna be here." "Man, I don't wanna see
no Miss America."

"There's Lola." The sky is blurred by magnesium flares
over the fishing boats.

"Shit, man, she looks awful white to me." We duck
when we hear the quick

metallic hiss of the mountain of amplifiers struck by
a flash of rain.

After the show's packed up & gone, after the choppers
have flown out backwards,

after the music & colors have died slowly in our heads,
& the downpour's picked up,

we sit holding our helmets like rain-polished skulls.

The Edge

When guns fall silent for an hour
or two, you can hear the cries

of women making love to soldiers.
They have an unmerciful memory

& know how to wear bright dresses
to draw a crowd, conversing

with a platoon of shadows
numbed by morphine. Their real feelings

make them break like April
into red blossoms.

Cursing themselves in ragged dreams
fire has singed the edges of,

they know a slow dying the fields have come to terms with.
Shimmering fans work against the heat

& smell of gunpowder, making money
float from hand to hand. The next moment

a rocket pushes a white fist
through night sky, & they scatter like birds

& fall into the shape their lives
have become.

"You want a girl, GI?"
"You buy me Saigon tea?"

Soldiers bring the scent of burning flesh
with them—on their clothes & in their hair,

drawn to faces in half-lit rooms.
As good-bye kisses are thrown

to the charred air, silhouettes of jets
ease over nude bodies on straw mats.

Donut Dollies

The three stood outside TOC
smiling, waiting with donuts & coffee
for the dusty-green platoon
back from a fire fight,
as the midday sun
fell through their sky-
blue dresses with Red Cross
insignias over their breasts,
like half-hearted cheerleaders.
But the GIs filed past them
with night-long tracer glare
still in their eyes
& the names of dead men
caught in their throats.
Across the hills a recoilless rifle

& mortar spoke to each other.
They followed a thousand-yard stare
until they walked out of boots & fatigues
& fled into the metal stalls
to shower off the night.
For days the donut dollies
were unable to stop shaking
their heads, like a ripple
trembling through horses.
Even back at the Officers' Club
they couldn't pull their eyes away
from the line of infantrymen
dragging their tired feet,
molded into a slow melody
inside bowed heads. They
were unable to feel the hands
slip under their uniforms & touch
money belts next to their pale skin.

Prisoners

Usually at the helipad
I see them stumble-dance
across the hot asphalt
with croaker sacks over their heads,
moving toward the interrogation huts,
thin-framed as box kites
of sticks & black silk
anticipating a hard wind
that'll tug & snatch them
out into space. I think
some must be laughing
under their dust-colored hoods,
knowing rockets are aimed
at Chu Lai, that the water's

evaporating & soon the nail
will make contact with metal.
How can anyone anywhere love
these half-broken figures
bent under the sky's brightness?
The weight they carry
is the soil we tread night & day.
Who can cry for them?
I've heard the old ones
are the hardest to break.
An arm twist, a combat boot
against the skull, a .45
jabbed into the mouth, nothing
works. When they start talking
with ancestors faint as camphor
smoke in pagodas, you know
you'll have to kill them
to get an answer.
Sunlight throws
scythes against the afternoon.
Everything's a heat mirage; a river
tugs at their slow feet.
I stand alone & amazed,
with a pill-happy door gunner
signaling for me to board the Cobra.
One day, I almost bowed
to such figures walking toward me,
& I can't say why.
From a half-mile away
trees huddle together,
& the prisoners look like
marionettes hooked to strings of light.

Jungle Surrender

after Don Cooper's painting

Ghosts share us with the past & future
but we struggle to hold on to each breath.

Moving toward what waits behind the trees,
the prisoner goes deeper into himself, away

from how a man's heart divides him, deeper
into the jungle's indigo mystery & beauty,

with both hands raised into the air, only
surrendering halfway: the small man inside

waits like a photo in a shirt pocket, refusing
to raise his hands, silent & uncompromising

as the black scout dog beside him. Love & hate
flesh out the real man, how he wrestles

himself through a hallucination of blues
& deep purples that set the day on fire.

He sleepwalks a labyrinth of violet,
measuring footsteps from one tree to the next,

knowing we're all somehow connected.
What would I have said?

The real interrogator is a voice within.
I would have told them about my daughter

in Phoenix, how young she was,
about my first woman, anything

but how I helped ambush two Viet Cong
while plugged into the Grateful Dead.

For some, a soft windy voice makes them
snap. Blues & purples. Some place between

central Georgia & Tay Ninh Province—
the vision of a knot of blood unravels

& parts of us we dared put into the picture
come together; the prisoner goes away

almost whole. But he will always touch
fraying edges of things, to feel hope break

like the worm that rejoins itself
under the soil . . . head to tail.

Eyeball Television

He sits crouched in a hole
covered with slats of bamboo,
recalling hundreds of faces
from *I Love Lucy, Dragnet,*
I Spy, & The Ed Sullivan Show.
A pinhole of light tells
when day comes. Sound
reaches him like honeybees
trapped in a boy's Coke bottle.
When he can't stop laughing
at *Roadrunner* on Channel 6
the sharp pain goes away.
Holding the world in focus
in his solitary cell, he sees
Spike Jones' one-man band

explode. Two minutes later
Marilyn Monroe is nude
on a round white sofa
that dissolves into a cloud.
Shaking his head to get her pose
right again, he finds himself
pushing vertical & horizontal hold
buttons, but only Liberace's
piano eases into the disconnected
landscape. He hears deliberate,
heavy footsteps of the guards
coming for him. The picture
fades into the sound of urine
dripping on his forehead,
as he tries to read the lips of Walter Cronkite.

The One-legged Stool

Semidarkness. A black POW is seated on a one-legged stool. He looks all round, slowly stands, then lets the stool hit the dirt floor. He's in a state of delirium, partly hallucinating. Periodically a shadow of a face appears at the peephole in the door.

You didn't see that. My stool never touched the floor, guard. I'm still sitting on my stool. It's all in your head. Would you just drag me out into the compound, then put a bullet through my brains for nothing? Do you call that honor? I never left my stool! It never touched the fucking floor! Look, I've been sitting here hypnotized by dawn crawling under the door like a bamboo viper. (*Pause.*) Sometimes there's a distant bird singing just for me. That's right. Just for me. I sit here on this one-legged stool, watching your eyes pressed against the face-window. Don't you know I'll never cooperate? No, don't care what you whisper into the darkness of this cage like it came out of my own head, I won't believe a word. Lies, lies, lies. You're lying. Those white prisoners didn't say what you say they said. They ain't laughing. Ain't cooperating. They ain't putting me down, calling me names like you say. Lies. Lies. It ain't the way you say it is. I'm American. (*Pause.*) Doctor King, he ain't dead like you say. Lies. How many times are you trying to kill me? Twice, three times, four, how many? You can't break me. Drops of water beating on my head for weeks, that didn't work. Bamboo under my fingernails, that didn't work either. The month I laid cramped in that body-cave of yours, with a pain running through me like a live wire, that didn't make me talk into your microphone. (*Pause.*) What you say? You gook, dink, slant-eyed sloe! That's right. I can get nasty too, just as cruel, you bastard. Standing there with your face in the window like a yellow moon that never goes down. I can give the devil hell. I can be Don Quixote fighting fields of windmills. You should've seen me at Khe Sanh! You think you're bad? Shit. Our machine gunner, Johnson, a kid we called Chi, he got hit. I took his M-60, walked that burning hill for a solid straight hour with the Pig. Charles didn't know what to do. I was dancing, swaying with that machine gun. (*Pause.*) You didn't see that. The hand's quicker than the eye. You didn't see that. I'm still sitting on my stool. I sleep, I live her on my damn stool. (*Pause.*) You've pitted me against them. Against those white troops over there behind those trees. I only half hear their voices through these bamboo walls. For my good, huh? You really think I believe that shit? I know how to protect myself, you can bet your life on that. I also know your games, VC. Anything to break a man, right? Anything to grind his mind to dust. But I know how to walk out of a nightmare backwards. I can survive. When you kicked me awake, then back into a stupor, did I break? Maybe I slipped back a few feet deeper into the darkness, but I didn't break. Maybe I pulled back into myself. Pulled back till there's nowhere to go. Sometimes it's like holding back a flood, but I'm still sanding here. Crouched in this place, just listening to my stupid heart. With you always two steps away, always so goddamn close, listening to my thoughts. Sometimes I can hear empty locust shells crack under my feet when I was a boy, but I'm not broken yet. (*Pause.*) I wasn't scratching for earthworms. I was sitting here, not batting an eyelid. I wasn't sniffing the ground like a dog on all fours. That wasn't me. Your eyes must be tricking you or something. Watch this. Do you see that dung beetle? Look! You see, the hands are quicker than the eyes. You didn't see me eat that bug, did you? No, don't think about how the dampness in here hurts. Just concentrate. (*Roars with laughter.*) You know what I was thinking? I was thinking a hundred ways I could bury you. Charlie, you can kill me, you can turn me into an animal, you can make me wish I was never born, but you can't break me. I won't cooperate. (*Pause.*) You didn't see that. I'm still sitting here on my stool. Name, rank— Sergeant First Class Thomas J. Washington. Serial number— 321–45–9876. Mission—try to keep alive. (*Pause.*) Yeah, VC. I've been through Georgia. Yeah, been through 'Bama too. Mississippi, yeah. You know what? You eye me worse than those rednecks. They used to look at me in my uniform like I didn't belong in it. (*Struts around in a circle.*) I'd be sharper than sharp. My jump boots spit-shined till my face was lost in them. You could cut your fingers on the creases in my khakis. My brass, my ribbons, they would make their blood boil. They'd turn away, cursing through their teeth. With your eyes pressed against the face-window, you're like a white moon over Stone Mountain. You're everywhere. All I have to go back to are faces just like yours at the door.

Short-timer's Calendar

Like a benediction of blue
feathers, minutes & seconds
moved me beyond who I was
before I knew I could snap,
seeing each hour worked down to salt
under a white grinding stone.
I'd lie awake listening to insects
closing another season,

& recounting tick marks
on the back of a lover's photograph—
where *now* meets *then*. Another day
gone, a few more young faces
dissolving from the formation.
Sometimes I wrestled their ghosts
in my sleep, with the Southern Cross
balanced on a branch weighing a cloud
of sparrows. Back in August
Sarge said, "If you want to stay
in one piece, don't hang around
short-timers. They just trip
over booby traps." It was like playing
tic-tac-toe with God. Each *x,*
a stitch holding breath together,
a map that went nowhere—
like lies told to trees.
I watched them grow into an ink blot,
an omen, a sign the dead could read.

Thanks

Thanks for the tree
between me & a sniper's bullet.
I don't know what made the grass
sway seconds before the Viet Cong
raised his soundless rifle.
Some voice always followed,
telling me which foot
to put down first.
Thanks for deflecting the ricochet
against that anarchy of dusk.
I was back in San Francisco
wrapped up in a woman's wild colors,
causing some dark bird's love call
to be shattered by daylight

when my hands reached up
& pulled a branch away
from my face. Thanks
for the vague white flower
that pointed to the gleaming metal
reflecting how it is to be broken
like mist over the grass,
as we played some deadly
game for blind gods.
What made me spot the monarch
writhing on a single thread
tied to a farmer's gate,
holding the day together
like an unfingered guitar string,
is beyond me. Maybe the hills
grew weary & leaned a little in the heat.
Again, thanks for the dud
hand grenade tossed at my feet
outside Chu Lai. I'm still
falling through its silence.
I don't know why the intrepid
sun touched the bayonet,
but I know that something
stood among those lost trees
& moved only when I moved.

To Have Danced with Death

The black sergeant first class
who stalled us on the ramp
didn't kiss the ground either.

When two hearses sheened up to the plane
& government silver-gray coffins
rolled out on silent chrome coasters,

did he feel better? The empty left leg
of his trousers shivered as another hearse
with shiny hubcaps inched from behind a building . . .

his three rows of ribbons rainbowed
over the forest of faces through
plate glass. Afternoon sunlight

made surgical knives out of chrome
& brass. He half smiled when
the double doors opened for him

like a wordless mouth taking black promises.
The room of blue eyes averted his.
He stood there, searching

his pockets for something:
maybe a woman's name & number
worn thin as a Chinese fortune.

I wanted him to walk ahead,
to disappear through glass,
to be consumed by music

that might move him like Sandman Sims,
but he merely rocked on his good leg
like a bleak & soundless bell.

Report from the Skull's Diorama

Dr. King's photograph
comes at me from *White Nights*
like Hoover's imagination at work,

dissolving into a scenario
at Firebase San Juan Hill:
our chopper glides in closer,
down to the platoon of black GIs
back from night patrol

with five dead. Down
into a gold whirl of leaves
dust-deviling the fire base.
A field of black trees
stakes down the morning sun.

With the chopper blades
knife-fighting the air,
yellow leaflets quiver
back to the ground, clinging to us.
These men have lost their tongues,

but the red-bordered
leaflets tell us
*VC didn't kill
Dr. Martin Luther King.*
The silence etched into their skin

is also mine. Psychological
warfare colors the napalmed hill
gold-yellow. When our gunship
flies out backwards, rising
above the men left below

to blend in with the charred
landscape, an AK-47
speaks, with the leaflets
clinging to the men & stumps,
waving to me across the years.

Combat Pay for Jody

I counted trip flares
the first night at Cam Ranh Bay,
& the molten whistle of a rocket
made me sing her name into my hands.
I needed to forget the sea
between us, the other men.
Her perfume still crawled
my brain like a fire moth,
& it took closing a dead man's eyes
to bring the war's real smell
into my head. The quick fire
danced with her nude reflection,
& I licked an envelope each month
to send blood money,
kissing her lipstick mouth-prints
clustering the perfumed paper,
as men's voices collected
in the gray weather I inhaled.
Her lies saved me that year.
I rushed to the word
Love at the bottom of a page.
One day, knowing a letter waited,
I took the last chopper back to Chu Lai,
an hour before the fire base was overrun
by NVA. Satchel charges
blew away the commander's bunker,
& his men tried to swim the air.
A week later when I returned
to Phoenix, the city hid her
shadow & I couldn't face myself
in the mirror. I asked her used-to-be
if it was just my imagination,
since I'd heard a man
could be boiled down to his deeds.
He smiled over his wine glass

& said, "It's more, man.
Your money bought my new Chevy."

Sunset Threnody

She's here again. There
leaning against the basement
window where the sun
crouches like a tiger.
Shaking the ice in her glass
to beckon the waitress
for another Tom Collins,
she knows an old wound starts to tingle
close to the heart.

Midwestern prom queen,
Army nurse, now working
the graveyard shift at St. Luke's
emergency ward, sweet thing
for every Vietnam vet.
How many faces are hers?
I've unhealed myself
for her eyes.

All the close calls
are inside my head
bright as a pinball machine,
& I'm a man fighting
with myself. Yes, no,
yes. I'm crouched there
in that same grassy gully
watching medevac choppers
glide along the edge
of the South China Sea,
down to where men run

with a line of green canvas
stretchers as twilight sinks
into the waves. I'm still
there & halfway to her
table where she sits
holding the sun
in her icy glass.

After the Fall

An afternoon storm has hit
the Pearl of the Orient
& stripped nearly everybody.
Bandoliers, miniskirts, tennis shoes,
fatigue jackets, combat boots—
city colors are bruised & polyester
suits limp down side streets.
Even the ragpicker is glad
to let his Australian bush hat
with the red feather float away.

Something deeper than sadness
litters the alleys like the insides
kicked out of pillows.
The old mama-san who always
collected scraps of yellow paper,
cigarette butts, & matchsticks
through field-stripped years
hides under her cardboard box.
Cowboys park new Harleys
along Lam Son Square

& disappear with gold in their mouths.
Dzung leaves the Continental Hotel
in a newspaper dress.

Hoping for a hard rain,
she moves through broken colors
flung to the ground,
mixing up the words to Trinh's
"Mad Girl's Love Song"
& "Stars Fell on Alabama,"
trying to bite off her tongue.

Saigon Bar Girls, 1975

You're among them
        washing off makeup
    & slipping into peasant clothes
        the color of soil.
            Chu nom lotus
rooted in singing blood,
    I know your story
        molded from ashes
        into a balled fist
            hidden in raw silk.
You're on Tu Do Street
    with whores. Unmirrored,
            they sigh & forget
        their lists of Mikes,
                        Bills, Joes, & Johns,
    as they shed miniskirts
        thinner than memories
denied, letting them fall
            into a hush
        at their feet—
        French perfume
pale as history, reverie
        of cloth like smoke rings
    blown at an electric fan.

Ho Xuan Huong,
 you can now speak.
  Those Top 40 hits
have been given to a gale
  moving out to sea,
    no match
for your voice shiny as a knife
against bamboo shoots.
  Bar girls give you
   their hard-earned stories
    & you pay them
    with green shadows
dancing nude around egrets
in paddies where lovers died.
    They stand like Lot's wife
     at plaintive windows
     or return to home villages
      as sleepwalkers, leaving
sloe gin glasses
kissed with lipstick.

Boat People

After midnight they load up.
A hundred shadows move about blindly.
Something close to sleep
hides low voices drifting
toward a red horizon. Tonight's
a black string, the moon's pull—
this boat's headed somewhere.
Lucky to have gotten past
searchlights low-crawling the sea,
like a woman shaking water
from her long dark hair.

Twelve times in three days
they've been lucky,
clinging to each other in gray mist.
Now Thai fishermen gaze out across
the sea as it changes color,
hands shading their eyes
the way sailors do,
minds on robbery & rape.
Sunlight burns blood-orange.

Storm warnings crackle on a radio.
The Thai fishermen turn away.
Not enough water for the trip.
The boat people cling to each other,
faces like yellow sea grapes,
wounded by doubt & salt.
Dusk hangs over the water.
Seasick, they daydream Jade Mountain
a whole world away, half-drunk
on what they hunger to become.

Bui Doi, Dust of Life

You drifted from across the sea
under a carmine moon,
framed now in my doorway
by what I tried to forget.
Curly-headed & dark-skinned,
you couldn't escape
eyes taking you apart.
Come here, son, let's see
if they castrated you.

Those nights I held your mother
against me like a half-broken

shield. The wind's refrain
etched my smile into your face—
is that how you found me?
You were born disappearing.
You followed me, blameless
as a blackbird in Hue
singing from gutted jade.

Son, you were born with dust
on your eyelids, but you bloomed up
in a trench where stones were
stacked to hold you down.
With only your mother's name,
you've inherited the inchworm's
foot of earth. *Bui doi.*
I blow the dust off my hands
but it flies back in my face.

Missing in Action

Men start digging in the ground,
propping shadows against trees
outside Hanoi, but there aren't
enough bones for a hash pipe.
After they carve new names
into polished black stone,
we throw dust to the wind
& turn faces to blank walls.

Names we sing in sleep & anger
cling to willows like river mist.
We splice voices on tapes
but we can't make one man
walk the earth again.
Not a single song comes alive
in the ring of broken teeth

on the ground. Sunlight
presses down for an answer.
But nothing can make that C-130
over Hanoi come out of its spin,
spiraling like a flare in green sky.

After the flag's folded,
the living fall
into each other's arms.
They've left spaces
trees can't completely fill.
Pumping breath down tunnels
won't help us bring ghosts
across the sea.

Peasants outside Pakse City
insist the wildflowers
have changed colors.
They're what the wind
& rain have taken back,
what love couldn't recapture.
Now less than a silhouette
grown into the parrot perch,
this one died looking up at the sky.

Losses

After Nam he lost himself,
   not trusting his hands
      with loved ones.

His girlfriend left,
    & now he scouts the edge of town,
      always with one ear

cocked & ready to retreat,
   to blend with hills, poised
      like a slipknot

becoming a noose.
   Unlike punji stakes,
      his traps only snag the heart.

Sometimes he turns in a circle
   until a few faces from Dak To
      track him down.

A dress or scarf in the distance
   can nail him to a dogwood.
      Down below, to his left,

from where the smog rises,
   a small voice reaches his ear
      somehow. No, never mind—

he's halfway back, closer to a ravine,
   going deeper into saw vines,
      in behind White Cove,

following his mind like a dark lover,
   away from car horns & backfire
      where only days are stolen.

Between Days

Expecting to see him anytime
coming up the walkway
through blueweed & bloodwort,
she says, "That closed casket
was weighed down with stones."

The room is as he left it
fourteen years ago, everything
freshly dusted & polished
with lemon oil. The uncashed
death check from Uncle Sam
marks a passage in the Bible
on the dresser, next to the photo
staring out through the window.
"Mistakes. Mistakes. Now,
he's gonna have to give them this
money back when he gets home.
But I wouldn't. I would
let them pay for their mistakes.
They killed his daddy, & Janet,
she & her three children
by three different men, I hope
he's strong enough to tell her
to get lost. Lord, mistakes."
His row of tin soldiers
lines the window sill. The sunset
flashes across them like a blast.
She's buried the Silver Star
& the flag under his winter clothes.
The evening's first fireflies
dance in the air like distant tracers.
Her chair faces the walkway
where she sits before the TV
asleep, as the screen dissolves
into days between snow.

Facing It

My black face fades,
hiding inside the black granite.
I said I wouldn't

dammit: No tears.
I'm stone. I'm flesh.
My clouded reflection eyes me
like a bird of prey, the profile of night
slanted against morning. I turn
this way—the stone lets me go.
I turn that way—I'm inside
the Vietnam Veterans Memorial
again, depending on the light
to make a difference.
I go down the 58,022 names,
half-expecting to find
my own in letters like smoke.
I touch the name Andrew Johnson;
I see the booby trap's white flash.
Names shimmer on a woman's blouse
but when she walks away
the names stay on the wall.
Brushstrokes flash, a red bird's
wings cutting across my stare.
The sky. A plane in the sky.
A white vet's image floats
closer to me, then his pale eyes
look through mine. I'm a window.
He's lost his right arm
inside the stone. In the black mirror
a woman's trying to erase names:
No, she's brushing a boy's hair

February in Sydney

Under the Harbour Bridge

America rhymes with Australia
as I watch the Southern Cross's
sequins fall. Fruit bats
& rifle birds brush
the sky vermilion & banksias
flare slow torches helping me to see
my blues on your canvas.
After Tooheys at the Fortune of War,
earth colors lead us to where
eyes edge along fault lines,
following us to the margin
to discover masks are faces
worn against such wistful nights.
The Ferris wheel blinks off
like St. Elmo's fire,
making the stars burn deeper.
Our hands blur over each other
as the last train to Wahroonga
rolls overhead like a thunderstorm
shaking the sandstone pillars.
When silence returns, it's three
times greater. The rise & fall
of waves, the rise & fall . . .
down at Pier One a woman's voice
bruises the air. Wherever I go
I find people who hurt
each other to feel alive.
Just when this shaky flotilla
is anchored by unhappiness,
an unseen hand lets years escape,
drawing us into Dreamtime, as spring
pulls us to the ground for a kiss.

The Man Who Carries the Desert
Around Inside Himself: For Wally

Desert dreamer, telepathic
sleepwalker over shifting sand,
your grandfather's on the last postcard
I airmailed to my mother.
Though he sees truer than you
this grog-scented night,
you remain in that skull-white landscape
like a figure burned into volcanic rock.
Reading footprints, straining not to walk
out of your body, you leave
a piece of yourself everywhere
you go, following some explorer's
sluggish boots like a slowmotion machine
stamping its imprint.
No rain for years, still
the labyrinth takes you home
to Alice Springs where gods
speak through blue-tongued lizards
& lost people become vivid
as Nosepeg's song cycles,
beyond wind-carved dunes
like humpback whales on the seafloor.
Atrocities of brightness
grow into a map of deaths
spread out like stars
as you read the debris
left by the sun & crows
where secret campsites
show through porcupine grass.
A cutting wind rides you down
like bushrangers, but you know
how to wrap your arms around
an anthill holding the midday
inside. Out of nothing

a slow rain glistens against silence
whispering to ghosts. Now
it's safe to cry away anger.
For you, the city's skyline
extends a lifetime into night.
Like spontaneous combustion, already
a wildfire of flowers
marches over the sand.

Rocks Push

A drizzle hangs in the air
like a torn photograph
of three or four tough guys
pieced together inside my head.
They ease up from the emulsion
of silver halides, with faith
in what lives under the whitewash
brushed over plague buildings.

Rocks Push, razor gang—
my imagination fires up
its black engine, & the car
creeping down a sidestreet
doesn't exist if I say so.
A foghorn shatters the stillness.
Everything's covered by a fine mist
from Fort Denison to the Observatory.

Faces play hide & seek, white & wet
as sandblasted gargoyles peering out of
the heart's rainy darkness.
Outside The Lord Nelson,
the night's festooned with play things
that swallow a man's spirit

& leave him dancing with silhouettes
till he falls drunk among roses.

Streetlights burn gauzy
& dim as Hell's Kitchen.
Cockney accents come with the wind.
I'm ready to turn my pockets inside out
& tell them I'm broke, that I'm as poor
& alone. Unwanted,
& a need to prove something to
women with corsets thrown on beds

lit by oil lamps, they bring back
trophies & stories of another's fear.
Did they forsee the flash of butterfly
knives in the hands of skinheads
bludgeoning the western suburbs?
East End
 Blackpool
  Woolloomooloo,
each blade sings about desire.

The Plea

Round about midnight
 the clock's ugly stare
hangs in mental repose
 & its antimagnetic second hand
measures a man's descent.
 The bottom falls out
of each dream—the silver spike
 in my hands & I'm on the floor.
The Alice in Malice
 does a little soft shoe
on my troubled heart.

Hot & heavy,
cool & cosmic honeydripper
    fingers play the missing notes
inbetween life & death
    round midnight. Lost
lovers in my empty doorway
    groove to a sweet pain
in the bruise-colored neon
    where my soul weaves
itself into *terra incognita*,
    into the blue & green
sounds of Botany Bay
    reflected like rozellas
through the big, black
    slow dance of waves grinding
against the shore. Thelonious
    & bright as that golden plea
of gospel under everything
    Monk wrung from the keys.
Round about midnight
    despair returns each minute
like a drop of moonshine
    elongating into rapture
moaned through Bird's mouthpiece
    in a soundproof room
where trust & love
    is white dust on the dark
furniture. Time is nothing
    but an endless bridge.
All those who thought
    they could use my body
for nowhere's roadmap
    I see their blank faces
float up from the whirlpool
    as the turntable spins.
Each undying note resounds.
    There's a cry in every pocket
& low swell of unhappy
    lust I've suffered,

& round about midnight the odor of sex
    & salvation quivers in each song
the wooden hammers
    strike from wire strings
like anger stolen back
    from the soil.

When Loneliness Is a Man

Laughing, with a TV's blue-static figures
    dancing through the air at 2 A.M.
with eight empty beer bottles lined up
    on the kitchen table, a full moon
gazing through the opened back door,
    his thick fingers drumming the pink
laminex, singing along with a rock video
    of soft porno, recounting dead friends
with a tally of his mistakes
    in front of him, after he's punched
the walls & refrigerator with his fist,
    unable to forget childhood's lonely
grass & nameless flowers & insects,
    crying for his black cat
hit by a car, drawing absent faces
    on the air with his right index finger,
rethinking lost years of a broken marriage
    like a wrecked ship inside a green bottle,
puffing a horn-shaped ceramic pipe,
    dragging his feet across the floor
in a dance with the shadow of a tree
    on a yellow wall, going to the wooden fence
to piss under the sky's marsupial stare,
    walking back in to pop the cap
on his last beer, hugging himself awake,
    picking up a dried wishbone

from the table & snapping it, cursing the world,
    softly whispering his daughter's name,
he disturbs the void that is
    heavy as the heart's clumsy logbook.

A Quality of Light

Two women in their twenties do a drunken
waltz. One wears a black
dress, opalescent under
the afternoon's ultraviolet,
& the other is in a see-
through sheath, curved
against the weak cloth,
crying, "Oh, is the Pope
here? Is he? Is he here?"
Four motorcycle cops
speed to a halt in shiny
leather & chrome glare.
She moves to a music
we touch in ourselves
sometimes, with her friend
shadowing her like a half-
forgotten thought. The sky
gleams off pails filled
with fresh-cut flowers.
Shopkeepers leave unbagged
apples & uncrated pears
to ripen in their sweet skins.

Italian,
Spanish, Greek.
Her white dress
sways in the heat,
merging with the Pope's
robe like metaphysics
& flesh. Innocence,
vulgarity, temptation,
spectacle, or what?
Hours later in bed,
I strain to hear him
say the word *Peace*
from his bulletproof
Popemobile, but only
the moon peers around
a corner of the window-
shade, transparent
as the dress, like a page
held up to sunlight
till it burns.

Gerry's Jazz

At fourteen you crawl through a hole
in the wall where they slip sly grog
into Ollie Ward's Maxine Cabaret,
& listen to a band play for gangsters.
You're on your way to Tom Ugly's
& El Rocco, & the guns on tables

can't stop you. Something
takes back part of childhood pain,
riding out long hours behind the trap
as the sonorous high hat
clicks a fraction between the cracks,
& then you're off on a trip:

Gene Krupa's *Wire Brush Stomp*
rains over the kit & sizzles like a tinroof
after you hired a blacksmith
to hammer a cymbol into shape.
You rap sticks against it & sound travels
through everyone like rings of water.

Cocky & skillful, you go
into a groove & dance the true pivot,
playing for jitterbug
contests at Katoomba & the Trocadero.
Going deeper into each song,
you rattle keys like Houdini locked in a trunk,

bending within a black echo.
"The difference
between the difference
is the difference," you holler
to a full moon hanging over
the steel mills of Wollongong.

Like an unknown voice rising
out of flesh, each secret
is buried beneath the skin,
& you feel they try to pick
your brain for them, to find
the rhythm of your heart,

as you swear the beat is stolen from the sea.
With empty flagons beside you at Fisherman's Bay,
you pat *Out of the Afternoon* upon your leg,
knowing you'll ride hope
till it's nothing but a shiny bone
under heavy light.

Boxing Day

> *"Burns never landed a blow.*
> *It was hopeless, preposterous, heroic."*
> —Jack London

This is where Jack Johnson
cornered Tommy Burns in 1908.
Strong as an ironbark
tree, he stood there
flexing his biceps
till he freed
the prisoner under his skin.
        The bell clanged
        & a profusion of voices
        shook the afternoon. Johnson
        jabbed with the power
        of an engine throwing a rod,
        & Burns sleepwalked
        to the spinning edge
of the planet like a moth
drawn to a burning candle.

He was dizzy as a drunken girl
tangoing with a flame tree
breaking into full bloom,
burdened by fruits of desire
& the smell of carnival.
	A currawong crossed the sun
	singing an old woman's cry.
	The referee threw in his towel
	in the fourteenth round & bookies
	scribbled numbers beside names
	madly, as twenty thousand rose
	into the air like a wave.
For years the razor-gang boys
bragged about how they would've KOed
Johnson, dancing & punching each day.
Eighty years later, the stadium's
checkered with tennis courts,
a plantation of pale suits
called White City.
	I hear Miles Davis' trumpet
	& Leadbelly's "Titanic."
	A bell's metal treble
	reverberates . . . the sunset
	moves like a tremble of muscle
	across Rushcutters Bay,
	back to the name Johnson
flashing over the teletype
when he danced The Eagle Rock,
drove fast cars & had a woman
on each arm, to Jesse Willard
pushing him down into a whirlpool's
death roll under white
confetti & cheers in Havana.

Protection of Moveable Cultural Heritage

Time-polished skulls of Yagan & Pemulwy
sit in a glass cage wired to a burglar alarm
in Britain, but the jaws of these two
resistance leaders haven't been broken
into a lasting grin for the empire.

Under fluorescent lamps they're crystal balls
into which one can gaze & see the past.
With eyes reflected into empty sockets
through the glass, I can't stop reading
an upside-down newspaper

headlining Klaus Barbie, Karl Linnas
& Bernhard Goetz. The skulls sit
like wax molds for Fear & Anger—
beheaded body-songs lament & recall
how windy grass once sang to the feet.

Now, staring from their display case,
they still govern a few broken hearts
wandering across the Nullarbor Plain.
Killed fighting for love of birthplace
under a sky ablaze with flying foxes

& shiny crows, they remember the weight
of chains inherited from the fathers
of bushrangers, how hatred runs into
the soul like red veins in the eye
or thin copper threads through money.

A Delicate Conspiracy

Our eyes meet: kookaburra
    & prey weaving through
a make-believe paradise
    outside the ANZ
Bank. Fourteen, fifteen, sixteen?
    Trapped like a pale moth
inside a naked globe,
    she reduces me to a three-minute chase
scene in her head. Anybody
    but herself in The Cross,
she's an envelope stuffed with hush money
    & torn open.
Having etched a tincture of darkness
    into herself, she's still pretty
as Sophia Loren, but I'm not interested
    in the soft music
she makes for strangers. Tonight
    I feel so mortal,
knowing desire only partly heals the spleen
    & one step is the blue
abyss. A pattern of stars
    cut into the black
dress she wears—a work of art
    by how it fits her.
She tries to look eighteen. Lipstick
    & polished nails,
dragging on a Kool slowly. I wish
    I could cut the thread
anchoring down her dreamworld.
    But she knows some guy
will walk over like a retired banker
    & whisper into her ear,
& she'll drift down the block
    like Psyche's persona,
her skin making the stars
    shine.

The Cops Call Him Charlie

An olive grove's his only country.
Without family or friends, fifty
years after the woman on the wharf
waved to him & the roots of acacia
embraced her, this old Greek's
moored in the tropic of Capricorn.
He digs into a sandpile
street workers left for Monday,
gazing at the faces of women
dodging confusion & wet cement.
They spin from the weight of his eyes.
His dirty clothes & grimy hands
flag down three petty officials
who write in their notebooks
& leave him talking to a lamppost.
Shoeless, with smudged eyeglasses
posed on an orange beanie,
he moves to the middle of the street
& leans on a shovel, surveying the scene
like a foreman, as cars screech & burn
rubber around him. I walk away, afraid,
wondering if we suffer the same illness:
Seeing without having to look.

Frank's Poem

In my mind, a curved tool
burns through crooked branches,
but you show me the marks
time & white ants
left inside the cylinder

of kerosene wood.
You place your lips to it
like a man who fears the unknown,
& circular breathe to unearth
sounds of some extinct totem

described by an old man
who died years ago.
Suddenly a monumental white noise
steals the quiet that brings
your night animal to life,

& you whisper the kadaitcha
in his shoes of emu feathers
might point the bone at your ribcage
for playing a didjeridoo
in city streets. Frank,

you can't say your other name,
unable to read rocks
& gum trees, born
between three worlds
like an unfinished man.

Blue Light Lounge Sutra for the Performance Poets at Harold Park Hotel

the need gotta be
so deep words can't
answer simple questions
all night long notes
stumble off the tongue
& color the air indigo
so deep fragments of gut
& flesh cling to the song

you gotta get into it
so deep salt crystallizes on eyelashes
the need gotta be
so deep you can vomit up ghosts
& not feel broken
till you are no more
than a half ounce of gold
in painful brightness
you gotta get into it
blow that saxophone
so deep all the sex & dope in this world
can't erase your need
to howl against the sky
the need gotta be
so deep you can't
just wiggle your hips
& rise up out of it
chaos in the cosmos
modern man in the pepperpot
you gotta get hooked
into every hungry groove
so deep the bomb locked
in rust opens like a fist
into it into it so deep
rhythm is pre-memory
the need gotta be basic
animal need to see
& know the terror
we are made of honey
cause if you wanna dance
this boogie be ready
to let the devil use your head
for a drum.

February in Sydney

Dexter Gordon's tenor sax
plays "April in Paris"
inside my head all the way back
on the bus from Double Bay.
Round Midnight, the '50s,
cool cobblestone streets
resound footsteps of Bebop
musicians with whiskey-laced voices
from a boundless dream in French.
Bud, Prez, Webster, & The Hawk,
their names run together riffs.
Painful gods jive talk through
bloodstained reeds & shiny brass
where music is an anesthetic.
Unreadable faces from the human void
float like torn pages across the bus
windows. An old anger drips into my throat,
& I try thinking something good,
letting the precious bad
settle to the salty bottom.
Another scene keeps repeating itself:
I emerge from the dark theatre,
passing a woman who grabs her red purse
& hugs it to her like a heart attack.
Tremolo. Dexter comes back to rest
behind my eyelids. A loneliness
lingers like a silver needle
under my black skin,
as I try to feel how it is
to scream for help through a horn.

Magic City

Venus's-flytraps

I am five,
   Wading out into deep
     Sunny grass,
Unmindful of snakes
   & yellowjackets, out
     To the yellow flowers
Quivering in sluggish heat.
   Don't mess with me
     'Cause I have my Lone Ranger
Six-shooter. I can hurt
   You with questions
     Like silver bullets.
The tall flowers in my dreams are
   Big as the First State Bank,
     & they eat all the people
Except the ones I love.
   They have women's names,
     With mouths like where
Babies come from. I am five,
   I'll dance for you
     If you close your eyes. No
Peeping through your fingers.
   I don't supposed to be
     This close to the tracks.
One afternoon I saw
   What a train did to a cow.
     Sometimes I stand so close
I can see the eyes
   Of men hiding in boxcars.
     Sometimes they wave
& holler for me to get back. I laugh
   When trains make the dogs
     Howl. Their ears hurt.
I also know bees
   Can't live without flowers.

I wonder why Daddy
Calls Mama honey.
  All the bees in the world
    Live in little white houses
Except the ones in these flowers.
  All sticky & sweet inside.
    I wonder what death tastes like.
Sometimes I toss the butterflies
  Back into the air.
    I wish I knew why
The music in my head
  Makes me scared.
    But I know things
I don't supposed to know.
  I could start walking
    & never stop.
These yellow flowers
  Go on forever.
    Almost to Detroit.
Almost to the sea.
  My mama says I'm a mistake.
    That I made her a bad girl.
My playhouse is underneath
  Our house, & I hear people
    Telling each other secrets.

The Whistle

1

The seven o'clock whistle
Made the morning air fulvous
With a metallic syncopation,
A key to a door in the sky—opening
& closing flesh. The melody
Men & women built lives around,

Sonorous as the queen bee's fat
Hum drawing workers from flowers,
Back to the colonized heart.
A titanous puff of steam rose
From the dragon trapped below
Iron, bricks & wood.
The whole black machine
Shuddered, blue jays & redbirds
Wove light through leaves
& something dead under the foundation
Brought worms to life.
Men capped their thermoses,
Switched off Loretta Lynn,
& slid from trucks & cars.
The rip saws throttled
& swung out over logs
On conveyer belts.
Daddy lifted the tongs
To his right shoulder . . . a winch
Uncoiled the steel cable
From its oily scrotum;
He waved to the winchman
& iron teeth bit into pine.
Yellow forklifts darted
With lumber to boxcars
Marked for distant cities.
At noon, Daddy would walk
Across the field of goldenrod
& mustard weed, the pollen
Bright & sullen on his overalls.
He'd eat on our screened-in
Back porch –red beans & rice
With ham hocks & cornbread.
Lemonade & peach jello.

The one o'clock bleat
Burned sweat & salt into afternoon
& the wheels within wheels
Unlocked again, pulling rough boards

Into the plane's pneumatic grip.
Wild geese moved like a wedge
Between sky & sagebrush,
As Daddy pulled the cable
To the edge of the millpond
& sleepwalked cypress logs.
The day turned on its axle
& pyramids of russet sawdust
Formed under corrugated
Blowpipes fifty feet high.
The five o'clock whistle
Bellowed like a bull, controlling
Clocks on kitchen walls;
Women dabbed loud perfume
Behind their ears & set tables
Covered with flowered oilcloth.

2

When my father was kicked by the foreman,
He booted him back,
& his dreams slouched into an aftershock
Of dark women whispering
To each other. Like petals of a black rose
In one of Busby Berkeley's
Oscillating dances in a broken room. Shadows,
Runagates & Marys.
The steel-gray evening was a canvas
Zigzagged with questions
Curling up from smokestacks, as dusky birds
Brushed blues into a montage
Traced back to *L'Amistad* & the psychosis
Behind *Birth of a Nation*.
With eyes against glass & ears to diaphanous doors,
I heard a cornered prayer.
Car lights rubbed against our windows,
Ravenous as snow wolves.
A brick fell into the livingroom like a black body,
& a riot of drunk curses
Left the gladioli & zinnias

Maimed. Double dares
Took root in night soil.
The whistle boiled
Gutbucket underneath silence
& burned with wrath.
But by then Daddy was with Uncle James
Outside The Crossroad,
Their calloused fingers caressing the .38
On the seat of the pickup;
Maybe it was the pine-scented moonglow
That made him look so young
& faceless, wearing his mother's powder blue
Sunday dress & veiled hat.

Playthings

I

I swung a switchman's lantern
Against dusk. One moment, a dull
Green; the next, somewhere
Between molybdate orange &
Bloodred. My Mason jar of lightning bugs
Flickered. The Rebel blew twice
Before stopping a mile away
At the depot, as silver coaches
Snaked like a whip of hot light.
I was never alone when the conductor
Yelled *Next stop, the Crescent City.*
Mama Mary was there to repeat
The lowdown: "It's ungodly.
Your Aunt Tim was sitting
In the depot one day & a joker
Strutted up to her & said,
'Lady, you're real lucky
With that five-dollar gold piece
Round your neck, 'cause I done

Left my dutch knife at home.'"
My half-dead lantern signaled
To the Dog Star, a screech owl
Hooted my name, Brer Rabbit
Gazed out of his thorny sanctuary,
& then my mother's voice
Was loud as a train whistle.
I flung down the jar,
Weaving through saw grass,
& tried to beat my shadow
Home.

                2

Mother taught me how
To snap off skinny, half-
Green reeds & whittle them clean
With penknives & shanks of glass
Till they were light as balsa.
We arranged triangles into
Hexagons. Looping cotton twine,
Mixing flour paste, we rolled out
Yards of pale butcher paper
Over a frame tall as a man.
Once she took off her red slip
& ripped it into a kite tail,
& later I almost couldn't see the boy
Hugging the black transformer
Like a war drum, as helmeted
Linemen worked him down
Off the singing wires.
I watched the big boys
Make their streamlined models
Dogfight over cornfields.
Laced with razorblades,
A dragon's tailspin
Slashed the late afternoon
Sky, as March bullied
Raintrees & a girl
In a crimson dress.

3

Round, woven out of pine
Straw, its dome-shaped lid
Like a Chinese hat.
When Grandmama held it in her big hands
She'd chant *Africa, Africa*.
The raised design smooth
As a scar on an old face.
Sunlight rushed into her bedroom
When she lifted the top.
Rhinestone combs, bracelets,
Rings stealing a secondhand halo,
A wooden token
She called a plug nickel:
Good for One Dance.
I'd turn the Gullah basket around
& around in my hands.
It was good work;
Someone's heart in it.
I tried to weave my own
But learned weeks later
The needles had to be green
It would take fifteen years
For Grandmama to say it was woven
By her Aunt Sarah who lived in Chicago
Forty years, passing.

4

I'd spit
On the sidewalk
& jab the popgun's
Pencil-size plunger—
Whittled from a foot
of mop handle –
till its tip
Flared soft
As a brush.
The barrel
Was eight inches of bamboo.

Chinaberries
Popped thirty feet
Into the air.
Vacuum & tension,
The sucking sound
Of the plunger
Drew the soul
Back
Into
Itself.

5

You cut a handle from a forked
Branch & peel away the bark,
Rounding & rasping it down to
True balance. You turn it over
In your hands to see if the feel
Is right. Next, you take out
An inner tube of red rubber;
Cut two strips straight as a surgeon,
Biting your bottom lip
& humming as you work.
Birds start to leave the trees
& powerlines. Cats & dogs hide
In their unlit worlds, under houses,
As you eye a stockpile of cast-iron
Shards arranged in a corner of the porch.
Sweat & dirt will polish the handle.
This isn't a store-bought slingshot,
What the boys in The Terrace call
Niggershooters. You have twine
& a stock notched just right.
For an ammo pocket you find a tongue
Inside the pair of keepsake shoes
Hidden in the back of your mother's
Closet, the alligator skin your grandfather tried
To break in before dying.

Yellow Dog Café

In a cerulean ruckus
Of quilts, we played house
Off the big room where
They laughed & slowdragged
Weekends. *The eagle flies*
On Friday. The jukebox pulsed
A rainbow through the papery walls.
We were paid a dollar to guard
Each other. I was eight
& S.C. Mae fourteen,
As we experimented with
The devil. Mill workers
Changed money in the briny
Glow of bootleg, overpowered
By the smell of collards, catfish
& candied yams. Granddaddy Gabriel
Worked the cash register
Beside his second wife, Rosie
Belle. I heard my mother
& father laugh like swimmers
Underwater. A raw odor
Of lilies & sweat filled the room;
My cousin's hands moved over me
Smooth & tough as a blues guitar.
Somebody swore they saw
A silhouette with a gasoline can
The night S.C. Mae ran away
With a woman's husband.
For weeks they sifted ashes
But the gutted studs & braces
Only leaned against the wind,
Weak as a boy & girl entwined
On the floor. That June
Granddaddy drove a busload
Up north: the growers paid him

A dollar a day for each pair of hands.
He wanted to rebuild those nights,
Their circle of blurred cards.
The bus grunted between orchards,
& by late August I had enough
Fire-blackened nickels & dimes
To fill a sock, but only a few pickers
Came back after a season of wine-stained
Greenbacks sewn inside coats
& taped to the soles of their feet.

Happiness

When I'd win the fight
Over whose turn it was,
I sat on the top doorstep,
Grinning out into the Fourth
Of July, turning the freezer
Handle. I rocked to a tune
In my head, satisfied
I could hear Satchmo's horn
On his birthday. "Dippermouth
Blues." Hydrangeas bloomed
Along the sidewalk & fence.
The freezer's wooden tub
Was packed with ice & salt,
Around a shiny cylinder
Filled with custard & peach
Slices. Caught up in the rhythm
Till an ache crawled
My arms. Fortissimo. Fire-
Works. The swim hole dynamited
A few days earlier, & voices
Rushed up now like loud
Hosannas. Hundreds of lanes

Snaked through oaks, wild fruit
& honeysuckle. Baskets overflowed
The bank. Big boys whistled at girls
& swandived from the tallest trees.
Small boys on the plankwalk
Jostled each other, springing up
& down like pogo sticks.
I turned the handle faster,
But the goat in the tree
Remained: Daddy Red forced
Me to stroke the throat
Before his butcher knife
Caught the sunlight.
The cry was a child's.
Silence belonged to gods.
There was no paradise, no
Cakewalk for demons hidden
In grass. Old Lazy Bones
Shook out his limbs & pinwheeled
A dustdevil's foxtrot. The air
Sweetened with the scent of goat
Cooking over a pit,
& as the icecream hardened
The hurt in my arms
Made me happy.

Seasons Between Yes & No

I

We stood so the day slanted
Through our dime-store magnifying glass.
Girls laughed & swayed, caught
On the wild edge of our scent.
A scorpion of sunlight crawled
Each boy's arm, as we took turns

Daring each other to flinch. Not
Knowing what a girl's smile did,
An oath stitched us to God.

2

Ice & wind cut through trees
Quick as Pompeian lava casting lovers
Into the arms of strange gods.
We brought in two robins,
& the heat from our hands made them fly
A few clumsy feet.
But half-drugged, rising out of hypnosis,
They broke their bodies
Against breath-fogged panes.

3

We held back curses,
Torturing each other with an adagio
Of silence. Little Faust
Games of the heart.
Bets. Dares. Sucker bait.
Romantic & obscene,
We held back cries,
Letting the mosquitoes suck
Till they popped like stars of blood through cloth.

Glory

Most were married teenagers
Working knockout shifts daybreak
To sunset six days a week—
Already old men playing ball
In a field between a row of shotgun houses
& the Magazine Lumber Company.
They were all Jackie Robinson

& Willie Mays, a touch of
Josh Gibson & Satchel Paige
In each stance & swing, a promise
Like a hesitation pitch always
At the edge of their lives,
Arms sharp as rifles.
The Sunday afternoon heat
Flared like thin flowered skirts
As children & wives cheered.
The men were like cats
Running backwards to snag
Pop-ups & high flies off
Fences, stealing each other's glory.
The old deacons & raconteurs
Who umpired made an *Out* or *Safe*
Into a song & dance routine.
Runners hit the dirt
& skid into homeplate,
Cleats catching light,
As they conjured escapes, outfoxing
Double plays. In the few seconds
It took a man to eye a woman
Upon the makeshift bleachers,
A stolen base or homerun
Would help another man
Survive the new week.

April's Anarchy

All five shades of chameleon
Came alive on the cross-hatched
Snakeskin, & a constellation
Of eyes flickered in the thicket
As quail whooped up from sagebrush.
I duck-walked through mossy slag

Where a turtledove's call
Held daylight to the ground.
Vines climbed barbed wire
& leapt blacktop,
Snuck down back alleys,
Disguised with white blossoms,
Just to get a stranglehold
On young Judas trees.
Thorns nicked my left ear.
A hum rushed through leaves
Like something I could risk
Putting my hands on.
What April couldn't fix
Wasn't worth the time:
Egg shell & dried placenta
Light as memory.
Patches of fur, feathers,
& bits of skin. A nest
Of small deaths among anemone.
A canopy edged over, shadowplaying
The struggle underneath
As if it never happened.

The Millpond

They looked like wood ibis
From a distance, & as I got closer
They became knots left for gods
To undo, like bows tied
At the center of weakness.
Shadow to light, mind to flesh,
Swamp orchids quivered under green hats,
Nudged by slate-blue catfish
Headed for some boy's hook
On the other side. The day's
Uncut garments of fallen chances

Stumbled among flowers
That loved only darkness,
As afternoon came through underbrush
Like a string of firecrackers
Tied to a dog's tail.
Gods lived under that mud
When I was young & sublimely
Blind. Each bloom a shudder
Of uneasiness, no sound
Except the whippoorwill.
They conspired to become twilight
& metaphysics, as five-eyed
Fish with milky bones
Flip-flopped in oily grass.

ᔕ

We sat there as the moon rose
Up from chemical water,
Phosphorous as an orange lantern.
An old man shifted
His three-pronged gig
Like a New Guinea spear,
So it could fly quicker
Than a frog's tongue or angry word.
He pointed to snapping turtles
Posed on cypress logs,
armored in stillness,
Slow kings of a dark world.
We knelt among cattails.
The reflection of a smokestack
Cut the black water in half.
A circle of dry leaves
Smouldered on the ground
For mosquitoes. As if
To draw us to them, like decoys
For some greater bounty,
The choir of bullfrogs called,
Singing a cruel happiness.

Sometimes I'd watch them
Scoot back into their tunnels,
Down in a gully where
The pond's overflow drained . . .
Where shrub oak & banyan
Grew around barbed wire
Till April oozed sap
Like a boy beside a girl
Squeezing honeycomb in his fists.
I wondered if time tied
Everything to goldenrod
Reaching out of cow manure for the sun.
What did it have to do
With saw & hammer,
With what my father taught me
About his world? Sometimes
I sat reading *Catcher in the Rye,*
& other times *Spider Man*
& *Captain Marvel.* Always
After a rain crawfish surfaced
To grab the salt meat
Tied to the nylon string,
Never knowing when they left
The water & hit the bottom
Of my tincan. They clung
To desire, like the times
I clutched something dangerous
& couldn't let go.

Immolatus

She had her feet in the trough,
Nosing into the golden corn,

When daddy did a half spin
& brought down the sledgehammer.
She sank to the mud.
An oak branch bowed
As they tightened the rope
To a creaky song of pulley wheels.
A few leaves left
For the wind to whip down,
They splashed hot water
& shaved her with blades
That weighed less each year.
Snow geese honked overhead
& Sirius balanced on a knifetip.
Wintertime bit into the ropy guts
Falling into a number-3 tub
That emptied out in a gray gush
Like the end of a ditch
Choked with slime & roses.
Something love couldn't make
Walk again. I had a boy's job
Lugging water from the pump
& filling the iron washpot.
I threw pine knots on the blaze.
Soon her naked whiteness
Was a silence to split
Between helpers & owner.
Liver, heart, & head
Flung to a foot tub.
They smiled as she passed
Through their hands. Next day
I tracked blood in a circle
Across dead grass, while fat
Boiled down to lye soap.

Banking Potatoes

Daddy would drop purple-veined vines
Along rows of dark loam
& I'd march behind him
Like a peg-legged soldier,
Pushing down the stick
With a V cut into its tip.

Three weeks before the first frost
I'd follow his horse-drawn plow
That opened up the soil & left
Sweet potatoes sticky with sap,
Like flesh-colored stones along a riverbed
Or diminished souls beside a mass grave.

They lay all day under the sun's
Invisible weight, & by twilight
We'd bury them under pine needles
& then shovel in two feet of dirt.
Nighthawks scalloped the sweaty air,
Their wings spread wide

As plowshares. But soon the wind
Knocked on doors & windows
Like a frightened stranger,
& by mid-winter we had tunneled
Back into the tomb of straw,
Unable to divide love from hunger.

The Smokehouse

In the hickory scent
Among slabs of pork

Glistening with salt,
I played Indian
In a headdress of redbird feathers
& brass buttons
Off my mother's winter coat.
Smoke wove
A thread of fire through meat, into December
& January. The dead weight
Of the place hung around me,
Strung up with sweetgrass.
The hog had been sectioned,
A map scored into skin;
Opened like love,
From snout to tail,
The goodness
No longer true to each bone.
I was a wizard
In that hazy world,
& knew I could cut
Slivers of meat till my heart
Grew more human & flawed.

The Steel Plate

They said Mister Dan
Came back from World War II
With a steel plate in his head.
Came back hooked
On Morphine & killed
His need with Muscat.
He came back a hero,
To a ramshackle house
Owned by the Rail Company,
Back to women who came & left
After each government check.

I would close my eyes to see
Metal reflect sunlight
Like a preacher's collection plate.
His tomatoes & sweet corn overtook
The backyard. Peach, plum,
& apricot blossoms deadened
Acid fumes of the papermill.
Fishing poles hung on nails from a wall.
Sometimes I could hear him
Singing a half mile away.
Maybe Creole or German.

But one Saturday he
Was pulled like a moon
Pulls water, dragged naked
Into the midnight street,
Dancing. The next morning
A rain of crushed blossoms
Just wasn't enough to cover
The vaporous smell of human
Feces outside his gate.
His impression in the dirt
Heavier than any white line.

I saw where the police
Blackjacked him to the ground.
Those lilies around that steel-
Gray casket would keep me away
From funerals. Mister Dan's
Dark-brown serge suit . . .
The round plate barely
Beneath a skin of powder
& hair glued into place,
Not able to stop or hide
The sun's gleamy blue search.

Sunday Afternoons

They'd latch the screendoors
& pull venetian blinds,
Telling us not to leave the yard.
But we always got lost
Among mayhaw & crabapple.

Juice spilled from our mouths,
& soon we were drunk & brave
As birds diving through saw vines.
Each nest held three or four
Speckled eggs, blue as rage.

Where did we learn to be unkind,
There in the power of holding each egg
While watching dogs in June
Dust & heat, or when we followed
The hawk's slow, deliberate arc?

In the yard, we heard cries
Fused with gospel on the radio,
Loud as shattered glass
In a Saturday-night argument
About trust & money.

We were born between Oh Yeah
& Goddammit. I knew life
Began where I stood in the dark,
Looking out into the light,
& that sometimes I could see

Everything through nothing.
The backyard trees breathed
Like a man running from himself
As my brothers backed away
From the screendoor. I knew

If I held my right hand above my eyes
Like a gambler's visor, I could see
How their bedroom door halved
The dresser mirror like a moon
Held prisoner in the house.

Looking for Choctaw

We put down our popguns
& cap pistols, & raised our hands
Into the air, hoping he'd step
From winterberry & hollyhock.
We flung ourselves in a circle
At sunset & fell in the dust,
But we couldn't trick him
Out. He'd walk in our footprints
When we were alone in the woods
Fishing or tracking a jackrabbit
Through wild-gray tobacco.
Heat figures waltzed to a killdeer
As we searched hollowed trees.
He remained in his unblinking
Stillness, years after toy guns
became real ones tucked into belts.
When we parked with our girlfriends
In our souped-up four-on-the-floor
Beside Mitch Creek & listened
To Fats Domino & The Shirelles
On WWEZ, we dared him to fight,
But he only left his breath
On windshields, as if nothing
Could hold him in this world.
Not even the fleshy hunger
Forged by what pulls
Greenness through a leaf.

Perhaps we betrayed mystery
So we could become shadows
Of dreamers, as fingers untangled
Saw vines & left us lost
To ourselves. Mama Mary
Was baking molasses tea cakes
Or stirring sugar into lemonade,
Deep in thought, when she turned
& I saw his face carved
Into hers.

Fleshing-out the Season

They said he lived in both houses.
That the black woman
Once worked as a maid
For his wife. The women
Sometimes met in town & talked
Like old friends, would hug & kiss
Before parting. They said
The man's father was a big-time
Politician in Jackson, Mississippi,
& owned a cotton gin,
& the Klan didn't dare hassle
Him. The black woman's house
Was a scaled-down replica
Of the other; both yards
A jungle of bougainvillea,
Azalea, & birds of paradise.
They said there's a picture
Of the three at Mardi Gras
Dancing in a circle of flambeaus.
In summer he always ate
Cones of raspberry ice cream,
& carried a fat ledger
From house to house. Alyce

Clover grew over his pathway.
He sent his white son to Vanderbilt,
The black one to Columbia.
He had read Blake aloud to them;
Pointed out Orion & Venus.
They said both women waited
To divide him. One sprinkled him
Over the Gulf of Mexico,
& the other put him under roots
Of pigweed beside the back gate—
Purple, amaranthine petals,
She wore in her hair on Sundays.

Blackberries

They left my hands like a printer's
Or thief's before a police blotter
& pulled me into early morning's
Terrestrial sweetness, so thick
The damp ground was consecrated
Where they fell among a garland of thorns.

Although I could smell old lime-covered
History, at ten I'd still hold out my hands
& berries fell into them. Eating from one
& filling a half gallon with the other,
I ate the mythology & dreamt
Of pies & cobbler, almost

Needful as forgiveness. My bird dog Spot
Eyed blue jays & thrashers. The mud frogs
In rich blackness, hid from daylight.
An hour later, beside City Limits Road
I balanced a gleaming can in each hand,
Limboed between worlds, repeating *one dollar*.

The big blue car made me sweat.
Wintertime crawled out of the windows.
When I leaned closer I saw the boy
& girl my age, in the wide back seat
Smirking, & it was then I remembered my fingers
Burning with thorns among berries too ripe to touch.

Yellowjackets

When the plowblade struck
An old stump hiding under
The soil like a beggar's
Rotten tooth, they swarmed up
& Mister Jackson left the plow
Wedged like a whaler's harpoon.
The horse was midnight
Against dusk, tethered to somebody's
Pocketwatch. He shivered, but not
The way women shook their heads
Before mirrors at the five
& dime—a deeper connection
To the low field's evening star.
He stood there, in tracechains,
Lathered in froth, just
Stopped by a great, goofy
Calmness. He whinnied
Once, & then the whole
Beautiful, blue-black sky
Fell on his back.

Gristmill

Black hands shucked
& shelled corn into a washtub
While a circle of ancient voices
Hummed "Li'l Liza Jane."
Daddy shouldered a hundred-pound sack
To Mister Adam's gristmill.
The place was a moment of
Inertia. A horde of rough shoes
Against a revolving dancefloor.
Navel to navel. Slip-
Socket to ball-
Bearing & cogwheel.
Gears dragged & caught,
& the machine's calibrated
Rhythm kicked in.
An orgasm of golden dust
Clung to the wooden floor,
To the grass & leaves
Outside. A field holler
Travelled out, coming back
With the same sweaty cries
Elvis stole from R & B,
Like a millstone worn
Bright. Smooth, white hands
Halved the meal & husk:
One for you, two for me.

History Lessons

I

Squinting up at leafy sunlight, I stepped back
& shaded my eyes, but couldn't see what she pointed to.

The courthouse lawn where the lone poplar stood
Was almost flat as a pool table. Twenty-five
Years earlier it had been a stage for half the town:
Cain & poor whites at a picnic on saint augustine
Grass. No, I couldn't see the piece of blonde rope.
I stepped closer to her, to where we were almost
In each other's arms, & then spotted the flayed
Tassel of wind-whipped hemp knotted around a limb
Like a hank of hair, a weather-whitened bloom
In hungry light. That was where they prodded him
Up into the flatbed of a pickup.

2

We had coffee & chicory with lots of milk,
Hoecakes, bacon, & gooseberrry jam. She told me
How a white woman in The Terrace
Said that she shot a man who tried to rape her,
How their car lights crawled sage fields
Midnight to daybreak, how a young black boxer
Was running & punching the air at sunrise,
How they tarred & feathered him & dragged the corpse
Behind a Model T through the Mill Quarters,
How they dumped the prizefighter on his mother's doorstep,
How two days later three boys
Found a white man dead under the trestle
In blackface, the woman's bullet
In his chest, his head on a clump of sedge.

3

When I stepped out on the back porch
The pick-up man from Bogalusa Dry Cleaners
Leaned against his van, with an armload
Of her Sunday dresses, telling her
Emmett Till had begged for it
With his damn wolf whistle.
She was looking at the lye-scoured floor,
White as his face. The hot words
Swarmed out of my mouth like African bees
& my fists were cocked,

Hammers in the air. He popped
The clutch when he turned the corner,
As she pulled me into her arms
& whispered, *Son, you ain't gonna live long.*

Temples of Smoke

Fire shimmied & reached up
From the iron furnace & grabbed
Sawdust from the pitchfork
Before I could make it across
The floor or take a half step
Back, as the boiler room sung
About what trees were before
Men & money. Those nights
Smelled of greenness & sweat
As steam moved through miles
Of winding pipes to turn wheels
That pushed blades & rotated
Man-high saws. It leaped
Like tigers out of a pit,
Singeing the hair on my head,
While Daddy made his rounds
Turning large brass keys
In his night-watchman's clock,
Out among columns of lumber & paths
Where a man & woman might meet.
I daydreamed some freighter
Across a midnight ocean,
Leaving Taipei & headed
For Tripoli. I saw myself fall
Through a tumbling inferno
As if hell was where a boy
Shoveled clouds of sawdust
Into the wide mouth of doubt.

Boys in Dresses

We were The Hottentot Venus
Draped in our mothers' dresses,
Wearing rouge & lipstick,
Pillows tucked under floral
& print cloth, the first day of spring,
As we balanced on high heels.
Women sat in a circle talking
About men, the girls off
Somewhere else, in other houses.
We felt the last kisses
Our mothers would give us
On the mouth. Medusa
Wound around our necks
As we wore out the day's
Cantillations. They gazed at us
& looked into their own eyes
Before the water broke, remembering
How we firstborn boys loved
Them from within, cleaved
Like silver on the backs of mirrors.
Would we grow into merciful
Men, less lead in our gloves?
That afternoon lives in the republic
Of our bones, when we were girlish
Women in a hermetic council
Of milky coffee & teacakes.
Dragonflies nudged window screens.
When we stepped out
Wearing an ecstasy of hues,
Faceless wolf whistles
& catcalls heated the air.
Azaleas buzzed as we went
House to house. Soon we'd be
Responsible for the chambered
Rapture honeycombed in flesh

& would mourn something lost.
It was harder than running
Naked down a double line
Of boys in those patriarchal woods,
Belts singing against our skin.

Nude Tango

While they were out buying Easter hats
With my brothers & sister,
I stole a third chocolate
Rabbit from the refrigerator
& tiptoed between two mirrors
Where the scent of my parents
Guarded the room. I swayed, bobbed,
Swayed, my shirt a white flag
When it landed on a bedpost.
Something I had to get past
In the pit of my belly.
What were my feet trying to do
When a shoe slid under the bed?
I tangoed one naked reflection
Toward another, creating a third,
As he sprung across the years
& pulled me into the woods:
If you say anything,
I'll kill your mama.
A ripped shirt pocket
Flapped like a green tongue.
Thistled grass bloodied my knees.
God was in the sunlight
Toying with the knife.
Milkweed surrounded us,
Spraying puffs of seeds,
& I already knew the word *cock*.

I shoved out a hip,
Threw my arms around
My image, & fell to the floor
To let it pass over
Like an animal traveling
Through our lives
To leave a mythic smell.

Touch

Goalposts were imaginary lines
East & West of a shotgun
House, as we trampled
Four-leaf clovers into rosin.
No clipping, no kidney jabs,
No roughing up the quarterback.
We huddled around the ball
Like a young tyrannosaurus
Lagging behind his brain.
You cut right.
You go left
& then zigzag
Right. I'll go up the middle,
& everybody else block. The snap
Propelled us like a battering ram,
As if the line between boy & girl
Could break easily as a wishbone.
Joined like centaurs, pleasure
To pain, we slapped hips & buttocks.
Names lay on our tongues
Like holy bread, sweet as Abishag,
& when we stood side by side
We were one, a shirtless
Juggernaut. Women & girls
Fanned at half-lit

Windows. Knowing our bodies
As well as Oedipus that season,
We faced ourselves, leaving
Shirts & skin on the grass.
Glazed with sweat & salt,
We butted heads till stars
Loomed over the redbuds.

Sugar

I watched men at Angola,
How every swing of the machete
Swelled the day black with muscles,
Like a wave through canestalks,
Pushed by the eyes of guards
Who cradled pump shotguns like lovers.
They swayed to a Cuban samba or Yoruba
Master drum & wrote confessions in the air
Saying *I been wrong*
But I'll be right someday.
I gazed from Lorenzo's '52 Chevy
Till they were nighthawks,
& days later fell asleep
Listening to Cousin Buddy's
One-horse mill grind out a blues.
We fed stalks into metal jaws
That locked in sweetness
When everything cooled down & crusted over,
Leaving only a few horseflies
To buzz & drive the day beyond
Leadbelly. At the bottom
Of each gallon was a glacier,
A fetish I could buy a kiss with.
I stared at a tree against dusk
Till it was a girl

Standing beside a country road
Shucking cane with her teeth.
She looked up & smiled
& waved. Lost in what hurts,
In what tasted good, could she
Ever learn there's no love
In sugar?

Albino

A field of blond sage
    Stood between us & them,
Where we planned ambushes
    With paperbags of gravel.

Sometimes their dark-skinned father
    Hugged & kissed their mother
Under the chinaberry tree
    In the backyard: an eclipse:

She was like a sheet of onionskin.
    We were sure this was how
White people were born,
    & they could see better than ghosts

At night. Some summer days
    We shot marbles with ballbearings
For hours before the first punch
    & the namecalling

Erupted. But by dusk
    We were back to quick kisses,
Hollering *You're It* & *Home*
    As we played hide & seek.

One morning in October
   Creola stepped from the trees
At the edge of a shortcut, the scent
   Of the season's last wild berries,

& we sank among the leaves
   Caught between green & gold.
She led me to their clubhouse
   Beside the creek, a betrayal

Of the genes. It was different
   From the time I was seven
In the half-empty barrel of hogfeed
   With Rosie Lee, when my mother

Lifted the lid & uncapped April.
   Maybe that escaped convict
Had found Creola & me playing hooky.
   Her eyes were pink

& startled as a rabbit's.
   An odor in the air made its own
Laws, as if the tongue was a latch
   Holding down a grace note.

The silence between birds
   Was heavy as a bell,
& here an insect could conjure
   A fugitive heartbeat's great noise.

Halloween, the Late Fifties

After ghosts & goblins
Were tricked home early,
Dragging cardboard moons in the dust,
We older boys became demons.

We munched Baby Ruths & Butterfingers
Before unearthing our midnight
Stash of inner-tube slingshots
Beside the opalescent millpond.

They uncoiled like water snakes
In our hands. We were ecstatic
With blue-gray cartons of rotten eggs
Resting like miniature bombs in silos.

For weeks we ransacked garbage dumps
For those perfect missiles to stockpile.
We ran through honeysuckle,
Taking shortcuts to the next roadblock

We'd construct with tree branches
& upturned garbage cans, unaware
Rear-view mirrors reflected our futures
Like bank robbers in parked Fords & Chevys.

Behind Batman & Dick Tracy masks
We were a blur of denim snagged
By berry bushes at the crossroad
Of an owl's soliloquy.

But we could depend
On mothers & sisters
To dapple iodine on cuts,
On love to get us out of trouble.

Men & women in bedrooms
Floated against pale window shades–
Stink bombs made in chemistry class
Exploded & oozed across verandahs.

We threw at our own houses.
We were the night's slow dance,
Free to think even the police
Didn't dare shoot.

Mismatched Shoes

A tiger shark
Swims from the mother stream,
Away from danger
Or hunger, to an unknown
Planet orbiting a dreamer's head.
My grandfather came from Trinidad
Smuggled in like a sack of papaya
On a banana boat, to a preacher's
Bowl of gumbo & jambalaya, to jazz;
The name Brown fitted him like trouble,
A plantation owner's breath
Clouding each filigreed letter.
He wore a boy's shoe
& a girl's shoe, with the taste
Of mango on his lips.
Gone was his true name
& deep song of Shango,
But for years it was whispered
Same as a poor man might touch
A lover's satin glove
From another life.
The island swelled in his throat
& calypso leapt into the air,
Only to be amputated
By the wind's white blade.
Yet, he could coo big, country women
& glide into an improvised
Jitterbug that tripped
Hearts. All-night blackjack
& moonshine in mill towns
Took him early. We had paid
Our death taxes, but my grandmother
Never stopped whispering his name.
I picked up those mismatched shoes
& slipped into his skin. Komunyakaa.
His blues, African fruit on my tongue.

My Father's Love Letters

On Fridays he'd open a can of Jax
After coming home from the mill,
& ask me to write a letter to my mother
Who sent postcards of desert flowers
Taller than men. He would beg,
Promising to never beat her
Again. Somehow I was happy
She had gone, & sometimes wanted
To slip in a reminder, how Mary Lou
Williams' "Polka Dots & Moonbeams"
Never made the swelling go down.
His carpenter's apron always bulged
With old nails, a claw hammer
Looped at his side & extension cords
Coiled around his feet.
Words rolled from under the pressure
Of my ballpoint: Love,
Baby, Honey, Please.
We sat in the quiet brutality
Of voltage meters & pipe threaders,
Lost between sentences . . .
The gleam of a five-pound wedge
On the concrete floor
Pulled a sunset
Through the doorway of his toolshed.
I wondered if she laughed
& held them over a gas burner.
My father could only sign
His name, but he'd look at blueprints
& say how many bricks
Formed each wall. This man,
Who stole roses & hyacinth
For his yard, would stand there
With eyes closed & fists balled,
Laboring over a simple word, almost
Redeemed by what he tried to say.

The Cooling Board

Prophet Johnson's white beard
Made the children run & hide,
& sometimes they chanted Santa
Santa. He'd lean on his cane,
Shake his head & say,
Lord, the devil's busy today.
Nobody dared light a cigarette
When the prophet was about.
He cursed women who wore lipstick
& called them Jezebels,
Caning the men who blasphemed
& played the dozens.
Because he read minds,
Teenagers would stare up
At the sky when he passed.
Over a hundred, his grey eyes
Were from the Old Testament
& the streetcorner his pulpit:
You can two-time Satan
But you can't lick the Holy Ghost.
Once he'd been a gambler,
Was trapped in a knife fight
& died on the doctor's table.
Women sang the blues from Fourth Street
To The Bottom, praying in a room
Scented with periwinkle & fuchsia,
Before he sat up on the cooling board
& requested a pigfoot
& a bottle of Colt 45.

Omen

The quart jar of silver dollars
Glowed in the windowless shed.
Daddy shook, pointing
To the blind demon
Guarding his poorbox
Like a ghost under a legendary
Tree where a black cat
Dogged the southern moon.
He stood frozen at the door,
Waiting for the coach whip
To stand on its tail
& whistle for a woman.
My right hand found a 2 × 4,
But I let it fall back
Against a barrel of hogfeed,
Happy in the swollen glands
Of my thirteenth year.
Daylight crawled across the floor
Where poison ivy looped
Up through a knothole.
Like a candle flame,
The snake's tongue darted
To the vibration
Of fear & breath. Still,
I don't know how or why
My body made one motion
As I popped off its head
& threw it at my father's feet.

Believing in Iron

The hills my brothers & I created
Never balanced, & it took years
To discover how the world worked.
We could look at a tree of blackbirds
& tell you how many were there,
But with the scrap dealer
Our math was always off.
Weeks of lifting & grunting
Never added up to much,
But we couldn't stop
Believing in iron.
Abandoned trucks & cars
Were held to the ground
By thick, nostalgic fingers of vines
Strong as a dozen sharecroppers.
We'd return with our wheelbarrow
Groaning under a new load,
Yet tiger lilies lived better
In their languid, August domain.
Among paper & Coke bottles
Foundry smoke erased sunsets,
& we couldn't believe iron
Left men bent so close to the earth
As if the ore under their breath
Weighed down the gray sky.
Sometimes I dreamt how our hills
Washed into a sea of metal,
How it all became an anchor
For a warship or bomber
Out over trees with blooms
Too red to look at.

Salomé

I had seen her
Before, nearly hidden
Behind those fiery branches
As she dove nude
Into the creek.
This white girl
Who moved with ease
On her side of the world
As if she were the only
Living thing. Her breasts
Rose like swamp orchids
On the water's rhythm
Along an old path—
Suckholes & whirlpools
Reaching down for years.
A hundred yards away
The black baptists
From Tree of Life
& Sweet Beulah
Dunked white-robed boys & girls.
The fishing cork danced
& then disappeared, but I couldn't
Move in my tall greenness.
A water snake crawled
Along the stunted oak
That grew half in water,
Half in earth. I knew
Salomé's brother, Cleanth,
Hung our cat with a boot lace
From a crooked fencepost—
Knew he pulled on the cat's
Hind legs, a smile on his face,
& it wouldn't be long before
He would join her in the creek
& they'd hold each other

Like Siamese twins at the State Fair,
Swimmers trapped under
A tyranny of roots, born
With one heart.

Between Angels & Monsters

Short & baldheaded,
He paced the line of black boys
Flexing their muscles
& pointed to the ones he wanted.
Caged lions & tigers
Stared out of a lush
Green, eyes pulsing
Like lights from a distant city.

When he pointed to me,
I stepped closer to the elephants.
They moved like they had a history of work,
& knew where to place their feet
To not cave-in platforms
Loaded with stakes & tarp
Heavy as Hannibal's rafts
Tailgating on a river.

Soon we were hammering down steel pegs
& tying-off ropes, as they nudged pylons
Into place. A new world
Swelled under the big top.
Outside, a woman in a stars-&-stripes bikini
Beckoned us. Near the aluminum trailers
A hundred colors heated the day
As women & men moved through doors,

A flash of bodies in bold windows.
A girl plucked a Spanish guitar
In the doorway of a tent
Where an armless man showed us
How he poured coffee & smoked
Chesterfields with his toes;
She placed a brush between his teeth
& he began painting a rose inside a bottle.

The baldheaded man was waving.
He gave each of us a free ticket
& a red T-shirt that said
The World's Greatest Circus.
We could hear the animal trainer's
Whip crack & bite into Saturday.
The smell of popcorn & chili dogs
Covered the scent of dung & dust.

A bouquet of flowers burst from a clown's trumpet.
We stood like obsidian panthers
In a corner of the white world.
It was as if our eyes had met
As she stepped off the highwire;
Her right foot hooked through a silver hoop—
Hanging like a limp flag
Over the invisible empire.

Poetics of Paperwood

Before dawn.   Before we knew women
We rolled into the woods   Could make us cry,
Just before blue jays   We'd dance-walk
Went crazy in the amber   Any hunk of wood
& jade light of dragonflies. Up to the red truck
I saw deer ease   We pushed on each other—

Back into the green
Future before double blades
Chopped the day loose.
I learned how to bed
Trees so they fell
Between an owl's nest &
    beehive.
A woodpecker tapped
Its syllabic drum
Like my father's finger
Against my heart
When I did something
Wrong. Junior, you
Kept the saw from
Bending in the wood
Like a whiplash.
I saw where locusts
Sang themselves out of
Translucent shells
Still clinging to
Whitman's Live-Oak.

Dropped & shoved,
It flew into place.
We ate lunch under
A flowered vine that looped
Down like a noose.
Sardines, crackers,
An orange Hi-C,
& a moon pie.
I raked my fingers
Through old leaves
& hundreds of insects
Lit the humus.
Junior, till after sunset
We pulled the crosscut
Through the pine like a seesaw
Of light across a map
Of green fungus.
We knew work
Was rhythm,
& so was love.

Slam, Dunk, & Hook

Fast breaks. Lay ups. With Mercury's
Insignia on our sneakers,
We outmaneuvered to footwork
Of bad angels. Nothing but a hot
Swish of strings like silk
Ten feet out. In the roundhouse
Labyrinth our bodies
Created, we could almost
Last forever, poised in midair
Like storybook sea monsters.
A high note hung there

A long second. Off
The rim. We'd corkscrew
Up & dunk balls that exploded
The skullcap of hope & good
Intention. Lanky, all hands
& feet . . . sprung rhythm.
We were metaphysical when girls
Cheered on the sidelines.
Tangled up in a falling,
Muscles were a bright motor
Double-flashing to the metal hoop
Nailed to our oak.
When Sonny Boy's mama died
He played nonstop all day, so hard
Our backboard splintered.
Glistening with sweat,
We rolled the ball off
Our fingertips. Trouble
Was there slapping a blackjack
Against an open palm.
Dribble, drive to the inside,
& glide like a sparrow hawk.
Lay ups. Fast breaks.
We had moves we didn't know
We had. Our bodies spun
On swivels of bone & faith,
Through a lyric slipknot
Of joy, & we knew we were
Beautiful & dangerous.

Sex, Magnolias, & Speed

No begging forgiveness
For my good aim,
For how the rock

Balanced in my hand
As I walked the bridge
Between football & home.
Someone mooned Orion
& a condom filled with piss
Burst at my feet.
Could the girls
Strapped into bucket seats
Make those boys into men?
The windshield glared like a helmet
On wheels, as chrome fins
Gutted the night
& circled back.
That spring I'd learned
A pivot, beginning in the guts
Behind the spleen.
The Chevy left skid marks.
The sky lay against sepia
Mill water where nothing lived
Among dead animals & blossoms.
At the end of the bridge
Below the Dairy Queen
Police lights splashed
Over magnolias & oaks,
But I walked straight ahead
Into the biography of light
& dark, even after they took me
Out to the white graveyard
& used their rubber hoses.

Knights of the White Camellia
& Deacons of Defense

They were in a big circle
Beside Mitch Creek, as it murmured

Like a murderer tossing in his sleep
Between a wife & daughter, demure
As Sartre's Respectable Prostitute
On a feathered bed in July.
The sacrament. A gallon
Jug of bootleg passed from hand
To hand. An orgy of nightbirds
Screeched under the guillotined
Moon that hung like a target
Reflected against each robe.
Bibles, icons, & old lies. Names
Dead in their mouths like broken
Treaties. A spired & cupolaed
Dominion for bloodhounds. Apparitions
Tied to the Lily-cross & Curse.

Next day, in the hard light,
In a show of force,
Dark roses outbloomed
Camellias, a radiance
Not borrowed from the gleam
Of gun barrels. Sons
& daughters of sharecroppers
Who made sawmills
& cotton fields hum for generations,
Encircled the slow-footed
Marchers like an ebony shield.
Bullhorns blared, German
Shepherds whined on choke chains,
& swaggering clubs throttled spring.
Resistance startled crepe myrtle
& magnolia, while a clandestine
Perfume diluted the tear gas.

Nocturne

The high-beam light swung
Through cypresses like a hundred
Copper wires hooked to a shadow
Tugging on the future. Boxcars
Clattered past like shutters closing, opening
A part of me into the unfinished
Night. Bloodhounds howled.
It was the blue inside
A stone, a cracker's stare.
I gazed so long at the horizon
I heard Big Joe Turner cry out
You a devil with nylon hose. Somewhere
Broonzy spat into a tin cup
Beside his bed, dying
Like my grandfather had
When my mother was eight.
Something held me up to dusk
When birds flew homeward
With straw & lice.
The train whistle left leaves shuddering
As the last drop of yellow disappeared.
Sixteen, I sat there
With a hard-on, sipping a Coke
& staring into the eyes of an Asian
Woman under a flame tree.

Butterfly-toed Shoes

We began at The Silver Shadow
Doing the Hully Gully,
Till we were dizzy with the scent
Of perfume on our hands. The jukebox

Blazed a path across the semi-dark
Dancefloor as we moved like swimmers
Against each other. April burned
Into the night, after the teenage club
Was padlocked & the scarred WWII
Vets who chaperoned went home
To wives. Some cars nosed into
Backwood lanes as wine bottles
Passed from hand to hand, girls
In their laps, but we sped off
Toward Dead Man's Curve
On two wheels, headed for The Plantation
Club slouched a half mile
Back into fragrant pines.
Off-duty deputy sheriffs guarded doors,
Protecting crap tables in the back room.
The place smelled of catfish
& rotgut. "Honey Hush"
Pulled us into its pulsebeat,
& somehow I had the prettiest woman
In the room. Her dress whirled
A surge of blue, & my butterfly-toes
Were copacetic & demonic.
Cream-colored leather
& black suede—my lucky shoes—
I could spin on those radiant heels,
No longer in that country town.
She'd loop out till our fingertips
Touched & then was back in my arms;
The hem of her dress snapped
Like a boy's shoeshine rag.
She was a woman who would take her time,
Unlike the girls an hour earlier.
We were hot colors rushing toward
The darkest corner, about to kiss,
When some joker cut in
& pulled her into his arms.
I was still swept on by the timbre
Of her breath, her body,

As I move to the jangle of three
Silver dollars my grandfather gave me
Five years earlier. I didn't see
The flash when her husband burst in.
Someone knocked the back door off its hinges,
& for a moment the shuffle of feet
Were on the deck of a Dutch man of War.
I'm still backing away
From the scene, a scintilla
Of love & murder.

Neon Vernacular

Fog Galleon

Horse-headed clouds, flags
& pennants tied to black
Smokestacks in swamp mist.
From the quick green calm
Some nocturnal bird calls
Ship ahoy, ship ahoy!
I press against the taxicab
Window. I'm back here, interfaced
With a dead phosphorescence;
The whole town smells
Like the world's oldest anger.
Scabrous residue hunkers down under
Sulfur & dioxide, waiting
For sunrise, like cargo
On a phantom ship outside Gaul.
Cool glass against my cheek
Pulls me from the black schooner
On a timeless sea—everything
Dwarfed beneath the papermill
Lights blinking behind the cloudy
Commerce of wheels, of chemicals
That turn workers into pulp
When they fall into vats
Of steamy serenity.

At the Screen Door

Just before sunlight
Burns off morning fog
Is it her, will she know
What I've seen & done,
How my boots leave little grave-stone

Shapes in the wet dirt,
That I'm no longer light
On my feet, there's a rock
In my belly? It weighs
As much as the story
Paul told me, moving ahead
Like it knows my heart.
Is this the same story
That sent him to a padded cell?
After all the men he'd killed in Korea
& on his first tour in Vietnam,
Someone tracked him down.
The Spec 4 he ordered
Into a tunnel in Cu Chi
Now waited for him behind
The screen door, a sunset
In his eyes, a dead man
Wearing his teenage son's face.
The scream that leaped
Out of Paul's mouth
Wasn't his, not this decorated
Hero. The figure standing there
Wasn't his son. Who is it
Waiting for me, a tall shadow
Unlit in the doorway, no more
Than an outline of the past?
I drop the duffle bag
& run before I know it,
Running toward her, the only one
I couldn't have surprised,
Who'd be here at daybreak
Watching a new day stumble
Through a whiplash of grass
Like a man drunk on the rage
Of being alive.

Moonshine

Drunken laughter escapes
Behind the fence woven
With honeysuckle, up to where
I stand. Daddy's running-buddy,
Carson, is beside him. In the time
It takes to turn & watch a woman
Tiptoe & pull a sheer blouse off
The clothesline, to see her sun-lit
Dress ride up peasant legs
Like the last image of mercy, three
Are drinking from the Mason jar.

That's the oak we planted
The day before I left town,
As if father & son
Needed staking down to earth.
If anything could now plumb
Distance, that tree comes close,
Recounting lost friends
As they turn into mist.

The woman stands in a kitchen
Folding a man's trousers—
Her chin tucked to hold
The cuffs straight.
I'm lonely as those storytellers
In my father's backyard
I shall join soon. Alone
As they are, tilting back heads
To let the burning ease down.
The names of women melt
In their mouths like hot mints,
As if we didn't know Old Man Pagget's
Stoopdown is doctored with
Slivers of Red Devil Lye.

Salt

Lisa, Leona, Loretta?
She's sipping a milkshake
In Woolworths, dressed in
Chiffon & fat pearls.
She looks up at me,
Grabs her purse
& pulls at the hem
Of her skirt. I want to say
I'm just here to buy
A box of Epsom salt
For my grandmama's feet.
Lena, Lois? I feel her
Strain to not see me.
Lines are now etched
At the corners of her thin,
Pale mouth. Does she know
I know her grandfather
Rode a white horse
Through Poplas Quarters
Searching for black women,
How he killed Indians
& stole land with bribes
& fake deeds? I remember
She was seven & I was five
When she ran up to me like a cat
With a gypsy moth in its mouth
& we played doctor & house
Under the low branches of a raintree
Encircled with red rhododendrons.
We could pull back the leaves
& see grandmama ironing
At their wide window. Once
Her mother moved so close
To the yardman we thought they'd kiss.
What the children of housekeepers

& handymen knew was enough
To stop biological clocks,
& it's hard now not to walk over
& mention how her grandmother
Killed her idiot son
& salted him down
In a wooden barrel.

Changes; or, Reveries at a Window Overlooking a Country Road, with Two Women Talking Blues in the Kitchen

Joe, Gus, Sham . . .
Even George Edward
Done gone. Done
Gone to Jesus, honey.
Doncha mean the devil,
Mary? Those Johnson boys
Were only sweet talkers
& long, tall bootleggers.
Child, now you can count
The men we usedta know
On one hand. They done
Dropped like mayflies—
Cancer, heart trouble,
Blood pressure, sugar,
You name it, Eva Mae.
Amen. Tell the truth,
Girl. I don't know.
Maybe the world's heavy
On their shoulders. Maybe
Too much bed hopping
& skirt chasing
Caught up with them.
God don't like ugly.

Heat lightning jumpstarts the slow
afternoon & a syncopated rainfall
peppers the tinroof like Philly Joe
Jones' brushes reaching for a dusky
backbeat across the high hat. Rhythm
like cells multiplying . . . language &
notes made flesh. Accents & stresses,
almost sexual. Pleasure's knot; to wrestle
the mind down to unrelenting white space,
to fill each room with spring's contagious
changes. Words & music, "Ruby, My Dear"
turned down on the cassette player,
pulsates underneath rustic voices
waltzing out the kitchen—my grandmama
& an old friend of hers from childhood
talking B-flat blues. Time & space,
painful notes, the whole thing wrung
out of silence. Changes. Caesuras.
Nina Simone's downhome cry echoes
theirs—Mister Backlash, Mister Backlash—
as a southern breeze herds wild, blood-
red roses along the barbed-wire fence.
There's something in this house, maybe

Look at my grandson
in there, just dragged in
From God only knows where.
He high tails it home
Inbetween women troubles.
He's nice as a new piece
Of silk. It's a wonder
Women don't stick to him
Like white on rice.
It's a fast world
Out there, honey
They go all kinda ways.
Just buried John Henry
With that old guitar
Cradled in his arms.
Over on Fourth Street
Singing 'bout hell hounds
When he dropped dead.
You heard 'bout Jack,
Right? He just tilted over
In prayer meeting.
The good & bad go
Into the same song.
How's Hattie? She
Still uppity & half
Trying to be white?
The man went off to war
& got one of his legs
Shot off & she wanted
To divorce him for that.
Crazy as a bessy bug.
Jack wasn't cold
In his grave before
She done up & gave all
The insurance money
To some young pigeon
Who never hit a lick
At work in his life.
He cleaned her out & left

those two voices & Satchmo's gold horn,
refracting time & making the Harlem
Renaissance live inside my head.
I can hear Hughes like a river
of fingers over Willie "The Lion" Smith's
piano, & some naked spiritual releases
a shadow in a reverie of robes & crosses.
Oriflamme & Judgment Day . . . undulant waves
bring in cries from Sharpeville & Soweto,
dragging up moans from shark-infested
seas as a blood moon rises. A shock
of sunlight breaks the moon & I hear
my father's voice growing young again,
as he says, "The devil's beating
his wife": One side of the road's rainy
& the other side's sunny. Imagination—
driftwood from a spring flood, stockpiled
by Furies. Changes. Pinetop's boogiewoogie
keys stack against each other like syllables
in tongue-tripped elegies for Lady Day
& Duke. Don't try to make any sense
out of this; just let it take you
like Pres's tenor & keep you human.
Voices of school girls rush & surge
through the windows, returning
with the late March wind; the same need
pushing my pen across the page.
Their dresses lyrical against the day's
sharp edges. Dark harmonies. Bright
as lamentations behind a spasm band
from New Orleans. A throng of boys
are throwing at a bloodhound barking
near a blaze of witch hazel at the corner
of the fence. Mister Backlash.
I close my eyes & feel castanetted
fingers on the spine, slow as Monk's
"Mysterioso"; a man can hurt for years
before words flow into a pattern
so woman-smooth, soft as a pine-scented

With Donna Faye's girl.
Honey, hush. You don't
Say. Her sister,
Charlene, was silly
Too. Jump into bed
With anything that wore
Pants. White, black,
Chinese, crazy, or old.
Some woman in Chicago
hooked a blade into her.
Remember? Now don't say
You done forgot Charlene.
Her face a little blurred
But she coming back now.
Loud & clear. With those
Real big, sad, gray eyes.
A natural-born hellraiser,
& loose as persimmon pie.
You said it, honey.
Miss High Yellow.
I heard she's the reason
Frank shot down Otis Lee
Like a dog in The Blue
Moon. She was a blood-
Sucker. I hate to say this,
But she had Arthur
On a short leash too.
Your Arthur, Mary.
She was only a girl
When Arthur closed his eyes.
Thirteen at the most.
She was doing what women do
Even then. I saw them
With my own two eyes,
& promised God Almighty
I wouldn't mention it.
But it don't hurt
To mention it now, not
After all these years.

breeze off the river Lethe. Satori-blue
changes. Syntax. Each naked string
tied to eternity—the backbone
strung like a bass. Magnolia
blossoms fall in the thick tremble
of Mingus's "Love Chant"; extended bars
natural as birds in trees & on powerlines
singing between the cuts—Yardbird
in the soul & soil. Boplicity
takes me to Django's gypsy guitar
& Dunbar's "broken tongue," beyond
god-headed jive of the apocalypse,
& back to the old sorrow songs
where boisterous flowers still nod on their
half-broken stems. The deep rosewood
of the piano says, "Holler
if it feels good." Perfect tension.
The mainspring of notes & extended
possibility—what falls on either side
of a word—the beat between & underneath.
Organic, cellular space. Each riff & word
a part of the whole. A groove. New changes
created. "In the Land of Obladee"
burns out the hell with flatted fifths,
a matrix of blood & language
improvised on a bebop heart
that could stop any moment
on a dime, before going back
to Hughes at the Five Spot.
Twelve bars. Coltrane leafs through
the voluminous air for some note
to save us from ourselves.
The limbo & bridge of a solo . . .
trying to get beyond the tragedy
of always knowing what the right hand
will do . . . ready to let life play me
like Candido's drum.

Work

I won't look at her.
My body's been one
Solid motion from sunrise,
Leaning into the lawnmower's
Roar through pine needles
& crabgrass. Tiger-colored
Bumblebees nudge pale blossoms
Till they sway like silent bells
Calling. But I won't look.
Her husband's outside Oxford,
Mississippi, bidding on miles
Of timber. I wonder if he's buying
Faulkner's ghost, if he might run
Into Colonel Sartoris
Along some dusty road.
Their teenage daughter & son sped off
An hour ago in a red Corvette
For the tennis courts,
& the cook, Roberta,
Only works a half day
Saturdays. This antebellum house
Looms behind oak & pine
Like a secret, as quail
Flash through branches.
I won't look at her. Nude
On a hammock among elephant ears
& ferns, a pitcher of lemonade
Sweating like our skin.
Afternoon burns on the pool
Till everything's blue,
Till I hear Johnny Mathis
Beside her like a whisper.
I work all the quick hooks
Of light, the same unbroken
Rhythm my father taught me

Years ago: *Always give*
A man a good day's labor.
I won't look. The engine
Pulls me like a dare.
Scent of honeysuckle
Sings black sap through mystery,
Taboo, law, creed, what kills
A fire that is its own heart
Burning open the mouth.
But I won't look
At the insinuation of buds
Tipped with cinnabar.
I'm here, as if I never left,
Stopped in this garden,
Drawn to some Lotus-eater. Pollen
Explodes, but I only smell
Gasoline & oil on my hands,
& can't say why there's this bed
Of crushed narcissus
As if gods wrestled here.

Praising Dark Places

If an old board laid out in a field
Or backyard for a week,
I'd lift it up with my finger,
A tip of a stick.
Once I found a scorpion
Crimson as a hibernating crawfish
As if a rainbow edged underneath;
Centipedes & unnameable
Insects sank into loam
With a flutter. My first lesson:
Beauty can bite. I wanted
To touch scarlet pincers—

Warriors that never zapped
Their own kind, crowded into
A city cut off from the penalty
Of sunlight. The whole rotting
Determinism just an inch beneath
The soil. Into the darkness
Of opposites, like those racial
Fears of the night, I am drawn again,
To conception & birth. Roots of ivy
& farkleberry can hold a board down
To the ground. In this cellular dirt
& calligraphy of excrement,
Light is a god-headed
Law & weapon.

A Good Memory

    1   *Wild Fruit*
I came to a bounty of black lustre
One July afternoon & didn't
Call my brothers. A silence
Coaxed me up into oak branches
Woodpeckers had weakened.
But they held there, braced
By a hundred years of vines
Strong & thick
Enough to hang a man.
The pulpy, sweet musk
Exploded in my mouth
As each indigo skin collapsed.
Muscadines hung in clusters,
& I forgot about jellybeans,
Honeycomb, & chocolate kisses.
I could almost walk on air
The first time I couldn't get enough

Of something, & in that embrace
Of branches I learned the first
Secret I could keep.

    2   *Meat*
Folk magic hoodooed us
Till the varmints didn't taste bitter
Or wild. We boys & girls
Knew how to cut away musk glands
Behind their legs. Good
With knives, we believed
We weren't poor. A raccoon
Would stand on its hind legs
& fight off dogs. Rabbits
Learned how to make hunters
Shoot at spiders when headlighting.
A squirrel played trickster
On the low branches
Till we were our own targets.
We garnished the animal's
Spirit with red pepper
& basil as it cooked
With a halo of herbs
& sweet potatoes. Served
On chipped, hand-me-down
Willow-patterned plates.
We weren't poor.
If we didn't say
Grace, we were slapped
At the table. Sometimes
We weighed the bullet
In our hands, tossing it left
To right, wondering if it was
Worth more than the kill.

    3   *Breaking Ground*
I told Mister Washington
You couldn't find a white man
With his name. But after forty years

At the tung oil mill, coughing up old dust,
He only talked butter beans & okra.
He moved like a sand crab.
Born half-broken, he'd say
If I didn't have this bad leg
I'd break ground to kingdom come.
He only stood erect behind
The plow, grunting against
The blade's slow cut.
Sometimes he'd just rock
Back & forth, in one place,
Hardly moving an inch
Till the dirt gave away
& he stumbled a foot forward,
Humming, "Amazing Grace."
Like good & evil woven
Into each other, rutabagas
& Irish potatoes came out
Worm-eaten. His snow peas
Melted on tender stems,
Impersonating failure.
To prove that earth can heal,
He'd throw his body
Against the plow each day, pushing
Like a small man entering a big woman.

   4   *Soft Touch*
Men came to her back door & knocked.
Food was the password. When switch engines
Stopped & boxcars changed tracks
To the sawmill, they came like Gypsies,
A red bandanna knotted at the throat,
A harmonica in the hip pocket of overalls
Thin as washed-out sky. They brought rotgut
Drought years, following some clear-cut
Sign or icon in the ambiguous
Green that led to her back porch
Like the Black Snake Blues.
They paid with yellow pencils

For crackling bread, molasses, & hunks
Of fatback. Sometimes grits & double-yolk
Eggs. Collard greens & okra. Louisianne
Coffee & chicory steamed in heavy white cups.
They sat on the swing & ate from blue
Flowered plates. Good-evil men who
Ran from something or to someone,
A thirty-year headstart on the Chicago hawk
That overtook them at Castle Rock.
She watched each one disappear over the trestle,
As if he'd turn suddenly & be her lost brother
Buddy, with bouquets of yellow pencils
In Mason jars on the kitchen windowsill.

5   *Shotguns*
The day after Christmas
Blackbirds lifted like a shadow
Of an oak, slow leaves
Returning to bare branches.
We followed them, a hundred
Small premeditated murders
Clustered in us like happiness.
We had the scent of girls
On our hands & in our mouths,
Moving like jackrabbits from one
Dream to the next. Brandnew
Barrels shone against the day
& stole wintery light
From trees. In the time it took
To run home & grab Daddy's gun,
The other wing-footed boys
Stumbled from the woods.
Johnny Lee was all I heard,
A siren in the flesh,
The name of a fallen friend
In their wild throats. Only Joe
Stayed to lift Johnny's head
Out of the ditch, rocking back
& forth. The first thing I did

Was to toss the shotgun
Into a winterberry thicket,
& didn't know I was running
To guide the paramedics into
The dirt-green hush. We sat
In a wordless huddle outside
The operating room, till a red light
Over the door began pulsing
Like a broken vein in a skull.

  6   *Cousins*
Figs. Plums. Stolen
Red apples were sour
When weighed against your body
In the kitchen doorway
Where late July
Shone through your flowered dress
Worn thin by a hundred washings.
Like colors & strength
Boiled out of cloth,
Some deep & tall scent
Made the daylilies cower.
Where did the wordless
Moans come from in twilit
Rooms between hunger
& panic? Those years
We fought aside each other's hands.
Sap pulled a song
From the red-throated robin,
Drove bloodhounds mad
At the edge of a cornfield,
Split the bud down to hot colors.
I began reading you Yeats
& Dunbar, hoping for a potion
To draw the worm out of the heart.
Naked, unable or afraid,
We pulled each other back
Into our clothes.

7 *Immigrants*

Lured by the cobalt
Stare of blast furnaces,
They talked to the dead
& unborn. Their demons
& gods came with black rhinoceros powder
In ivory boxes with secret
Latches that opened only
Behind unlit dreams.
They came as Giuseppe, Misako,
& Goldberg, their muscles tuned
To the rhythm of meathooks & washboards.
Some wore raw silk,
A vertigo of color
Under sombrous coats,
& carried weatherbeaten toys.
They touched their hair
& grinned into locked faces
Of nightriders at the A & P.
Some darker than us, we taught them
About *Colored* water fountains & toilets
Before they traded sisters
& daughters for weak smiles
At the fish market & icehouse.
Gypsies among pines at nightfall
With guitars & cheap wine,
Sunsets orange as Django's
Cellophane bouquets. War
Brides spoke a few words of English,
The soil of distant lands
Still under their fingernails.
Ashes within urns. The Japanese plum
Fruitless in our moonlight.
Footprints & nightmares covered
With snow, we were way stations
Between sweatshops & heaven.
Worry beads. Talismans.
Passacaglia. Some followed
Railroads into our green clouds,

Searching for friends & sleepwalkers,
But stayed till we were them
& they were us, grafted in soil
Older than Jamestown & Osceola.
They lived in back rooms
Of stores in The Hollow,
Separated by alleyways
Leading to our back doors,
The air tasting of garlic.
Mister Cheng pointed to a mojo
High John the Conqueror & said
Ginseng. Sometimes zoot-suited
Apparitions left us talking
Pidgin, Tagalog & Spanish.
We showed them fishing holes
& guitar licks. Wax pompadours
Bristled like rooster combs,
But we couldn't stop loving them
Even after they sold us
Rotting fruit & meat,
With fingers pressed down
On the scales. We weren't
Afraid of the cantor's snow wolf
Shadowplayed along the wall
Embedded in shards of glass.
Some came numbered. *Geyn*
Tzum schvartzn yor. Echoes
Drifted up the Mississippi,
Linking us to Sacco, Vanzetti,
& Leo Frank. Sometimes they stole
Our Leadbelly & Bessie Smith,
& headed for L.A. & The Bronx,
As we watched poppies bloom
Out of season, from a needle
& a hundred sanguine threads.

    8   *A Trailer at the Edge of a Forest*
A throng of boys whispered
About the man & his daughters,

How he'd take your five dollars
At the door. With a bull terrier

At his feet, he'd look on. Fifteen
& sixteen, Beatrice & Lysistrata

Were medicinal. Mirrors on the ceiling.
Posters of a black Jesus on a cross. Owls

& ravens could make a boy run out of his shoes.
Country & Western filtered through wisteria.

But I only found dead grass & tire tracks,
As if a monolith had stood there

A lifetime. They said the girls left quick
As katydids flickering against windowpanes.

9   *White Port & Lemon Juice*
At fifteen I'd buy bottles
& hide them inside a drainpipe
Behind the school
Before Friday-night football.
Nothing was as much fun
As shouldering a guard
To the ground on the snap,
& we could only be destroyed
By another boy's speed
On the twenty-yard line.

Up the middle on two, Joe.
Eddie Earl, you hit that damn
Right tackle, & don't let those
Cheerleaders take your eyes off
The ball. We knew the plays
But little about biology
& what we remembered about French
Was a flicker of blue lace
When the teacher crossed her legs.

Our City of Lights
Glowed when they darkened
The field at halftime
& a hundred freejack girls
Marched with red & green penlights
Fastened to their white boots
As the brass band played
"It Don't Mean A Thing."
They stepped so high
The air tasted like jasmine.

We'd shower & rub
Ben-Gay into our muscles
Till the charley horses
Left. Girls would wait
Among the lustrous furniture
Of shadows, ready to
Sip white port & lemon juice.
Music from the school dance
Pulsed through our bodies
As we leaned against the brick wall:

Ernie K-Doe, Frogman
Henry, The Dixie Cups, & Little Richard.
Like echo chambers,
We'd doo-wop song after song
& hold the girls in rough arms,
Not knowing they didn't want to be
Embraced with the strength
We used against fullbacks
& tight ends on the fifty.

Sometimes they rub against us,
Preludes to failed flesh,
Trying to kiss defeat
From our eyes. The fire
Wouldn't catch. We tried
To dodge the harvest moon
That grew red through trees,

In our Central High gold-
&-blue jackets, with perfect
Cleat marks on the skin.

    10   *The Woman Who Loved Yellow*
Mud puppies at Grand Isle,
    English on cue balls, the war
        Somewhere in Southeast Asia—
            That's what we talked about
For hours. She wore a yellow blouse
    & skin-tight hiphuggers,
        & would read my palm
            At the kitchen table: *Your lifeline*
Goes from here to here. Someday you'll fall
In love & swear you've been hoodooed.
        Mama Mary would look at us
            Out of the corner of an eye,
Or frame our faces in a pot lid
    She polished over & over. After she crossed
        The road, I'd throw a baseball
            Till my arms grew sore,
Floating toward flirtatious silhouettes.
    A few days home, her truck-driver
        Husband would blast a tree of mockingbirds
            With his shotgun, & then take off
For Motor City or Eldorado.
    She'd stand at our back door
        Like a dress falling open. Sometimes
            We'd go fishing at the millpond;
I kept away the snakes,
    We baited hooks with crickets.
        A forked willow branch
            Held two bamboo poles
As we unhooked the sky. Breasts
    & earlobes, every fingerprinted
        Curve. When we rose, goldenrod
            Left our tangled outline on the grass.

Birds on a Powerline

Mama Mary's counting them
Again. Eleven black. A single
Red one like a drop of blood

Against the sky. She's convinced
They've been there two weeks.
I bring her another cup of coffee

& a Fig Newton. I sit here reading
Frances Harper at the enamel table
Where I ate teacakes as a boy,

My head clear of voices brought back.
The green smell of the low land returns,
Stealing the taste of nitrate.

The deep-winter eyes of the birds
Shine in summer light like agate,
As if they could love the heart

Out of any wild thing. I stop,
With my finger on a word, listening.
They're on the powerline, a luminous

Message trailing a phantom
Goodyear blimp. I hear her say
Jesus, I promised you. Now

He's home safe, I'm ready.
My traveling shoes on. My teeth
In. I got on clean underwear.

Fever

I took orders, made my trail
Of blood, & you want me
To say it was right.
I go into the desert
Thistle, till I'm stopped
Like an obsidian statue.
The slow rise of below
Sea level to the Rockies,
Where I sleepwalk among
Headshops with false doors
Outside Red Rocks. I weigh my life
Against the evening sky
Orange as dinosaur dung
In scraggly ravines,
Before putting an ear to Cheyenne Mountain
To divine Ute horses,
Chief Joseph. Bombs rest
On springs to absorb a direct hit,
But I only hear my body
Talking to Venus. Breasts
Against the thinnest cloth
This side of heaven.
She rides a cloud horse,
Blowing a soundless whistle
Till I float off like a balloon
Cut loose. A ganglion
Of blossoms pushes through
April like a blood clot.
Odyssey in winding cells,
Into what divides & equals
The axis. Some nights I lie
Awake, staring into a promised land.
A cold wind out of Wyoming
Works the mind, like waves
Against stone, sand & willpower.
I don't know if I can ride

Out the slack, can just float
Along a precipice. I can't
Trust my hands with loved ones,
The drum under my skin
Driven by a burning field. Trees
Stand like a death squad
Hemmed in by juniper & yucca.
Wanderlust, beds where
Unhealing is a religion.
I pray for those who work
Earth down to a blank stare
Up at the Colorado sky.
I thought I could learn
To hold these people, love
Their scary laughter & strength
With children & animals.
They accept heartworms
& infection like gods;
Making me remember
That if I'd stayed home
I would've killed
Someone I love. My father
Stood apart, wounded
By what I had seen.
America, no brass bands,
No confetti. Please
Put away your pinwheels
& tin whistles. What I know
Now can lay open desire
With the right look.
Jill's perfume uncoils a noose
& I am rain beating a leaf;
Anita, a friend's wife, light
Burning paper, untying me
From the hot thread of a blues
Song. *Another man done gone*
Echoes from the prairie,
A penance flesh pays to doubt.

I can't outrun the throng
Of voices like the full moon
In a rearview mirror.
I want to be punched to the floor
In Hillbilly Heaven, as Luanne
Leans over the pool table
In a low-cut dress.
I know how to line up
The balls like a sniper
& not blink; breathe in,
Hold it till the heart
Slows down. The click
Of white ball against black
A kiss. In the Garden of the Gods
We make love under Pleiades,
With Balanced Rock
Gazing like an old mystic,
Where hundreds of birds
Flash in empty eyesockets.
Sugar Dee rolls in on her Harley
From Vegas, wearing silver boots
& gold tassels, & we lie
In each other's arms
Monday to Thursday. Linda,
Roma, Holly, Jan, Peaches—
I drain fears into them
But they can't raise the dead
In my eyes. The barbs fit
Like commas between names,
Worlds, ways of seeing.
If it wasn't for each daybreak
I'd stay here, staked like a star
In the back of the brain.
My shadow would keep watch
Where the coyote's loneliness
Shines like lice in fur.
Smoke edges into scrub oak
& aspen, & the map misleads

Like shark's teeth in the mountains.
I need to know simple things
Again, the hard facts
Alongside innocence.
You can hug flags into triangles,
But can't hide the blood
By tucking in the corners.
I can now see legs & arms
Wound in concertina wire,
The few who fell when I aimed.
One woman leads to the next
Excuse, names like teethmarks,
Everything connected to a sapper
With a grenade in his hand.

Little Man Around the House

Mama Elsie's ninety now.
She calls you whippersnapper.
When you two laugh, her rheumatism
Slips out the window like the burglar
She hears nightly. Three husbands
& an only son dead, she says,
I'll always be a daddy's girl.
Sometimes I can't get Papa's face
Outta my head. But this boy, my great-
Great-grandson, he's sugar in my coffee.

You look up from your toy
Telescope, with Satchmo's eyes,
As if I'd put a horn to your lips.
You love maps of buried treasure,
Praying Mantis, & Public Enemy . . .
Blessed. For a moment, I'm jealous.
You sit like the king of trumpet

Between my grandmama & wife,
Youngblood, a Chesire cat
Hoodooing two birds at once.

—for Ladarius

Songs for My Father

I told my brothers I heard
You & mother making love,
Your low moans like blues
Bringing them into the world.
I didn't know if you were laughing
Or crying. I held each one down
& whispered your song in their ears.
Sometimes I think they're still jealous
Of our closeness, having forgotten
We had to square off & face each other,
My fists balled & cocked by haymakers.
That spring I lifted as many crossties
As you. They can't believe I can
Remember when you had a boy's voice.

∽

You were a quiet man
Who'd laugh like a hyena
On a hill, with your head
Thrown back, gazing up at the sky.
But most times you just worked
Hard, rooted in the day's anger
Till you'd explode. We always
Walked circles around
You, wider each year,
Hungering for stories

To save us from ourselves.
Like a wife who isn't touched,
We had to do something bad
Before you'd look into our eyes.

                  ∾

We spent the night before Easter
Coloring eggs & piling them into pyramids
In two crystal punch bowls.
Our suits, ties, white shirts, shoes,
All lined up for the next day.
We had memorized our passages
From the bible, about the tomb
& the angel rolling back the stone.
You were up before daybreak,
In the sagebrush, out among goldenrod
& mustard weed, hiding the eggs
In gopher holes & underneath roots.
Mother always argued with you,
Wondering why you made everything so hard.

                  ∾

We stood on a wooden platform
Facing each other with sledgehammers,
A copper-tipped sieve sunken into the ground
Like a spear, as we threaded on five foot
Of galvanized pipe for the pump.
As if tuned to some internal drum,
We hammered the block of oak
Placed on top of the pipe.
It began inching downward
As we traded blows—one for you,
One for me. After a half hour
We threaded on another five foot. The sweat
Gleamed on our shirtless bodies, father
& son tied to each other until we hit water.

Goddamn you. Goddamn you.
If you hit her again I'll sail through
That house like a dustdevil.
Everyone & everything here
Is turning against you,
That's why I had to tie the dog
To a tree before you could chastise us.
He darted like lightning through the screen door.
I know you'll try to kill me
When it happens. You know
I'm your son & it's bound to happen.
Sometimes I close my eyes till I am
On a sea of falling dogwood blossoms,
But someday this won't work.

I confess, I am the ringleader
Who sneaked planks out of the toolshed,
Sawed & hammered together the wagon.
But I wasn't fool enough to believe
That you would've loved our work.
So, my brothers & I dug a grave
In the corner of the field for our wagon
That ran smooth as a Nat King Cole
Love ballad. We'd pull it around
The edge of our world & rebury it
Before the 5 o'clock mill whistle blew.
I bet it's still there, the wood gray
& light as the ribs of my dog Red
After somebody gunned him down one night.

You banged a crooked nail
Into a pine slab,
Wanting me to believe

I shouldn't have been born
With hands & feet
If I didn't do
Your kind of work.
You hated my books.
Sometimes at dusk,
I faced you like that
Childhood friend you trained
Your heart to always run
Against, the horizon crimson
As the eyes of a fighting cock.

∽

I never asked you how you
Passed the driver's test,
Since you could only write
& read your name. But hell,
You were good with numbers;
Always counting your loot.
That Chevy truck swerved
Along back roads night & day.
I watched you use wire
& sunlight to train
The strongest limbs,
How your tongue never obeyed
The foreman, how the truck motor
Was stunted, frozen at sixty.

∽

You wanted to fight
When I told you that a woman
Can get rid of a man
With a flake of lye
In his bread each day.
When you told her what I said
I bet the two of you made love

Till the thought flew out of your head.
Now, when you stand wax-faced
At the door, your eyes begging
Questions as you mouth wordless
Songs like a red-belly perch,
Assaying the scene for what it is,
I doubt if love can part my lips.

∾

Sometimes you could be
That man on a red bicycle,
With me on the handlebars,
Just rolling along a country road
On the edge of July, honeysuckle
Lit with mosquito hawks.
We rode from under the shady
Overhang, back into sunlight.
The day bounced off car hoods
As the heat & stinking exhaust
Brushed against us like a dragon's
Roar, nudging the bike with a tremor,
But you steered us through the flowering
Dogwood like a thread of blood.

∾

You lean on a yard rake
As dry leaves & grass smolder
In a ditch in mid March,
Two weeks before your sixty-first
Birthday. You say I look happy.
I must be in love. It is 1986,
Five months before your death.
You toss a stone at the two dogs
Hooked together in a corner of the yard.
You smile, look into my eyes
& say you want me to write you a poem.

I stammer for words. You
Toss another stone at the dogs
& resume raking the leafless grass.

        ~

I never said thanks for Butch,
The wooden dog you pulled by a string.
It was ugly as a baldheaded doll.
Patched with wire & carpenter's glue, something
I didn't believe you had ever loved.
I am sorry for breaking it in half.
I never meant to make you go
Stand under the falling snowflakes
With your head bowed on Christmas
Day. I couldn't look at Butch
& see that your grandmother Julia,
That old slave woman who beat you
As if that's all she knew, had put love
Into it when she carved the dog from oak.

        ~

I am unlike Kikuji
In Kawabata's *Thousand Cranes*,
Since I sought out one of your lovers
Before you were dead.
Though years had passed
& you were with someone else,
She thought I reminded her
Of a man she'd once known.
She pocketed the three dollars.
A big red lampshade bloodied
The room, as if held by a mad
Diogenes. Yes, she cried out,
But she didn't sing your name
When I planted myself in her.

~

You spoke with your eyes
Last time I saw you, cramped
Between a new wife & a wall. You couldn't
Recognize funeral dirt stamped down
With dancesteps. Your name & features half
X-ed out. I could see your sex,
Your shame, a gold-toothed pout,
As you made plans for the next house you'd build,
Determined to prove me wrong. I never knew
We looked so much like each other. Before
I could say I loved you, you began talking money,
Teasing your will with a cure in Mexico.
You were skinny, bony, but strong enough to try
Swaggering through that celestial door.

Thieves of Paradise

Mcmory Cave

A tallow worked into a knot
of rawhide, with a ball of waxy light
tied to a stick, the boy
scooted through a secret mouth
of the cave, pulled by the flambeau
in his hand. He could see
the gaze of agate eyes
& wished for the forbidden
plains of bison & wolf, years
from the fermented honey
& musty air. In the dried
slag of bear & bat guano,
the initiate stood with sleeping
gods at his feet, lost
in the great cloud of their one
breath. Their muzzles craved
touch. How did they learn
to close eyes, to see into
the future? Before the Before:
mammon was unnamed & mist
hugged ravines & hillocks.
The elders would test him
beyond doubt & blood. Mica
lit the false skies where
stalactite dripped perfection
into granite. He fingered
icons sunlight & anatase
never touched. Ibex carved
on a throwing stick, reindeer
worried into an ivory amulet,
& a bear's head. Outside,
the men waited two days
for him, with condor & bovid,
& not in a thousand years
would he have dreamt a woman
standing here beside a man,

saying, "This is as good
as the stag at Salon Noir
& the polka-dotted horses."
The man scribbles *Leo loves*
Angela below the boy's last bear
drawn with manganese dioxide
& animal fat. This is where
sunrise opened a door in stone
when he was summoned to drink
honey wine & embrace a woman
beneath a five-pointed star.
Lying there beside the gods
hefty & silent as boulders,
he could almost remember
before he was born, could see
the cliff from which he'd fall.

Out There There Be Dragons

Beyond King Ptolemy's dream
outside the broken
girdle of chance, beyond
the Lighthouse of Pharos
in a kingdom of sea turtles,
nothing can inter or outrun
a stormy heart. Beyond galleon
& disappearing lovers, a flame
flounces behind a glass crab
to signal a craggy reef
in the Bay of Alexandria.
Beyond archipelagos of drizzle
& salt, Armageddon & hellfire,
bearded seals turn into Helen's
mermaids sunning on a white beach
beside Paris, where blotches of ink
map omens. Beyond Atlantis

uncovered by desert winds
phantom armies ride against,
necklace of shark teeth
adorn virgins. When earth
dilates, the known magnifies
till unknowns tincture silk,
till pomegranates bleed
redemption into soil.
Sirens cry across dark
waters, as anguelle becomes air,
beyond the mapmaker's omphalos
where hydra first mounted Venus.

The Song Thief

                    Up there
in that diorama of morning
light through springtime branches,
how many feathered lifetimes
sifted down through green
leaves, how many wars sprung up
& ended before the cowbird figured out
laws of gravity in Cloudcuckooland,
before the songbird's egg
was nudged from its nest?
Maybe a flock followed a herd
of heifers across a pasture,
pecking wildflower seed
from fresh dung
when the first urge of switcheroo
flashed in their dirt-colored heads.
What nature of creature comforts
taught the unsung cells this art,
this shell game of odds
& percentages in the serpent's leafy
Babylon? Only the cowbird's mating song

fills the air until their young
are ravenous as five
of the seven deadly sins
woven into one.

Wet Nurse

The shadow of a hilltop
    halves an acropolis
in the head of a serf's
    descendant. Heimdall's horn
at the gates of Asgard
    pulses beneath prayers
for wealth. April unhinges
    rings in the cottonwood
till sap seethes from each slow
    hour. A sliver of whalebone
slips from the mother's satin corset
    as the dark-skinned nurse
unbuttons her floral blouse
    & unhooks her cheap bra.
The child swallows a lament,
    & his rich father nods
to a reproduction of Da Vinci's
    Madonna Litta to answer
silence, to quieten his fear
    of the primal in the wife's
smile. But what isn't desired
    stays a hard-green or grows
too sweet for the tongue.
    A cry, a wet trigger—
agog. Not enough milk
    left for her own child,
each nipple's an eyedropper
    of rage & beatitude.

Ode to a Drum

Gazelle, I killed you
for your skin's exquisite
touch, for how easy it is
to be nailed to a board
weathered raw as white
butcher paper. Last night
I heard my daughter praying
for the meat here at my feet.
You know it wasn't anger
that made me stop my heart
till the hammer fell. Weeks
ago, I broke you as a woman
once shattered me into a song
beneath her weight, before
you slouched into that
grassy hush. But now
I'm tightening lashes,
shaping hide as if around
a ribcage, stretched
like five bowstrings.
Ghosts cannot slip back
inside the body's drum.
You've been seasoned
by wind, dust & sunlight.
Pressure can make everything
whole again, brass nails
tacked into the ebony wood
your face has been carved
five times. I have to drive
trouble from the valley.
Trouble in the hills.
Trouble on the river
too. There's no kola nut,
palm wine, fish, salt,
or calabash. Kadoom.

Kadoom.   Kadooom.   Ka-
doooom.   Kadoom.   Now
I have beaten a song back into you,
rise & walk away like a panther.

Eclogue at Daybreak

His unlidded eyes a wish
always coming true,
as his body slithered
from a sheath of skin
half-alive on the grass
like a final lesson on escape.
He moved only when other things
strayed beyond suspicion.
The worlds inside sleep
couldn't hold him. In an arcade
somewhere in a marketplace
he was Houdini reincarnated
in a box. Soon came the hour
he was created for: a woman,
free-footed as Isadora
in sashes, draped his body
over hers. An apprentice
placed an apple in her left hand
& lush gardens sprouted across
three canvases. Her smooth skin,
how his wedge-shaped head
lingered between her breasts,
left him drowsy. The clocks
sped up. A cruel season
fell across their pose
as they began a slow dance.
She reshaped the pattern of skulls
on his yellow skin, a deep

falling inside him when her hips
quivered & arms undulated,
stealing the pleas of prey.

Genealogy

We were almost unreal.
    If you don't believe me,
  let the wind open the *Journals*

of the House off Burgesses
    so you can hear it whisper
  lessons of the soil through maple

& birch. We buried
    ourselves in holes, shelter
  we could wrestle free of earth

& wood held in place by snow,
    this last door nailed shut
  with icicles. Rations dwindled

to eight ounces of meal
    & a pint of peas a day,
  working with maggots & cobwebs.

That winter a man salted down guilt,
    feeding upon his wife
  till she was only a head.

You can erase Sir Thomas Smith
    from your genealogical charts;
  our ancestors stole handfuls of oats

& were chained to trees,
    starved or broken
  slowly on the wheel,

& here's our coat of arms.
    This crossbone. This boar
  wreathed with hemlock & laurel.

Kosmos

Walt, you shanghied me to this
oak, as every blood-tipped leaf
soliloquized "Strange Fruit"
like the octoroon in New Orleans

who showed you how passion
ignited dogwood, how it rose
from inside the singing sap.
You heard primordial notes

murmur up from the Mississippi,
a clank of chains among the green
ithyphallic totems, betting your heart
could run vistas with Crazy Horse

& runaway slaves. Sunset dock
to whorehouse, temple to hovel,
your lines traversed America's
white space, driven by a train whistle.

       ∽

Believing you could be three places
at once, you held the gatekeeper's daughter,
lured by the hard eyes of his son,
on a voyage in your head

to a face cut into Mount Rushmore.
You knew the curse in sperm
& egg, but had faith in the soil,
that it would work itself out

in generations, springs piercing bedrock.
Love pushed through jailhouses, into bedrooms
of presidents & horse thieves,
oil sucked into machines in sweatshops

& factories. I followed from my hometown
where bedding an oak is bread on the table;
where your books, as if flesh, were locked
in a glass case behind the check-out desk.

            ◇

Wind-jostled foliage—a scherzo,
a bellydancer adorned in bells.
A mulatto moon halved into yesterday
& tomorrow, some balustrade

full-bloomed. But you taught home
was wherever my feet took me,
birdsong over stockyards or Orient,
fused by handshake & blood.

Seed & testament, naked
among fire-nudged thistle,
from the Rockies to below
sea level, to the steamy bayous,

I traipsed your footpath.
Falsehoods big as stumbling blocks
in the mind, lay across the road,
beside a watery swoon.

I'm back with the old folk
who speak your glossolalia of pure
sense unfolding one hundred years.
Unlocked chemistry, we're tied to sex,

spectral flower twisted out of
filigreed language & taboo
stubborn as crabgrass. You slept
nude under god-hewn eyes & ears.

Laughter in trees near a canebrake,
I know that song. Old hippie,
before Selma & People's Park,
your democratic nights a vortex

of waterlilies. The skin's cage
opened, but you were locked inside
your exotic Ethiopia. Everything
sprung back like birds after a shot.

Confluence

I've been here before, dreaming myself
backwards, among grappling hooks of light.

True to the seasons, I've lived every word
spoken. Did I walk into someone's nightmare?

Hunger quivers on a fleshly string
at the crossroad. So deep is the lore,

there's only tomorrow today where darkness
splinters & wounds the bird of paradise.

On paths that plunge into primordial
green, Echo's laughter finds us together.

In the sweatshops of desire men think
if they don't die the moon won't rise.

All the dead-end streets run into one
moment of bliss & sleight of hand.

Beside the Euphrates, past the Tigris,
up the Mississippi. Bloodline & clockwork.

The X drawn where we stand. Trains
follow rivers that curve around us.

The distant night opens like a pearl
fan, a skirt, a heart, a drop of salt.

When we embrace, we are not an island
beyond fables & the blue exhaust of commerce.

When the sounds of River Styx punish
trees, my effigy speaks to the night owl.

Our voices break open the pink magnolia
where struggle is home to the beast in us.

All the senses tuned for the Hawkesbury,
labyrinths turning into lowland fog.

Hand in hand, feeling good, we walk
phantoms from thc floating machinc.

When a drowning man calls out,
his voice follows him downstream.

Palimpsest

Modern Medea
Apex, triangle . . . a dead child
on the floor between his mother
& four slavecatchers in a Cincinnati hideout.
Blood colors her hands

& the shadow on the wall
a lover from the grave.
She sacrificed her favorite
first. He must've understood,

stopped like a stone figure.
Where's the merciful weapon, sharp
as an icepick or hook knife?
We know it was quick,

a stab of light. Treed
as if by dogs around an oak—
she stands listening to a river
sing, begging salt for her wounds.

Meditations on a Smoothing Iron
They touched fingers to tongues,
& then tapped you with wet kisses.
You've outlasted five women
who pressed white shirts of bankers,

preachers, bartenders, & thieves.
You left an imprint on a pair of trousers
when he pulled her away & embraced her.
You smoothed the silk underwear

of a thirteen-year-old who died
in childbirth. You're the weapon
Three Fingers was done in with.
McGrory wiped off every smudge.

You left Memphis, headed for Ohio,
pushed by hard times. For thirty years
you were a doorstop, & then a Saturday-morning
yardsale made you a debutante's paperweight.

Basiliqué
I dip a twig into a glass of rosé
& the daughter of that Alabama judge
struts through the door,
Rene Depestre. The dead rise

when gods bend me into this
Yanvalou, & nightbirds
sing in the redbuds.
There's no medicine

to cure her of me.
No lies to cut the potion.
I am Papa-Legba
from the backwoods,

& the cock's blood
metamorphoses my hands
into five-pointed stars
holding down the night.

Mercy
Old Lady Emma's calling her dog
Pepper again. I can see skidmarks
where somebody's car tried to brake.
Her voice a high-pitched reed flute.

All day she sings out his name,
but he can't rise from where
I stamped down the red clay.
Can't push away the creek-polished stones.

I told her some boy
from The Projects walked off
with Pepper, that he's bound
to break free & come home.

Leaning on her oak-limb
cane, she wants me to go search
the neighborhood. It'll take half the night
to walk up & down the streets, calling.

    Diorama
Terra incognita—crosshairs
& lines on the atlas—anywhere
have-nots outnumber raintrees along avenues
igniting skylines, marrying the dead

to the unborn. The meek. The brain
an Orwellian timemachine where *Boyz
N the Hood* drifts into a Fagin school.
They look for Wild Maggie Carson,

Crazy Butch, the Little Dead Rabbits,
Plug Uglies, & Daylight Boys. No one
escapes the concentric shotgun blast.
Circles reach back to Hell's Kitchen

& out to Dorchester, coldcocking
the precious sham of neon. The night
sways like a pinball machine on a warped floor
slowdragged smooth by Love & Hate in each other's arms.

    Red Dust
Gargoyled angels ride
the backs of black men
who hurl their bodies
on exploding grenades,

who vaporize into unquestioned
mist & syllables of names,
who rise like curses & prayers
entwined in broken earth

& fall into smoky-red
cerecloth. An answer
coils around wounded branches.
After fragments of bone

settle on leaves, & birds
reclaim their songs, the world
moves again. Someone speaks
& the army ants go to work.

Descendants of the Dragon
Tanks push till day breaks from night
in Tiananmen Square, as gardens uproot
& bleed a map only the blind follow. The dead
hold each other in broken arms like a fire-gutted

rock 'n' roll dancehall. Chrysanthemum
& lotus take root again, womb to earth,
until human & animal wail as one
outside The Forbidden City.

A line of students falls
beneath a dancing paper dragon. Spent
ammo casings refract lodestone. Flames
push aside a river of voices & singe

trees along The Bamboo Curtain.
Somewhere a seismograph knows now is
the time to drop a bronze ball
into the frog's mouth.

Shape & Sound

Mallets ring out over the Hawkesbury
as they teach stone to worship human posture,
how to be one with hold & abandonment. Below
Wondabyne's sculpture garden a one-carriage railway

crouches in the thigh of the valley. A whistle cuts
like a blade, & the twelve sentinels of Gosford quiver
as commuters wave. Curses have fallen where hands
from Katmandu use two SRA nails to sign the air.

Sculptors from Papua New Guinea, Bulgaria, Nepal,
France, stand with Aussies at the Gateway of Peace.
The song of iron & wood persuades a seven-ton block
to grow into a woman who calls out to passing boats,

a new friend embraced into the world. The stone
figures listen to river music like hands fashioning
lovers in dark curves—in the right angle of a Greek
dead on the ground.

Gutbucket

I'm back, armed
with Muddy's mojo hand.
Take your daughters & hide them.
Redbuds cover the ground

like Lady Day's poppies
kissed beyond salvation & damnation:
so pretty in their Easter dresses
this day of the flower eater.

I'm fool enough to believe
loneliness can never tango me into
oblivion again. I've swayed to Lockjaw,
Trane, Pepper, & Ornette,

& outlived the cold whiteness
of Head Power in Shinjuku.
I know if you touch beauty right
a bird sings the monkey to you.

    A Call from the Terrace
Old bile in young fruit
puckers the mouth shut.
Her voice on the phone: *I see you*
sometimes from our window

when you're grafting roses.
I bet you can't guess
what my left hand's doing now?
Faces you've known forever

glide by like jack-o'-lanterns,
living to make your life miserable,
kissing pedigreed dogs & cats to sleep
behind padlocked doors.

Inheritors pace-off stolen land.
The dead fertilize the interminable
future, flowers drawing psychosis
up through their roots.

    Pain Merchant
Twelve blues songs
distilled, every
letdown focused through eyes
looking into mine. Pestilence

clusters at the base of the spine
the way a tumor flowers. An owl
laments. Each breath takes me back
to the Nile. I am the last stonemason

in Khufu's chamber, locking out
daylight & greed, just before
ascending. I taste each breath.
What did I do to be so black & blue?

fades. I don't care what you say,
with your bright pills & capsules,
I am going to teach Mr. Pain
to sway, to bop.

In Love with the Nightstalker
To kiss death, to sleep
with a persona,
to make love
to Satan & his square-jawed effigies

smiling from *Esquire* & *GQ*.
His double profile in a bedroom mirror:
Crescent, knife in a father's hand.
With so much fear, there's no

orgasm. The brain: a cruel king
ogles from a stone tower.
Or, a dog goes down
on all fours,

crawling in the dust. I stop
& wag my tail. Whining for bread
held out in his left hand, I come forth,
eyes fixed on his right fist cocked like a hammer.

Note to Pavese
I'm in the corner of your right
eye, that black man in a bar
drinking your lush red wine.
As your dream women pass before us,

this one beauty floats into night
mystery—*la donna dalla voce rauca.*
A dress so bright, the place darkens
like a headless rooster across the floor.

Maybe flesh wasn't made to possess.
Sure as Hannibal jostled stone gates,
if you're Mediterranean, Africa sings
in your blood & sperm. Late nights,

as you translated Melville & Faulkner,
did classic fear crawl into you? I don't
know why she came nude to the door, why
she said we'd been making love for days.

 Russian Phantasia
The lovers fall asleep after a fifth
of vodka, watching reruns of *Dallas,*
Fantasy Island & *I Led Three Lives.*
The night's punched black & blue.

Now, they can see Pushkin's
love-sick Evgeny in Petrograd
the moment the Neva leaps
its banks, can hear him cursing

& shaking a balled fist
at Peter the Great's statue.
The bronze horse springs
like an acetylene torch.

They're with Evgeny, caught-up
in the plot, but even ghosts are forbidden
to venture down into catacombs
like ghettoes fenced-in by freeways.

The Modern World

The mind tortures a traitor.
You want to daydream hummingbirds
in larkspur, but all you can see
is the bitch eating her puppies

under the house. You're unsure
if Honey loves you a year later.
The mirrors face each other
so she falls into your arms

when you push her away.
Snow fills the hourglass
as you read Mandelstam's letters
to Gorky about clothes. Be thankful

you whisper. Another bomb-shaped
question glides overhead like the
Hindenburg. You load the gun
when you think you're unloading it.

Nighthawks

Dusk lit paths quicker
than stars on gunmetal. Swift
as bats condemned to dart through
the mind's blue hoops. Smooth

as a boy's flashy hands over a girl's
boyish hips. Shirley Ruth & I knew
where to find each other, hugging
the ground in a place ghosts hid.

Our brothers counted us out
as we kissed under branches of a fig
tree huddled into a wide skirt
against summer grass. Night-

hawks scissored in & out of pines
& oaks, as if pulling silver thread
through a black cloth of loopholes,
a drunk's signature on a quitclaim deed.

Triangles
It's one of those things.
Like drawing a line in the dust
& pointing a chicken's beak
to it. How the hypnosis

works, I don't know.
It's like placing three pans
of dog food on the floor
equally apart.

Triangles are torture.
The dog is condemned
to walk in a circle
till he drops dead.

This is Dante's first cycle,
rings looped inside each other
like a sorcerer's bracelet, a heart
divided into trinity by good & evil.

Balance
I kill a part
so the other lives;
unlike the snake
chopped in half,

rejoining itself among
nightshade. Otherworldly
green—amazed by what
logic weaves as one—

how the sky's balanced
by the ground underfoot.
I think of Count Basie,
what he knew

to leave out. Leverage
determines the arc,
& everything else is
naked grace.

Mumble Peg

We stood in a wide-legged
dare, three country boys
triangulating a circle
in April, lines scored in clay.
With the snap of a wrist
bright-handled knives spun
& pierced each other's plot.
Tied to earth, we couldn't run
for the snowball wagon
anymore. The blades marked
our places, as we swaggered
toward the old man
hunched over his metal scoop
singing across the block of ice.
His row of bottles huddled
in slots like a rainbow
under the canopy & he'd grab
the right flavor without looking,
as if his body didn't need a mind
to guide it. After the sweet air
wore off, we returned to our knives
to homestead spring. Dragonflies
stitched the day with a blue-

green blur. Like Pascal
tossing a coin into the air,
our bodies posed questions
while girls skipped rope
till clay hardened into reddish stone.
They leapt so high they answered
the day as we stood in the silent
council of our pocketknives.
If a boy could no longer stand
like a one-legged crane on the land he owned,
he lost it all. But the winner
always looked the loneliest
in his circle at sunset.
If no one could see us
as the brain divided hemispheres
in the garden, what would we own?
A faint Venus burned the sky
as we bet each girl a kiss
if we guessed the color of her underwear.

Ia Drang Valley

To sleep here, I play dead.
My mind takes me over the Pacific
to my best friend's wife nude
on their bed. I lean over
& kiss her. Sometimes the spleen
decides what it takes to bridge
another night. The picture
dissolves into gray as I fight,
cussing the jumpcut that pulls me back
to the man in a white tunic,
where I'm shoved against the wall
with the rest of the hostages.
The church spire hides

under dusk in the background,
& my outflung arms shadow bodies
in the dirt. I close my eyes
but Goya's *Third of May* holds
steady, growing sharper. I stand
before the bright rifles,
nailed to the moment.

Cenotaph

An owl hoots my dead friend's name
from a high branch, gossiping
about how I dreamt his sister
nude beside me in Chu Lai,
how sometimes their faces
were one. I can't escape
his voice & her onyx eyes
montaged into a hot season.
Maybe she'd see Judas
if we embraced. Or believe
she's hugging her brother,
kissing him back into this world.
Denial is a cardinal flying backwards,
as if the ambush were shooting stars
along a paddie dike. Blackberries
color our lips. The times we played
Buffalo Bill & Sitting Bull,
he'd fall like a shadow in a cenotaph,
but my teasing never failed to raise
his eyelids. I know his mother
tried to pull the flag to the floor
& pry open the coffin. There's no verb
to undo the night he hit the booby trap,
& I know shame would wear me like a mask
against a century of hot morning light
if I didn't slowdrag to Rockin' Dopsie.

The Trapper's Bride

She's from Bengal or Kashmir,
holding James Dean's hand
in *East of Eden*. I wonder
if I'm a eunuch in her head,
as we face this Indian warrior
selling his daughter for guns,
red flannel, beads, tobacco,
& blankets. The green sky
& pale horse counterpoint
the bride's bemusement.
What about the other woman
half nude on the ground
in a red garment, like hush
& rage brushed over primer?
The trappers sit like Jesus
& a shepherd in rawhide,
years from their future
on a hill of buffalo skins
at Michigan Carbon Works.
We survey the vista of golds
& dark accents. She says, "Oops,"
when our eyes meet, as she leans
forward in a lowcut blouse, almost
touching the canvas. Yes,
he knew how to work with light.
A bruise seethes into the lost
colors of our mute rendezvous.

Eclogue at Twilight

The three wrestle in the grass
five or ten minutes, shaking blooms

& winged seeds to the ground.
The lioness lays a heavy paw on the jackal's chest,
almost motherly. His mate
backs off a few yards. Eyeball
to eyeball, they face each other
before she bites into his belly
& tugs out the ropy entrails
like loops of wet gauze.
Time stops. She'd moved
through the tall yellow sage
as they copulated,
stood only a few feet
away, enveloped in the scent
that drew them together.
When they first saw her
there, they couldn't stop.
Is this how panic & cunning
seethe into the bloodstream?
Without the power to forgive,
locked in ritual, the fight
began before they uncoupled.
A vulture, out of the frame,
draws an unbroken spiral
against the plains & sky.
Black quills scribble
slow as the swing of a hypnotist's
gold chain. For a moment, it seems
she's snuggling up to the jackal.
Maybe the wild aroma of sex
plagues the yellow grass.
A drizzle adds its music
to the background,
& a chorus of young girls
chants from across the hills.
For a man who stumbles
on this scene, with Hegel
& awe in his head, he can't
say if his mouth is opened
by the same cry & song.

The Tally

They're counting nails,
barrels of salt pork,
sacks of tea & sugar,
links of hemp, bolts of cloth
with dead colors, the whole
shape & slack of windy sails
down to galley planks
& clapboard hued by shame.
They're raising & lowering
an anchor clustered with urchins,
wondering if sandstone
can be taught a lesson
if inscribed with names & proclamations.
Snuff, powdered wigs—
redcoats run hands over
porcelain & silverware.
They're uncrating hymnals,
lace, volumes of Hobbes,
Rousseau, & kegs of rum.
Rats scurry across the deck
down the wharf, & a gaggle
of guinea fowl calls to lost sky
from a row of slatted boxes.
Knives & forks, wooden pegs,
balls of twine, vats of tallow,
& whet stones. They're counting women
& men: twenty-two prostitutes, ten
pickpockets, one forger, countless
thieves of duck eggs & black bread.
A soldier pries open a man's fists
to tally twelve marigold seeds—
here for lobbing off a half pound
of butter. Deck hands winch in
the drag of lines. A young officer
surveys the prettiest women, before

stashing *The Collected Quotations
of Pythagoras* for the governor.
Albatross perched on the mast
await another burial at sea,
shadowing a stoic nightingale
in a bamboo cage mended with yarn
where a red-headed woman kneels,
whispering his song to him.

Heroes of Waterloo

Here's the pub they conked
drunks over the head & shanghaied
them on carts rolled down shafts
to the quay. After schooners
of cider, I see the half-dazed
waking to sea monsters
outside The Heads.

Your hands anchor me to the antipodes
as "Stormy Monday Blues"
drowns the mermaid's lament,
& suddenly a man wants to bop
me over the head. The night
steals memories from sandstone
walls the convicts cut.

Larrikins shout middies of Strongbow
& point to the trapdoor
where Captain Hook hides
on the other side of jetlag.
But with your fingertips
at the nape, the blood's sextant,
I can't move beyond the body's true north.

Wokanmagulli

I searched all morning
for them along George Street,
paced The Rocks, corridors
of an invisible cellblock,
but only their absence
made them known. Later,
the surf of Botany Bay
licked out cups of sandstone.
In the Royal Botanic Gardens
I curled up in a cave
as if it waited one thousand
years for me. I weighed my body
against phantoms as car horns
shattered the afternoon.
Trees & flowers had eyes
like stones buried in a riverbed.

Why wasn't I happy
at parties where silhouettes
believed my fingers were jazz
riffs? Couldn't I have been
calm as dragonhead
under shaded glass
at the herbarium?
But when I felt the hearts
of bushrangers beat under
a plot of six shades of grass
like seeds of locoweed left
in the soil by the First Fleet,
it hurt not to speak.

Gnarled figs & ghost gums
slouched into a corroboree
of ring-barked old men.
My grandfather stood before me.
A nude peered from a fire

of waterlilies, but I had to look
through his eyes to see her
smile chiseled in Greek
marble. I tore off
their metal tags,
& my tongue weighed more
than I could balance
as I renamed them
for dead loved ones.

Waratah

Love & pain converge
    to the point of a yellow
  pencil pressed against paper.

At the angle you sit
    the Centrepoint Tower
  is a gigantic lampshade

retrieving your face
    from that old world
  breaking through oils.

Something disturbs the calm
    like a hand through water,
  unromantic as a corpse

hugging a bloated sack
    of poisoned flour slumped
  bedside a billabong.

That green in the sky
    isn't there till dark
  eases across the canvas.

It isn't the Beaujolais
        stealing thoughts on death
    & slamming twilight up

against the buildings.
        The Medusa tongues
    on the kitchen table

pull us into a frame
        to create tension
    that keeps them alive.

New Gold Mountain

Families & dreams chained
to merchants back in Hong Kong,
men drifted to Hsin Chin Shan.

Sails clouded Guichen Bay
quick as brush strokes
against an unreal sky,
vipers in a field of skeletons.

They worked tailings in stamp mills
at Bendigo & Rocky River
before their stores & joss houses

burned down to a pouch of dust.
Blue distance & green mystery
of *Chinatown in Creswick*
highlighted by burnt orange.

Cobb & Co stagecoached horses
into anthills, trying to outrun
the vigilante's dustdevils

whose anger & indigo ignited
kerosene lanterns at Burrangong.
They clawed the earth to get
to suns inside rock, proving

the good in some men
can only half fill
a gold thimble.

White Lady

Something to kill songs
& burn the guts, to ride
& break the hippocampus.
Something to subdue
the green freedom of crows
at Slaughterhouse Creek.
Milk mixed with gin or metho—
something to finish the job
guns & smallpox blankets
didn't do, to prod women
& seduce gods to dance
among trees, letting silver bark
uncurl into an undressed season.
Something to undermine those who
refuse to dangle brass breastplates
from their necks like King Billy.

Something to erase the willy wagtail
from vesperal leaves. No one
can sniff the air & walk miles
straight to water anymore.
Their heads fill with wings
& then they touch down again
like poisoned butterflies

bumping into bougainvillea.
Fringe dwellers languish,
piles of old clothes under gums.
White Lady is their giddy queen,
her arms flung around sleeping
children, ruling dreams
with an iron scepter,
her eyes screwed into them
like knots in bloodwood.

Meditations on a Dingo

The smell of ubiquitous
blood on grass rekindles
the morning she chewed off
her leg. Sniffing left
& right, she plunges into a ravine.
If this is a man's totem,
he must cross the river
of amnesia. In a labyrinth
of familiar scents, nosing
her way around milk thistle,
she eyes her three-footed tracks
printed like stars in clay.
Another ewe has been herded
into the corner of a fence,
& repose wounds the sky.

Can she take a stone in her mouth
& drop it to spring a trap,
before eating the bait
under a pregnant moon? Sunrise
creeps over sandstone. Before
the fever breaks, you're on a hill
cradling a Winchester.

She's there, a few feet
from the rock you're standing
on. You think about the woman
you haven't touched for weeks,
before calling out to Beatrice.
Abetted by a mirage, as you
squeeze the trigger, a shadow
shakes blossoms from a bush.

Report from the Lucky Country

No, please! Then night
scabs over. Is it a call
for help, or a magpie
drugged with starlight?
They goaded him in drunk,
leaning against his totem.
But now he trembles
& pisses on the cell floor,
as cries echo over grasstrees
& wind down to Cat Camp Creek,
Garibaldi Rock—meeting other cries
from South Florida, Transvaal,
Santiago, etching a blue map.
What they want him to sing
can't fit into his mouth.
Green tree frogs & stars are
good listeners, spreading out
till human dust grows into one
compendious anthem. *No,*
please! resounds. Bear hugs
& hammerlocks tilt the world
inside his head. But he won't
climb into a noose, won't lift
himself like a swan diver

off The Gap. That same
Cyclops stares through
the bars, a Tasmanian tiger
telling what his silence means
to the cricket in tussock.

In the Mirror

Joey, you're behind shades
borrowed from Teach on page 67
of *The Australian Woman's Mirror*
March 29, 1961. Under the canopy

of a wide hat, with notebook & pencil,
you gaze out across the Kimberleys,
one step from the corner of time
crawling from a rainbow serpent's cave.

Less than the Crown of Thorns
along the Great Barrier Reef,
I look to see if a crack's started
in the black porcelain of your face.

No, I haven't swum the Fitzroy
near the Liveringa Sheep Station
or felt as small as you, Joey,
under the bigness of your sky,

but I hope you've outlasted
pages I found in the Opportunity Shop
where silver moths began years ago
to eat away your name.

The Piccolo

"There's Ayisha,"
you say, pointing to a wall
yellowing with snapshots
& theatre posters, her face
wakes Piaf & Lady Day
on the jukebox, swelling this
12×12 room. A voice
behind the espresso machine
says Ayisha's in town,
& another says No,
she's back in New York.
Everyone's like Ehrich
Weiss in a tiger cage,
a season to break
things & make ourselves
whole. Someone puffs a J
rolled in perfumed paper,
& in my head I'm scribbling
you a love note, each word
sealed in amber. A cry
seethes from a semi-dark
corner, hidden like potato
eyes in a root cellar. My lips
brush your right cheek.
It's St. Valentine's Day,
but there's no tommy gun
in a violin case from Chicago
because it is your birthday.
You buy another sweet
for me, & when I take a bite
I taste desire. Another
dollar's dropped into the box:
Bud Powell's "Jor-Du"
fills The Piccolo,
& we move from one truth

to the next. Fingers
on the keys, on the spine.
Passion & tempo. We kiss
& form the apex that knows
what flesh is, the only
knot made stronger
by time & pressure.

John Says

I'm more medicine
        than man. His hair
a white roar on the corner
        of Roslyn & Darlinghurst.
I'm thinking yellow
        skirts grow shorter
when streets are sad.
        On tonight's furlough
from the psychiatric ward,
        he throws his baseball cap
to the sidewalk & recites
        "Kubla Khan." Working
the crowd closer, he segues
        into "Snowy River" &
"Marriage" in Lear's voice.
        After years of Thorazine,
Hamlet & Caliban still
        share his tongue. Coins
rain into his upturned cap,
        & the crowd drifts toward
The Love Machine
        & McDonald's, before
he scoops up the money
        & dashes to a milkbar
across the street. Sometimes

among blossoms, we imprison
each other with what we know
       & don't say beneath the moon's
striptease. John's back
       sitting near the footpath.
Between sips of Coke,
       he talks about Strasberg
& his birth on Australia Day,
       as his pink artificial leg
glows like a nude doll.
       A week later at Rozelle,
we're on a red arched bridge
       Japanese POWs erected
in a garden of flame trees.
       He tells almost the same story
Harry told about the LSD
       one Friday night in April,
what God kept telling him.
       Harry said an axe was used,
but John says he cut off a leg
       with a power saw. The trees
ignite the brook. A smile
       flashes among the goldfish,
& he says, *This is what love made me do.*

Corners of Night

Their love for Mickey Mouse
& Sleeping Beauty, for blue
jeans & cosmic pinball
backdrops the black rain
of Little Boy & Fat Man.
Madame Butterfly's kimono
branches into cherry trees
as Japanese in *America's Cup*

T-shirts gaze into strip clubs
& Lebanese take-aways.
But no trick photography
can erase *White Australia*
till it's a subtitle for Kabuki
masks. Two young men from Osaka
fire flashbulbs at a blonde
posed beneath the Norgen-
Vaaz ice cream sign,
draped in a T-shirt mini.
She seems to know everything
about gods, how to reverse
Circe's curse. The men pay
five dollars a pose, as she
tucks each bill between her breasts,
saying, "I don't sleep
with the enemy." They smile
& bow. She slips a foot
in & out of a red shoe.
Silhouettes burn into stone
walls & earth. Three years
later, standing a block away
from the ice cream sign,
she goes back. Now,
with shadows washing out
as much of her face
night's mercy can undo,
they'll know how light
corrupts the body of an angel
who stands on a city corner
to make a street musician
play his sax three times harder.

Messages

They brand themselves with hearts
& dragons, *omni vincit amor*
wreathing the handles of daggers,
skulls with flowers between teeth,
& dotted lines across throats
saying *c-u-t-a-l-o-n-g-h-e-r-e*.
Epigraphs chiseled into marble
glisten with sweat.
Madonna quivers on a bicep
as fingers dance over a pinball machine.
Women pose with x's drawn through names
to harden features & bring knifethrowers
into their lives. A stripper in the neon
doorway of The Pink Pussycat
shows how the tattoo artist's hands
shook, as if the rose
were traced on her skin
with carbon paper & colored-in by bad luck . . .
red as a lost cartographer's ink.
A signature under her left nipple.

Visitation

Dad was saying they've duplicated us
for eons & can read minds,
& there are two elders
who know where their portraits
hide in a cave of red ochre,
that all we have to do is
watch the animals to know
if they desire to govern the air.
That's the year Lucy MacPherson
broke my heart, the moment I knew

my bargi, Gran, was dead. Outside
Cape Tribulation, I circled midnight
paths, afraid I'd disappear. Now
this doesn't go back to Goodah
when he lost his sacred fire
in Oola-pikka's whirlwind
& the lyrebird spoke of gods.
Carried away by Lucy's big smile
& sway of her hips, my feet
couldn't touch earth.
I felt her eyes from an afternoon
thicket, & till then I never broke
a horse with so much ease.
Beneath the Southern Cross,
I saw a Girramay man hanging in gaol
by his belt. Dad removed the spell
when he gripped my shoulder,
telling about the sky gods
who took people aboard ships
& made x-ray drawings. The Seven
Sisters grew so young, I was there
chanting witchetty grubs from the soil.
A scrub-hen shook a fig tree at sunset
when I woke singing the Honey Ant's
love song. A flying fox's shadow ran me home.

Bennelong's Blues

You're here again, old friend.
You strut around like a ragtag redcoat
bellhop, glance up for a shooting star
& its woe, & wander in & out the cove
you rendezvoused with Governor Phillip
after Wil-le-me-ring speared him beside a beached
whale. We've known each other for years.

You're unchanged. But me, old scapegoat,
I never knew I was so damn happy
when we first met. Each memory
returns like heartbreak's boomerang.
You didn't tell me you were a scout,
a bone pointer, a spy,
someone to stand between new faces
& gods. I didn't know your other four
ceremonial names, hero in clownish clothes,
till another dead man whispered into my ear.

Quatrains for Ishi

When they swoop on you hobbled there
almost naked, encircled by barking dogs
at daybreak beside a slaughterhouse
in Oroville, outside Paradise,

California, draped in a canvas scrap
matted with dung & grass seed,
slack-jawed men aim rifles
at your groin. *Wild Man*

hums through telegraph wires,
as women from miles around
try to tame your tongue
by cooking family recipes

& bringing bowls of ambrosia
to the jail. Hungry & sick,
lonely & scared, you never touch
the food. Not even the half-breeds

can open your mouth with Wintu,
Spanish, & Maidu. Days pass
till an anthropologist faces you
with his list of lost words,

rolling them off his tongue
like beads of old honey. But you
are elsewhere, covering your head
with a mourning cap of pine pitch,

in earshot of Wild Horse Corral,
as winds steal prayers of the dead
from Kingsley Cave. It takes
more than years of moonlight

to torch bones down to ashes
to store in a rock cairn
at Mill Creek. You are there,
Ishi, with the last five men

strong enough to bend bows,
with the last twelve voices
of your tribe. When you hear
the anthropologist say *siwini,*

the two of you dance
& bang your hands against
the wooden cot, running fingers
along the grain of yellow pine.

On Main Street, where gold
fever left the air years ago,
you're now The Wild Man of Oroville
beside a new friend. When the train

whistles, you step behind a cottonwood
shading the platform, afraid of The Demon
your mother forbade you to venture near.
What is it, does a voice call to you

out of windy chapparal,
out of Wowunupo mu terna,
to urge you back? Down
that rainbow of metal light

& sparks—then ferried across
Carquinez Straits—to the Oakland Mole.
The Golden Gate frames water
meeting sky, as a trolley car

lumbers upill to your new home
at the Museum of Anthropology.
Here, in this ancient dust
on artifacts pillaged from Egypt

& Peru, I know why a man like you
laughs with one hand over his mouth.
Also, I know if I think of you
as me, you'll disappear. Ishi,

you're like a Don Juan
siting beside Mrs. Gifford
calling birds. Who's Miss Fannie
in this photo from St. Louis?

Friend, what can you say
about these stone charms
from Lone Pine & England,
& are you still going to Chico

for that *Fiesta Arborea?*
How about this Sierra Club
walk from Buena Vista Park?
Here's another sack of acorns,

a few bundles of buckeye, hazel
shoots & alder. There's a sadness
in these willow branches, but no mock
orange. Pine needles have taught me

humility, & I'll never string
a bow or chip a blade from a block
of obsidian. The salmon harpoon
glides through the air as if

your mind entered the toggles
& shaft. I walk backwards
into Bear's Hiding Place
like you showed me—coming when

gone, on the other side of the river
standing here beside you, a snare
of milkweed coiled on the ground
like a curse inside a dream.

Back in your world of leaves,
you journey ten thousand miles
in a circle, hunted for years
inside the heart, till you wake

talking to a shadow in a robe
of wildcat pelts. Here
the day's bright as the purse
you carry your sacred tobacco in.

Your lungs are like thumbprints
on a negative, with you at a hospital
window as workmen walk girders:
All a same monkey-tee. I know why

a man doesn't sleep with the moon
in his face, how butter steals
the singing voice, & how a frog
cures a snakebite. At the museum

in your counting room, we gaze
down at the divided garden, past
bearded phantoms on streetcorners
perfumed with incense & herbs,

signaling the hills closer
where eucalyptus stores up oils
for a new inferno in the Sutro
Forest. Here's your five hundred

& twenty half dollars
saved in thirteen film cases—
your unwound watch now ticks
as the pot of glue hardens

among your arrows & knots
of deer sinews. March 25
at noon is as good a time to die
as to be born. A bluish sun

conspires to ignite the pyre
of bone awls & pendants of Olivella
shells, as a bear stands in Deer Creek
waving a salmon at the sky.

       —for Luzma

The Glass Ark

*(Two paleontologists working inside a glassed-in cubicle at La
Brea Tar Pits)*

M: How could you hear him
     When we were making love?

W: Voices rise.

M: Over love making?

W: Last week, you said
   You loved how birdsongs
   Drifted into the bedroom.

M: I didn't hear anything.

W: I heard him say, Please
   Don't. Don't hurt me,
   Martin.

M: I didn't hear anything
   But your love moans.

W: I'm going to tell
   What I heard.
   Every sigh.
   Every plea.
   Everything.

M: Where would I be?

W: Are you worried about
   Your Miss Whatshername?

M: We hear things.
   We see things.
   We make the clavicle
   Into an angel.

W: A window's bottom sash
   Swells with memories.

M: Sometimes you can read salvation
   Beneath sage brush & cypress,
   But wonder how anyone
   Ever dreamt these bones
   Were their livestock
   That wandered off a blind path.

W: Maybe if I were La Brea Woman,
   Nothing but a carbon-dated skull
   You can hold like a crystal ball
   & ask unfathomable questions,
   You'd count each seashell
   On my necklace a thousand times.

M: I heard a mourning dove
   Caught there, singing
   From a place
   Deep as regret's
   Tar pit.

W: Can they read
   The lies
   On our lips
   Through glass?

M: They stroll in,
   Thinking of Noah's Ark,
   But leave here knowing
   This is no place
   To come & argue with God.

W: We bury things
   Like dogs bury bones,
   & sneak back under moonglow
   To boxes of dirt & absence.

M: I used to have nightmares
   When I first started here.
   Too many animal shadows
   In limbo, stopped
   On the edge.

W: Waiting for the *Cathartes aura,*
   For a turkey vulture
   To tangle his beak
   In death.

How can you listen to bones
Speak to ice flowers,
& not hear his voice
Begging for help last night?

M: We were making love,
As Chet Baker's horn
Filled the bedroom.

W: You can't stop me
From hearing him.

M: We could always make love
Right here beneath this
Row of high-intensity lights.
Can you see our faces
In the frontpage
Of *The L. A. Times*,
Is that your desire?

W: Why didn't we yell down,
Why did we wait for sirens
To crimson the windowpanes?

M: It was a night lie,
Like a paper airplane pulled
To a furnace of neon
& avarice

W: You have no backbone.

M: It isn't my backbone
You're condemned to praise,
Sweetheart.

W: I've been sleeping
With a stranger for three months.

M: I heard nothing.

W: I want you . . .
    I want you to brave
    Daylight, to be
    Heroic as midnight,
    To pull me into your arms
    & make me feel
    I'm not insane.

M: You're not insane.

W: I see the dead man
    Kneeling in dust,
    While he begs Martin
    Not to kill him.

M: You're not insane.

W: Why didn't you stop?

M: I couldn't.

W: You wouldn't . . .
    Wouldn't let me up.

M: I couldn't.

W: Why are their faces pressed
    Against the glass?
    Are they reading lips?
    Why is there no privacy
    In this world?

M: I heard him say,
    Please stop,
    Martinez.

W: Do you say kerosene
    When I say Pleistocene?

M: He said *Martinez*.

W: Liar.

M: Martinez.

W: Do you hear *Equus occidentalis* if—
   When I say Angel Margolis?

M: Please.

Nude Interrogation

Did you kill anyone over there? Angelica shifts her gaze from the
Janis Joplin poster to the Jimi Hendrix, lifting the pale muslin
blouse over her head. The blacklight deepens the blues when the
needle drops into the first groove of "All Along the Watch-
tower." I don't want to look at the floor. *Did you kill anyone?
Did you dig a hole, crawl inside, and wait for your target?* Her
miniskirt drops into a rainbow at her feet. Sandalwood incense
hangs a slow comet of perfume over the room. I shake my head.
She unhooks her bra and flings it against a bookcase made of
plywood and cinderblocks. *Did you use an M-16, a hand-
grenade, a bayonet, or your own two strong hands, both thumbs
pressed against that little bird in the throat?* She stands with her
left thumb hooked into the elastic of her sky-blue panties. When
she flicks off the blacklight, snowy hills rush up to the windows.
*Did you kill anyone over there? Are you right-handed or left-
handed? Did you drop your gun afterwards? Did you kneel be-
side the corpse and turn it over?* She's nude against the falling
snow. *Yes.* The record spins like a bull's eye on the far wall of
Xanadu. *Yes,* I say. *I was scared of the silence. The night was too
big. And afterwards, I couldn't stop looking up at the sky.*

The Poplars

Half in Monet's colors, headlong into this light, like someone
lost along Daedalus' footpath winding back into the brain,
hardly here. Doubts swarm like birds around a scarecrow—
straw pulled from underneath a work cap.

Church bells alloy the midwest sky. How many troubled feet
walked this path smooth? Is it safe to go back to Chu Lai? She's
brought me halfway home again, away from the head floating
down into my out-stretched hands.

I step off the path, sinking into one-hundred-years of leaves. Like
trapped deer, we face each other. Her hand in his. His blue eyes.
Her Vietnamese face. Am I a ghost dreaming myself back to flesh?

I stand in the skin's prison. A bluejay squawks till its ragged song
pulls me out into the day burning like a vaporous temple of joss
sticks. June roses in beds of mulch and peat moss surround me. I
hear her nervous laughter at my back, among the poplars.

I can't hear my footsteps. I stop, turn and gaze at the lovers
against an insistent green like stained glass. I walk toward a car
parked near the church. Birds sing and flit in the raucous light. I
hear the car's automatic locks click, sliding like bullets into the
chamber of a gun.

On Third Street, the morning's alive with coeds hurrying into the
clangor of bells, Saturday night asleep beneath their skin. Flow-
ers herd them toward Jesus—cutworms on the leaves, at the
roots.

Surgery

Every spring, sure as the dogwood's clockwork, someone hack-
saws off Odysseus' penis. And it lies dumbly at his feet, a door-

knocker to a limestone castle, the fountain spraying out a Medusa halo. In this watery mist, with a contrary sunlight glinting the bronze, there's only an outline of Eumaeus handing a quiver of arrows and a bow to him. Rivulets of water make the penis tremble, as if it were the final, half-alive offering to the gods.

Fifty yards past the fountain, on the other side of the quad, I step among lotus-eaters sunning in each other's arms. Mockingbirds and jays squabble overhead, dive-bombing Dutch elms. This unholy racket doesn't faze sunbathers and tree surgeons. As if they're fathering their destruction, branches fall into a pile, and the workmen pack beetle-eaten crevices with a white medicine, something like mortar—whiter than flesh.

I stop beneath an elm and clutch a half-dead branch. Momentarily, there's an old silence thick as memory. Claymores pop. Rifles and mortars answer, and then that silence again, as the slow light of tripflares drifts like a thousand falling handkerchiefs, lighting the concertina woven with arms and legs of sappers. Flares tied to little parachutes like magnolia blooming in the wounded air.

The sunbathers retreat into their abodes and the workmen feed the last branches into a big orange machine. The fountain's drained, and a man kneels before Odysseus. He holds the penis in one hand and a soldering torch in the other, his face hidden behind a black hood, beading a silver seam perfect enough to mend anyone's dream.

Phantasmagoria

The two prisoners slump like baskets of contraband rice, blue sky pushing past. The doorgunner rocks his M-60, drifts on a cloud, and the day's whole machine shakes like a junkie's hand.

"*Anh hieu?* You understand, VC? *Lai-dai, lai-dai!*"

When the sergeant drags papa-san to the chopper door, I see J. L. and Philly face-down in the rice paddie. Smoke curls like a dragon in the trees, and the wind's anger whips the old man like a flag for a phantom ship. "Can you fly motherfucker, you some kinda gook angel?"

He dances, holds on, knowing the boy will talk when he lets go.

∾

He glides along air, on magic, on his Honda, shooting American officers with a .45. Saigon nights hide this Tiger Lady, eyes like stones on a river bottom. In his breezy *ao dai* he's a cheap thrill, gunning his motorcycle, headed for a tunnel in the back of his mind lit by nothing but blood, just a taillight outdistancing the echo.

∾

We slept side by side in the sand-bagged bunker, with arms around each other, too scared to see black and white. We didn't know how deeply hearts took sides on foreign shores, that only the metallic whine of rockets broke down barriers.

We'd lay down a fire that melted machineguns, but back in The World we threw up fences laughter couldn't shake. The bridge we rigged with our bodies, did we know it would crumble into dust and light?

When we stepped off the plane, you kissed the ground and disappeared. I put on my time-woven mask. But wherever you are, please know I won't say I heard you cry out in your sleep those burning nights—like you didn't hear me.

∾

In the Ville Cholon, you can buy photos of your sister in bed with the yardman back in Muskogee. Spanish fly, counterfeiting plates of $20 bills, mother-of-pearl stash boxes, 9mm tie-clasp pistols, stilettos, M-16s packed in Cosmoline, French ticklers, snakeskin belts and boots, girlie magazines, German hand grenades, pieces of cardboard you scratch to sniff the perfume of round-eyed women, pirated editions of *War and Peace* and Genet's *Les Negres*, tapes by The Mothers of Invention, baseball cards, Mickey Mouse watches, and bubblegum machines rigged to explode months later. Subscriptions for Ten Easy Lessons in Writing Successful Love Letters in three colors of disappearing ink, chromeplated AK-47s, Alicante knives playing with sunlight, silver coke spoons and needles, a French perfume called Loneliness in a Bright Bottle, subway maps of New York City, secret diagrams of The Kremlin and Pentagon in Day-Glo, mink-lined gloves, cartons of Zippos, and snapshots of your dead buddies in Kodak living color.

∽

Bikinied women tattooed with 900 numbers dance between third downs and beer ads. They take him back to an afternoon at L.A. International Airport as he gazes at his hands, fascinated by the moons on his fingernails.

He looks up. She uncrosses her legs. Her miniskirt opens like a pearl fan, a blur of shuffled cards. He could fly to Peoria, or go to The Big Apple to see the Statue of Liberty. Maybe she's looking past him, beyond the day's swift colors of tropical fish.

She's shampooing his hair, letting her fingers trail down his torso. A cloud of lather engulfs him. He feels the jungle's sweat and dirt let go, and memories whirl down the drain. Her touch drives blood to his fingertips, his scalp, his cock.

Another fumble and a replay. Another beer ad. More 900 numbers—lookalikes of Susie Wong and Eartha Kitt writhe on a red sofa. First and ten on the twenty-yard line. Halfback around the left flank, and another yard gained.

The soap burns his eyes. The room dances. An animal sound runs through him when he hears the motel door slam shut. He stumbles over to the nightstand and holds up her forty dollars, but his wallet and AWOL bag are gone. He stands there half-soaped, calling every woman's name he's ever known.

The kick's good. Cheerleaders cartwheel and toss batons into the air. Their glittered bodies turn into strobes and the afternoon becomes a chessboard. He's lost another fifty bucks on the Wildcats.

She'll discover the snapshots of his girlfriends, Eloise and Mary, back in Peoria. The nude of the fifteen-year-old he stayed with a week in Hong Kong. A pack of rubbers sealed in milky oil. The lock of his mother's hair that kept him alive in Danang. She'll find socks and underwear, shaving cream and a razor, and a handkerchief monogrammed with his dead grandfather's initials.

Three minutes left in the game. He's thinking, All the Wildcats need is an interception. No more timeouts left. He has seen miracles happen before. From his highschool days, he can feel in his body that they are about to run the wishbone.

Maybe she'll hang the Pentax around her neck. But as she peers closer, inside the AWOL bag's right pocket, she'll find what looks like two apricot halves. As he pictures her lifting them to her face, her red lips only inches away, he smiles. She won't know the scent, but she'll hear all the phantom voices of the rice paddie.

∾

He leaves his Purple Heart under her negligee in a dresser drawer, and hitchhikes the mesa's burning rim. His footsteps blur the living and the dead, as faces float up from the jungle, each breath unstitching the landscape. He counts telephone poles to fall asleep in Blanco, conjuring-up a woman in Bac Ha.

No, it wasn't easy to let his girlfriend and Jody walk into that motel back in Phoenix. Why hadn't he been as merciful with the boy beside the ammo cache when he stepped into daylight? For weeks he walks around with his hands shoved deep into his pockets, gazing up at the Rockies, till feeling steals back to his fingers.

Girl, we were out celebrating Willie's promotion at The Plant.
Candlelight, champagne, roses, a hundred-dollar dinner at The
Palace. You won't believe how fast it came over him. In a finger
snap. A cornered look grew on his face when a Vietnamese wait-
ress walked over to our table. First, I thought he was making eyes
at her. You know how Willie is. She was awful pretty. But with no
warning he started to shout. The man raised hell for an hour, talk-
ing about ground glass in the food. He didn't even know who I
was. Girl, it took three cops with a straitjacket to carry him away.

A Summer Night in Hanoi

When the moviehouse lights click off and images flicker-dance
against the white walls, I hear Billie's whispered lament. *Ho Chi
Minh: The Man* rolls across the skin of five lynched black men,
branding them with ideographic characters.

This scene printed on his eyelids is the one I was born with. My
face is up there among the poplar leaves veined into stained
glass. I'm not myself here, craving a mask of silk elusive as his
four aliases.

He retouches photographs, paints antiques, gardens, cooks pas-
tries, and loves and hates everything French. On his way to
Chung-king to talk with Chiang K'ai-shek about fighting the
Japanese, as day runs into night, he's arrested and jailed for four-
teen months. Sitting here in the prison of my skin, I feel his
words grow through my fingertips till I see his southern skies and
old friends where mountains are clouds. As he tosses kernels of
corn to carp, they mouth silent O's through the water.

Each face hangs like swollen breadfruit, clinging to jade leaves.
How many eyes are on me, clustered in the hum of this dark the-
atre? The film flashes like heat lightning across a southern night,

and the bloated orbs break open. Golden carp collage the five faces. The earth swings on a bellrope, limp as a body bag tied to a limb, and the moon overflows with blood.

A Reed Boat

The boat's tarred and shellacked to a water-repellent finish, just sway-dancing with the current's ebb, light as a woman in love. It pushes off again, cutting through lotus blossoms, sediment, guilt, unforgivable darkness. Anything with half a root or heart could grow in this lagoon.

There's a pull against what's hidden from day, all that hurts. At dawn the gatherer's shadow backstrokes across water, an instrument tuned for gods and monsters in the murky kingdom below. Blossoms lean into his fast hands, as if snapping themselves in half, giving in to some law.

Slow, rhetorical light cuts between night and day, like nude bathers embracing. The boat nudges deeper, with the ease of silverfish. I know by his fluid movements, there isn't the shadow of a bomber on the water anymore, gliding like a dream of death. Mystery grows out of the decay of dead things—each blossom a kiss from the unknown.

When I stand on the steps of Hanoi's West Lake Guest House, feeling that I am watched as I gaze at the boatman, it's hard to act like we're the only two left in the world. He balances on his boat of Ra, turning left and right, reaching through and beyond, as if the day is a woman he can pull into his arms.

Buried Light

A farmer sings about the Fourth Moon, as a girl and boy push rice shoots under slush, their hands jabbing like quick bills of long-legged birds. Their black silk clothes shine in watery light.

Afternoon crouches like three tigers, the sun a disc against a dream of something better. The water buffalo walks with bowed head, as if there's a child beneath his hide, no longer a mere creature willed to the plow.

Mud rises, arcing across the sun. Some monolithic god has fallen to his knees. Dead stars shower down. It was there waiting more than twenty years, some demonic egg speared by the plowshare. Mangled legs and arms dance in the muddy water till a silence rolls over the paddie like a mountain of white gauze.

The Hanoi Market

It smells of sea and earth, of things dying and newly born. Duck eggs, pig feet, mandarin oranges. Wooden bins and metal boxes of nails, screws, ratchets, balled copper wire, brass fittings, jet and helicopter gadgets, lug wrenches, bolts of silk, see-through paper, bamboo calligraphy pens, and curios hammered out of artillery shells.

Faces painted on coconuts. Polished to a knife-edge or sealed in layers of dust and grease, cogs and flywheels await secret missions. Aphrodisiacs for dream merchants. A silent storm moves through this place. Someone's worked sweat into the sweet loaves lined up like coffins on a stone slab.

She tosses her blonde hair back and smiles down at everyone. Is it the squid and shrimp we ate at lunch, am I seeing things? An adjacent stall blooms with peacock feathers. The T-shirt wavers like a pennant as a sluggish fan slices the humidity.

I remember her white dress billowing up in a blast of warm air from a steel grate in New York City, reminding me of Miss Firecracker flapping like a flag from an APC antenna. Did we kill each other for this?

I stop at a table of figurines. What was meant to tear off a leg or arm twenty years ago, now is a child's toy I can't stop touching.

Maybe Marilyn thought she'd erase herself from our minds, but she's here when the fan flutters the T-shirt silkscreened with her face. The artist used five shades of red to get her smile right.

A door left ajar by a wedge of sunlight. Below the T-shirt, at the end of two rows of wooden bins, a chicken is tied directly across from a caged snake. Bright skin—deadly bite. I move from the chicken to the snake, caught in their hypnotic plea.

Shrines

A few nightbirds scissor dusk into silhouettes . . . distant voices harmonize silences. Thatched houses squat against darkness, and the squares of light grow through doorways like boxes inside boxes. They've driven ancestors deeper into the jungles, away from offerings of rice and children's laughter. There's no serpent to guard these new shrines. The cameraman has tried to make an amputee whole again, as if he can see through a lover's eyes. Everything's paralyzed at twilight, except the ghostly jitterbug-flicker of videos from Hong Kong, Thailand, and America, with spellbound faces in Hanoi, Haiphong, Quang Tri, wherever electricity goes. The abyss is under the index finger on the remote control. As if losing the gift of speech, they fall asleep inside someone else's dream.

Frontispiece

Walden Pond's crowded this Saturday afternoon, cars backed up
to the main highway. There's an air show overhead. The Blue
Angels zoom and zigzag prankish patterns across the flyway.
With a sharp U-turn, we're heading to where the Redcoats first
fell in Concord. I can already see rows of stone the militia hid be-
hind, like teeth grinning up from the ground.

A blond boy poses with a minuteman in a triangular hat. His fa-
ther aims the camera. Can the three Vietnamese visitors see how
our black hair makes the boy cower from something he reads in
the father's face? The minuteman is dressed in garb the color of
low hills. Before he retells the battle here, he says he received two
Silver Stars in Danang. The Vietnamese take turns wearing the
minuteman's hat and aiming his musket. A thread of smoke ties
trees to sky, and when The Blue Angels break the sound barrier
we duck and cover our heads with our hands.

At the souvenir shop, I buy *The Negro in the American Revolu-
tion* and give it to Thieu. His eyes dart from the book's fron-
tispiece to my face: Jordan Freeman's killing Major William
Montgomery at the Battle of Groton Heights. Huu Thinh studies
the image also, and says that the American poets he likes best are
Langston Hughes and Whitman.

Le Minh walks out into a tussle of tall grass surrounding a
wooden bridge, and we follow her striped sun hat. Her high heels
sink into the sandy soil that's held together by so many tiny white
roots. Burrs cling to her nylons. Now it isn't hard to imagine her
filling bomb craters along the Ho Chi Minh Trail or reading Jack
London in some Laotian jungle. She's ahead of us. On a path
that winds back like apparitions imprinted on the living, as if we
need to quick-march through grass to prove we outfoxed time.

She climbs into the car, and begins to pick cockles off her stock-
ings. We speed up like shadows overtaking men, smiling and
huffing as if we've been making love an hour.

Breasts

Our fingers played each other like a blue guitar, teaching the body how hands made the brain grow beyond the cave's light and fortress. You smelled of sassafras and Louisiana honeysuckle, but your breasts were two Moorish peaks on the edge of Xanadu. As a goldfish reflects the size of its glass bowl or weedy pond, that summer my hands grew to fit curves.

I still have a lumberjack or stevedore's hands. And Cousin, you remain silent as sin. Each embrace held blood's yoke. Kissed down to a blue feeling, we both fell for life and death. So many mouths, so many kisses, from twelve to the grave . . . the left breast, the right breast, a split between never again. But, no, I still can't believe God and Satan wrestle each other in every pound of flesh.

After your brother told me, I stood there and tried out the entire horoscope on my tongue, as if I needed to hold a stone in each hand to anchor myself under that red sky. Yes, I stood there like Judas, missing what I almost had—the bread and wine never tasted beneath the yellow trees. Still, I can't blame my hands for flying up to clutch a piece of heaven.

The Deck

I have almost nailed my left thumb to the 2 × 4 brace that holds the deck together. This Saturday morning in June, I have sawed 2 × 6s, T-squared and levelled everything with three bubbles sealed in green glass, and now the sweat on my tongue tastes like what I am. I know I'm alone, using leverage to swing the long boards into place, but at times it seems as if there are two of us working side by side like old lovers guessing each other's moves.

This hammer is the only thing I own of yours, and it makes me feel I have carpentered for years. Even the crooked nails are going in straight. The handsaw glides through grease. The toenailed stubs hold. The deck has risen up around me, and now it's strong enough to support my weight, to not sway with this old, silly, wrong-footed dance I'm about to throw my whole body into.

Plumbed from sky to ground, this morning's work can take nearly anything! With so much uproar and punishment, foot-work and euphoria, I'm almost happy this Saturday.

I walk back inside and here you are. Plain and simple as the sun-light on the tools outside. Daddy, if you'd come back a week ago, or day before yesterday, I would have been ready to sit down and have a long talk with you. There were things I wanted to say. So many questions I wanted to ask, but now they've been answered with as much salt and truth as we can expect from the living.

Ghost Video

In the Golden Triangle Café, I see two waitresses tiptoe and reach for plates and teapots with scenes of Van Lang and Au Lac glazed in aquamarine. When they glide from behind the rice paper screen angled between the kitchen and dining tables, their mouths peel open like poppies.

If I tilt my head to the left, there are three men in a side room. Two old faces play Mah-Jongg with two absent friends. They move to a song behind a closed door. Two defeated soldiers three arms and three legs—dressed in jungle fatigues. There's no mercy or pride left in the faded cloth. Cigarette smoke curls up from each dark mouth, hanging like question marks. If they were in Cu Chi or Hue, they'd find words for the images in their heads. And the teenager beside them, what has he learned from these two as he sits hypnotized by a video? He's slumped in his chair, as if the last dream has been drained from him. The Mah-Jongg players bathe their hands in the video's wounded reflec-tion. The boy has fallen in love with the actress, a ghost girl who walks through fortress walls.

The women stroll with teacups on their heads. The landmines never explode. Some days they brush each other with rice powder. After they've rehearsed beneath the kitchen's naked bulb, in a peppery mist of onion and garlic, they walk out into the world in miniskirts, with smiles stolen from the two concubines who knelt before Sun Tzu.

Phantom Limbs

When you take her into your wounded embrace, a bra clasp unhooks itself. A leg, an arm—the piano in your mother's living room three blocks away still plays boogiewoogie when you shuffle in. After you returned, love slipped out a side door. But you knew the librarian with the bifocals, Miss Nancy, always had a crush on you. She sent you pecan cookies for a year, and you shared them with your squad till the point man hit a booby trap on the Ho Chi Minh Trail.

Your missing hand itches. You can hear your grandmother say, "I'm gonna get some money today." Your feet wander off together and leave you lost in soap operas and morphine. You're still strong enough not to wish you were someone else. You tell the guys at The Golden Day, "If that new waitress sits in my lap, I'll bet my other arm and leg she'll know I'm still one hundred per cent man."

Two dogs couple under a cottonwood, and Johnny four doors down throws stones at them. And there goes Mrs. Carson in her leopard-skin coat, talking to herself. A part of you waits in a brass urn on a windowsill. With women, this is a conversation-piece. As you sit there, balancing a plate on your knee, thinking about sprinkling the finest-ground pepper on your pizza, you gaze down at the avenue.

Dream Animal

He's here again. Is this hunger I smell, something like wildflowers and afterbirth tangled in sage? I press down on each eyelid to keep him here: otherwise, otherwise . . . But he always escapes the lair. Don't care how much I dance and chant rain across the mountains, it never falls on his back. Tiger or wolf, he muzzles up to me, easy as a Christbird walking across lily pads. As if he slipped out of a time machine, his phantom prints disappear at the timberline. I'm on all fours, with my nose almost pressed to the ground. A few galah feathers decorate clumps of tussock. Ants have unlocked the mystery of a bearded dragon, as they inch him toward some secret door. I close my eyes again. Somewhere a kookaburra laughs. In this garden half-eaten by doubt and gunpowder, honeyeaters peck the living air. And here he stands beneath the Southern Cross, the last of his kind, his stripes even brighter in this dark, nocturnal weather.

Testimony

I

He hopped boxcars to Chitown
late fall, just a few steps
ahead of the hawk. After
sleepwalking to the 65 Club,
he begged Goon for a chance
to sit in with a borrowed sax.
He'd paid his dues for years
blowing ravenous after-hours
till secrets filled with blues
rooted in Mississippi mud;
he confessed to Budd Johnson
that as a boy playing stickball,
sometimes he'd spy in a window
as they rehearsed back in K. C.

It was Goon who took him home,
gave him clothes and a clarinet.
Maybe that's when he first
played laughter & crying
at the same time. Nights
sucked the day's marrow
till the hibernating moon grew
fat with lies & chords. Weeks
later, with the horn hocked,
he was on a slow Greyhound
headed for the Big Apple,
& "Honeysuckle Rose"
blossomed into body language,
driven by a sunset on the Hudson.

II

Washing dishes at Jimmy's
Chicken Shack from midnight
to eight for nine bucks a week
just to hear Art Tatum's keys,
he simmered in jubilation
for over three months. After
a tango palace in Times Square
& jam sessions at Clark Monroe's,
in the back room of a chili house
on "Cherokee," he could finally play
everything inside his head,
the melodic line modulating
through his bones to align itself
with Venus & the Dog Star.

Some lodestone pulled him
to Banjo's show band on the highway
till Baltimore hexed him: a train
ticket & a telegram said a jealous
lover stabbed his father to death.
He followed a spectral cologne
till he was back with Hootie,
till that joke about chickens

hit by a car swelled into legend.
Now, he was ready to squeeze
elevenths, thirteenths,
every silent grace note
of blood into each dream
he dared to play.

III
Purple dress. Midnight-blue.
Dime-store floral print
blouse draped over a Botticellian
pose. Tangerine. He could blow
insinuation. A train whistle
in the distance, gun shot
through the ceiling, a wood warbler
back in the Ozarks at Lake
Taneycomo, he'd harmonize
them all. Celt dealing in coal
on the edge of swing. Blue
dress. Carmine. Yellow sapsucker,
bodacious "zoot suit with the reet
pleats" & shim sham shimmy.

Lime-green skirt. Black silk
petticoat. Velveteen masterpiece &
mindreader, twirling like a spotlight
on the dance floor. Yardbird
could blow a woman's strut
across the room. "Alice in
Blue" & "The Lady in Red"
pushed moans through brass.
Mink-collared cashmere & pillbox.
Georgia peach. Pearlized facade
& foxtrot. Vermillion dress. High
heels clicking like a high hat.
Black-beaded flapper. Blue satin.
Yardbird, he'd blow pain & glitter.

IV

Moving eastward to the Deep
South with Jay McShann,
on trains whistling into dogwood
& pine, past shadows dragging balls
& chains, Bird landed in jail
in Jackson for lallygagging
on the front porch of a boardinghouse
with the lights on. For two days
he fingered a phantom alto
till "What Price Love" spoke
through metal & fluted bone.
The band roared through the
scent of mayhaw & muscadine,
back into Chicago & Detroit.

When the truckload of horns
& drums rolled into Manhattan,
Bird slid behind the wheel.
The three-car caravan
followed, looping Central Park
till a mounted policeman
brandished his handcuffs.
Days later, after moving into the Woodside,
after a battery of cutting contests,
Ben Webster heard them & ran downtown
to Fifty-second Street & said
they were kicking in the devil's door
& putting the night back
together up at the Savoy.

V

Maybe it was a day like today.
We sat in Washington Square Park
sipping wine from a Dixie cup
when Bird glimpsed Anatole
Broyard walking past & said,
"He's one of us, but he doesn't
want to admit he's one of us."

Maybe it was only guesswork
contorted into breath. We sat
staring after Anatole until he
disappeared down Waverly Place.
Bird took a sip, shook his head,
& said, "Now, that guy chases
heartbreak more than I do."

Maybe it was a day like today.
We were over at Max's house
as Bird talked Lenny
before Bruce was heard of,
telling a story about a club owner's
parrot squawking the magic word.
Maybe it was sunny or cloudy
with our tears, like other days
when Max's mama slid her key
into the front-door lock. Bird
would jump up, grab the Bible
& start thumbing through pages,
& Mrs. Roach would say, "Why
aren't you all more like Charlie?"

        VI
If you favor your left
hand over the right, one
turns into Abel & the other
into Cain. Now, you
take Ikey, Charlie's half-brother
by an Italian woman, their father
would take him from friend
to friend, saying, "He's got good
hair." Is this why Charlie
would hide under his bed & play
dead till his mother kissed him
awake? No wonder he lived
like a floating rib
in a howl whispered through brass.

Always on the move, Charlie
traversed the heart's nine rings
from the Ozarks to le Boeuf
sur le Toit in Montmartre.
Though he never persuaded himself
to stay overseas, his first day
in Stockholm glowed among fallen
shadows. Always on some no-man's
land, he'd close his eyes
& fly to that cluster of Swedes
as he spoke of his favorite artist:
"Heifetz cried through his violin."
Charlie could be two places at once,
always arm-wrestling himself in the dark.

VII
Like a black cockatoo
clinging to a stormy branch
with its shiny head rocking
between paradise & hell,
that's how Yardbird
listened. He'd go inside
a song with enough irony
to break the devil's heart.
Listening with his whole body,
he'd enter the liquid machine
of cow bells & vibes,
of congas & timbales,
& when he'd raise his alto
a tropic sun beamed into the club.

Machito & his Afro-Cuban
Orchestra peppered the night
till Yardbird left ash in the bell
of his horn. He swore Africa
swelled up through the soles
of his feet, that a Latin beat
would start like the distant
knocking of tiny rods & pistons

till he found himself mamboing.
He must've known this is
the same feeling that drives
sap through mango leaves,
up into the fruit's sweet
flesh & stony pit.

  VIII
He was naked,
wearing nothing but sky-
blue socks in the lobby
of the Civic Hotel in Little Tokyo,
begging for a quarter
to make a phonecall. The Chinese
manager led him back to his room,
but minutes later a whiff of smoke
trailed him down the staircase.
This was how six yellow pills
sobered him up for a recording
session. He was naked, & now
as fireman extinguished the bed
cops wrestled him into a straitjacket.

Camarillo's oceanic sky opened
over his head for sixteen months
when the judge's makeshift bench
rolled away from his cell door.
Eucalyptus trees guarded this
dreamtime. Yardbird loved
working his hands into the soil
till heads of lettuce grew round
& fat as the promises he made
to himself, lovers, & friends.
Saturday nights he'd blow
a C-melody sax so hard
he'd gaze into the eyes of the other patients
to face a naked mirror again.

IX

I can see him, a small boy
clutching a hairbrush.
This is 852 Freeman
Street, just after his father
took off on the Pullman line
with a porter's jacket
flapping like a white flag.
A few years later, he's astride
a palomino on Oliver Street
where a potbellied stove
glowed red-hot as a nightclub
down the block. Rudee Vallee
& late nights on Twelfth
haven't marked him yet.

When I think of Bird, bad
luck hasn't seethed into his body,
& Kansas City isn't Tom's
Town. This is before the silver
Conn bought on time, before Rebecca's
mother rented the second-floor,
before prophecies written on his back
at the Subway Club by Buster & Prez
on "Body & Soul," long before
Jo Jones threw those cymbals
at his feet, before benzedrine
capsules in rotgut & the needle's
first bite, before he was bittersweet
as April, when he was still Addie's boy.

X

My darling. My daughter's death
surprised me more than it did you.
Don't fulfill funeral proceeding until
I get there. I shall be the first
one to walk into our chapel.
Forgive me for not being there

with you while you were at
the hospital. Yours most sincerely,
your husband, Charlie Parker.
Now, don't say you can't hear
Bird crying inside these words
from L. A. to New York,
trying to ease Chan's pain,
trying to save himself.

My daughter is dead.
I will be there as quick
as I can. My name is Bird.
It is very nice to be out here.
I am coming in right away.
Take it easy. Let me be the first
one to approach you. I am
your husband. Sincerely,
Charlie Parker. Now, don't
say we can't already hear
those telegraph keys playing Bartok
till the mockingbird loses its tongue,
already playing Pree's funeral song
from the City of Angels.

    XI
I believe a bohemian girl
took me to Barrow Street
to one of those dress-up parties
where nobody's feet touched
the floor. I know it was months
after they barred Bird
from Birdland. Months
after he drank iodine,
trying to devour one hundred
black roses. Ted Joans
& Basheer also lived there,
sleeping three in a bed
to keep warm. A woman dusted
a powdered mask on Bird's face.

I remember he couldn't stop
talking about Dali & Beethoven,
couldn't stop counting up gigs
as if tallying losses: the Argyle . . .
Bar de Duc . . . the Bee Hive . . .
Chanticleer . . . Club de Lisa . . .
El Grotto Room . . . Greenleaf Gardens . . .
Hi De Ho . . . Jubilee Junction . . .
Le Club Downbeat . . . Lucille's Band Box . . .
The Open Door . . . St. Nick's . . . Storyville.
I remember some hepcat talking about
vaccinated bread, & then Bird began
cussing out someone inside his head
called Moose the Mooche. I remember.

     XII

Bird was a pushover, a soft
touch for strings, for the low
& the high, for sonorous catgut
& the low-down plucked ecstasy
of garter belts. He loved
strings. A medley of nerve endings
ran through every earth color: sky
to loam, rainbow to backbone
strung like a harp & cello.
But he never wrung true blues
out of those strings, couldn't
weave the vibrato of syncopated
brass & ghosts
till some naked thing cried out.

Double-hearted instruments breathed
beneath light wood, but no real flesh
& blood moaned into that unbruised
surrender. Did he think Edgard
Varese & Stefan Wolpe could help
heal the track marks crisscrossing
veins that worked their way back
up the Nile & down the Tigris?

Stravinsky & Prokofiev. Bird
loved strings. Each loveknot
& chord stitched a dream to scar
tissue. But he knew if he plucked
the wrong one too hard, someday a nightmare
would break & fall into his hands.

XIII

They asked questions so hard
they tried to hook the heart
& yank it through the mouth.
I smiled. They shifted
their feet & stood there
with hats in hands, hurting
for headlines: *Baroness Pannonica* . . .
I told then how I met my husband
at Le Touquet airport, about decoding
for De Gaulle, about my coming-out ball.
I said I heard a thunderclap,
but they didn't want to hear
how Charlie died laughing
at jugglers on the Dorsey show.

The Stanhope buzzed with innuendo.
Yes, they had him with a needle
in his arm dead in my bathroom.
They loved to hear me say that
he was so sick he refused a shot
of gin. I told them his body
arrived at Bellevue five hours
later, tagged John Parker.
I told them how I wandered
around the Village in circles,
running into his old friends,
that a cry held down my tongue
till I found Chan, but they only
wanted us nude in bed together.

They wanted to hold his Selmer
to put lips to the mouthpiece,
to have their pictures snapped
beneath *Bird Lives! Bird Lives!*
scrawled across Village walls
& subway trains. Three women
sang over his body, but no one read
The Rubaiyat of Omar Khayyam
aloud. Two swore he never said
"Please don't let them bury me
in Kansas City." Everyone
has a Bird story. Someone
said he wished for the words
Bird recited for midnight fixes.

Someone spoke about a letter
in *Down Beat* from a G.I.
in Korea who stole back
a recording of "Bird in Paradise"
from a dead Chinese soldier's hand.
Someone counted the letters in his name
& broke the bagman's bank. Maybe
there's something to all this
talk about seeing a graven image
of Bird in Buddha & the Sphinx.
Although half of the root's gone,
heavy with phantom limbs, French
flowers engraved into his horn
bloom into the after-hours.

Blessing the Animals

Two by two, past
the portals of paradise,
camels & pythons parade.

As if on best behavior,
civil as robed billy goats
& Big Bird, they stroll
down aisles of polished stone
at the Feast of St. Francis.
An elephant daydreams, nudging
ancestral bones down a rocky path,
but won't venture near the boy
with a white mouse peeking
from his coat pocket. Beyond
monkeyshine, their bellows
& cries are like prayers
to unknown planets & zodiac
signs. The ferret & mongoose
on leashes, move as if they know
things with a sixth sense.
Priests twirl hoops of myrrh.
An Australian blue cattle dog
paces a heaven of memories—
a butterfly on a horse's ear
bright as a poppy outside
Urbino. As if crouched
between good & bad, St. John
the Divine grows in quintessence
& limestone, & a hoorah of Miltonic
light falls upon alley rats
awaiting nighttime. Brother
ass, brother sparrowhawk,
& brother dragon. Two
by two, washed & brushed down
by love & human pride,
these beasts of burden
know they're the first
scapegoats. After sacred
oils & holy water, we huddle
this side of their knowing
glances, & they pass through
our lives, still loyal to thorns.

Rhythm Method

If you were sealed inside a box
within a box deep in a forest,
with no birdsongs, no crickets
rubbing legs together, no leaves
letting go of mottled branches,
you'd still hear the rhythm
of your heart. A red tide
of beached fish oscillates in sand,
copulating beneath a full moon,
& we can call this the first
rhythm because sex is what
nudged the tongue awake
& taught the hand to hit
drums & embrace reed flutes
before they were worked
from wood & myth. Up
& down, in & out, the piston
drives a dream home. Water
drips till it sculpts a cup
into a slab of stone.
At first, no bigger
than a thimble, it holds
joy, but grows to measure
the rhythm of loneliness
that melts sugar in tea.
There's a season for snakes
to shed rainbows on the grass,
for locust to chant out of the dunghill.
Oh yes, oh yes, oh yes, oh yes
is a confirmation the skin
sings to hands. The Mantra
of spring rain opens the rose
& spider lily into shadow,
& someone plays the bones
till they rise & live
again. We know the whole weight

depends on small silences
we fit ourselves into.
High heels at daybreak
is the saddest refrain.
If you can see blues
in the ocean, light & dark,
can feel worms ease through
a subterranean path
beneath each footstep,
Baby, you got rhythm.

The Parrot Asylum

His vest of fifty pockets
woven from black nylon mesh
nestles against his skin,
snug as a WWII moneybelt.
His head is still up
in a tall eucalyptus,
gazing out over Kakadu
National Park. His body
throbs as if one hundred eyes
press against his ribcage—
a milkmaid's brood
between warm breasts.
He tries to daydream himself
into The Master Egg Thief
headline again, in a new Lexus
with a Madonna look-alike
speeding down a Dallas freeway.

It'll take years, maybe
two or three girlfriends
later, for him to arrive here
& linger like Pisthetairos

before this dome-shaped aviary
matted with red-tailed
cockatoo feathers. Once,
this one called Lily
knew more words than a child:
bloody . . . fool . . . our song . . .
Flicking raven hair
out of her eyes, Dr. Charcot,
the bird psychologist, says
that Parker's "Ornithology"
used to make them chatter
human voices. But now
they only gaze at the floor
or slant their heads sideways,
pecking the last fluff
from their pale bodies,
never facing the sun,
never speaking to the jester's
godlike shadow on the wall.

The Thorn Merchant's Daughter

When she cocks her head
the last carrier pigeon's ghost
cries out across a cobalt sky.
The glossy snapshot of her
draped in a sun-blanched dress
before a garden of stone phalluses
slants crooked in its gold frame.
She looks as if she's tiptoed
out of *Innocence Choosing Love
over Wealth*. A Janus-headed
figure tarries at a junction
with twelve versions of hell
& heaven. She's transfixed

by bluejays pecking dewy figs
down to the meaty promise of a heart.
She's *Mary Magdalen in the Grotto*,
& was eyeing Lee Morgan at Slugs'
when the pistol flash burned
through his solo. Her aliases
narrate tales from Nepal & Paris,
Texas, from Bathsheba to the woman
flaming like poppies against sky
at the theatre with John
Dillinger. To see her
straight, there's no choice
but to walk with a limp.

The Monkey House

He pressed his face against the bars,
watching the biggest male macaque
mount a statuesque female.
She gazed at the cage floor
& he looked up past
rafters of leaves & fiberglass,
squinting toward a sundial.
They were rocking back & forth,
grunting a chorus of muffled laughs.
A father covered his daughter's eyes
with both hands, but let his two sons look.
An old woman kept tugging
her husband's sleeve
as he stood munching Cracker
Jacks, searching for the toy
pistol or spinning top
at the bottom of the box.
He watched, stroking his beard,
a hundred yards away from the crowd

eating noontime sandwiches & sipping
thermoses of coffee. Joggers worked
the air with arms & legs,
& it seemed to him the monkeys
were making love to the rhythms
of the city. Also, he still can't
say why, but he was running
the term *ethnic cleansing* over
& over in his mind, like a stone
polishing itself in a box of sand.
There were tears in his eyes,
& he felt like he'd returned
to the scene of a crime.
When their bodies began to tremble
down to a split second, the other
monkeys began to slap the male
& beat his head like a drum.
Then, lost among the absurd
clocks, he turned to watch
leaves as they began to fall.

Dolphy's Aviary

We watched Baghdad's skyline
ignite, arms & legs entwined
as white phosphorus washed over
our bedroom, the sounds of war
turned down to a sigh. It was one
of those nights we couldn't let go
of each other, a midwestern storm
pressing panes till they trembled
in their sashes. Eric Dolphy
scored the firmament splitting
to bedrock, as the wind spoke
tongues we tried to answer.
At first, we were inside

muted chords, inside an orgasm
of secrets, & then cried out,
"Are those birds?" Midnight
streetlights yellowed the snow—
a fleeting ghost battalion
cremated in the bony cages
of tanks in sand dunes. Dolphy said
"Birds have notes between our notes . . ."
I could see them among oak rafters
& beams, beyond the burning cold,
melodious in cobweb & soot.
Like false angels up there
in a war of electrical wires
& bat skeletons caked with excrement,
we in winding sheets of desire
as their unbearable songs
startled us down.

Crack

You're more jive than Pigmeat
    & Dolemite, caught by a high note
  stolen from an invisible saxophone.

I've seen your sequinned nights
    pushed to the ragged end
  of a drainpipe, swollen fat

with losses bitter as wormwood,
    dropped tongues of magnolia
  speaking a dead language.

You're an eyeload, heir
    to cotton fields & the North
  Star balancing on a needle.

Where's the loot, at Scarlett O'Hara's
        or buying guns for the Aryan Nation?
    The last time I saw you, fabulous

merchant of chaos, you were beating days
        into your image as South African
    diamonds sparkled in your teeth.

Cain's daughter waits with two minks
        in a tussle at her throat,
    fastened with a gold catch.

You pull her closer, grinning up
        at barred windows, slinky
    as a cheetah on a leash.

You're the Don of Detroit,
        gazing down from your condo
    at the night arranged into a spasm

band, & groupies try to steady hands
        under an incantation of lights,
    nailed to a dollarsign & blonde wig.

Desire has eaten them from the
        inside: the guts gone, oaths
    lost to a dictum of dust

in a worm's dynasty. Hooded
        horsemen ride out of a Jungian
    dream, & know you by your mask.

I see ghosts of our ancestors
        clubbing you to the ground.
    Didn't you know you'd be gone,

condemned to run down a John
        Coltrane riff years from Hamlet,
    shaken out like a white sleeve?

Bullbats sew up the evening
     sky, but there's no one left
   to love you back to earth.

No-Good Blues

1

I try to hide in Proust,
Mallarme, & Camus,
but the no-good blues
come looking for me. Yeah,
come sliding in like good love
on a tongue of grease & sham,
built up from the ground.
I used to think a super-8 gearbox
did the job, that a five-hundred-dollar suit
would keep me out of Robert Johnson's
shoes. I rhyme Baudelaire
with Apollinaire, hurting
to get beyond crossroads & goofer
dust, outrunning a twelve-bar
pulsebeat. But I pick up
a hitchhiker outside Jackson.
Tasseled boots & skin-tight
jeans. You know the rest.

2

I spend winter days
with Monet, seduced
by his light. But the no-good
blues come looking for me.
It takes at least a year
to erase a scar
on a man's heart. I come home nights
drunk, the couple next door
to keep me company, their voices

undulating through my bedroom wall.
One evening I turn a corner
& step inside Bearden's *Uptown
Sunday Night Session*. Faces
Armstrong blew from his horn
still hanging around the Royal Gardens—all
in a few strokes, & she suddenly leans out of
a candy-apple green door & says,
"Are you from Tougaloo?"

        3
At The Napoleon House
Beethoven's *Fifth* draws shadows
from the walls, & the no-good blues
come looking for me. She's here,
her left hand on my knee.
I notice a big sign
across the street that says
The Slave Exchange.
She scoots her chair closer.
I can't see betrayal
& arsenic in Napoleon's hair—
they wanted their dying emperor
under the Crescent City's
Double Scorpio. But nothing
can subdue these African voices
between the building's false floors,
this secret song from the soil
left hidden under my skin.

        4
Working swing shift at McGraw-
Edison, I shoot screws
into cooler cabinets as if I were born
to do it. But the no-good blues come
looking for me. She's from Veracruz,
& never wears dead colors of the factory,
still in Frida Kahlo's world of monkeys.
She's a bird in the caged air.

The machines are bolted down
to the concrete floor,
everything moves with the same big
rhythm Mingus could get out of
a group. Humming the syncopation
of punch presses & conveyor belts,
work grows into our dance
when the foreman
hits the speed-up button
for a one-dollar bonus.

5

My hands are white
with chalk at The Emporium
in Colorado Springs, but the no-good
blues come looking for me. I miscue
when I look up & see sunlight
slanting through her dress
at the back door. That shot
costs me fifty bucks.
I let the stick glide along the V
of two fingers, knowing men who
wager their first born to conquer
snowy roller coasters & myths.
I look up, just when
the faith drains out of
my right hand. It isn't
a loose rack. But more like—
well, I know I'm in trouble
when she sinks her first ball.

6

I'm cornered at Birdland
like a two-headed man hexing
himself. But the no-good blues
coming looking for me. A prayer
holds me in place,
balancing this sequinned
constellation. I've hopped boxcars

& thirteen state lines to where
she stands like Ma Rainey.
Gold tooth & satin. Rotgut
& God Almighty. Moonlight
wrestling a Texas-jack.
A meteor of desire burns
my last plea to ash. Blues
don't care how many tribulations
you lay at my feet, I'll go
with you if you promise
to bring me home to Mercy.

Sandhog

They tango half the night
before he can believe she isn't
Eurydice. The bandonean
& violin cornet pull them into an embrace
in an Eden burdened with fruits
out of season. He wants to punch
walls or elbow the pug-nosed bouncer,
Quasimodo, whose eyes caress Angelina
as they ascend. He tells himself
he isn't afraid of anything
or anyone, that he lives to work
in the abyss where a small stone can kill
if nudged free by a steel-toed boot.

The yellow cage on a whiny cable drags
the sun down. Almost in each other's arms,
hardhats descend into the caisson
where the air's giddy, humming "Sentimental
Journey," in the fraternity of sons
who follow fathers down past
omens: *Never take love this deep*

into the ground. He can hear her
say, "I can't endure a one-night
stand," as she pulls away & grabs
her beaded purse. Accents echo
through this inverted Tower of Babel
till nirvana grows into the East Tunnel.
With Angelina in his head, *Fire
in the hole* means a starry night.

The Wall

> *But you shall shine more bright in these contents*
> *Than unswept stone, besmeared with sluttish time.*
> —William Shakespeare

Lovenotes, a bra, lipstick
kisses on a postcard, locks
of hair, a cerulean bouquet,
baseball gloves broken in
with sweat & red dirt,
a fifth of Beefeaters,
everything's carted away.
Before it's tagged & crated,
a finger crawls like a fat slug
down the list, keeping record
for the unborn. All the gunshots
across America coalesce here
where a mother sends letters
to her son. As time flowers
& denudes in its whorish work,
raindrops tap a drumroll
& names fade till the sun
draws them again out of granite nighttime.

A Story

She says he was
telling a dirty joke
about Asian women
working in a sweatshop
in Orange County, sewing
Ku Klux Klan robes & hoods
for The Redneck Discount
somewhere in South Carolina,
as Mary Blake sang "Bright
Blue Rose" on the jukebox,
when the whine of airbrakes
& raw squeal of Goodyear tires
signalled the rig's thunderous
crash through the Sundowner's
neon facade, that it's funny
how no one else was hurt
when the truck uprooted
the big redbud out front
& showered the whole day
with flowers & bone.

What Counts

I thumb pages, thinking onion
or shreds of garlic
flicked into my eyes.
Maybe the light's old,
or the earth begs every drop
of water it dares to caress.
I leaf through the anthology,
almost unconscious, unaware
I'm counting the dead faces
I've known. Two Roberts—
Hayden & Duncan. Dick

Hugo. Bill Stafford &
Nemerov. Here's Etheridge's
"Circling the Daughter"
again, basic as a stone
dropped into a creek,
a voice fanning out
circles on delta nights.
Anne's haze-eyed blues
at dusk in a bestiary
behind her "reference
work in sin." If we were
ever in the same room,
it isn't for the living
to figure out. Unearthly
desire makes man & woman
God's celestial wishbone
to snap at midnight. Pages
turn on their own & I listen:
*Son, be careful what you
wish for.* Do I want my name
here, like x's in the eyes
of ex-lovers? I'm thankful
for the cities we drank
wine & talked about swing
bands from Kansas City
into the after hours
under green weather
in this age of reason.

Woebegone

We pierce tongue
& eyebrow, foreskin
& nipple, as if threading wishes
on gutstring. Gold bead

& question mark hook
into loopholes & slip
through, We kiss
like tiny branding irons.
Loved ones guard words
of praise, & demigods mortgage
nighttime. Beneath bruised
glamor, we say, "I'll show
how much I love you by
how many scars I wear."
As we steal the last
drops of anger, what can we
inherit from Clarksdale's blue
tenements? Medieval & modern,
one martyr strokes another
till Torquemada rises.
We trade bouquets
of lousewort, not for the red
blooms & loud perfume,
but for the lovely spikes.

Strands

If you had asked
after my fifth highball,
as I listened to Miles' midnight
trumpet, in Venus De Milo's embrace,
I would have nodded
Yes, as if I didn't
own my tongue. *Yes,*
I believe I am
flesh & fidelity
again. I washed lipstick
off the teacup, faced
your photo to the wall,

swept up pieces of goodtime
moshed with dustballs,
& haggled with myself
over a bar of lemon soap.
Yes, I could now feel
luck's bile & desire
sweetened by creamy chocolates,
& I would have bet
my Willie Mays cards
a strand of your hair
clinging to an old Thelonious T-shirt
could never make me fall apart
at this bedroom window
beneath a bloodred moon.

Anodyne

I love how it swells
into a temple where it is
held prisoner, where the god
of blame resides. I love
slopes & peaks, the secret
paths that make me selfish.
I love my crooked feet
shaped by vanity & work
shoes made to outlast
belief. The hardness
coupling milk it can't
fashion. I love the lips,
salt & honeycomb on the tongue.
The hair holding off rain
& snow. The white moons
on my fingernails. I love
how everything begs
blood into song & prayer

inside an egg. A ghost
hums through my bones
like Pan's midnight flute
shaping internal laws
beside a troubled river.
I love this body
made to weather the storm
in the brain, raised
out of the deep smell
of fish & water hyacinth,
out of rapture & the first
regret. I love my big hands.
I love it clear down to the soft
quick motor of each breath,
the liver's ten kinds of desire
& the kidney's lust for sugar.
This skin, this sac of dung
& joy, this spleen floating
like a compass needle inside
nighttime, always divining
West Africa's dusty horizon.
I love the birthmark
posed like a fighting cock
on my right shoulder blade.
I love this body, this
solo & ragtime jubilee
behind the left nipple,
because I know I was born
to wear out at least
one hundred angels.

Index of Titles and First Lines

Yusef Komunyakaa, originally from Bogalusa, Louisiana, has published more than eleven books. Newly published is *Blue Notes: Essays, Interviews, and Commentaries* (University of Michigan Press) and *Talking Dirty to the Gods* (poems, Farrar, Straus & Giroux). Among his other titles are *Thieves of Paradise* (Wesleyan), a finalist for the 1999 National Book Critics Circle Award; *Neon Vernacular: New and Selected Poems 1977–1989* (Wesleyan), winner of the 1994 Pulitzer Prize; and *Magic City* and *Dien Cai Dau* (Wesleyan). Komunyakaa has written the libretto *Slip Knot*, commissioned by Northwestern University, in collaboration with the opera's composer, T. J. Anderson. Besides the CD recording *Love Notes from the Madhouse* (8th Harmonic Breakdown, 1998), jazz-related releases feature Komunyakaa's poem celebrating Charlie Parker's life on *Testimony* (Australian Broadcasting Corporation, 2 CDs), and lyrics on *Thirteen Kinds of Desire* sung by jazz singer Pamela Knowles (Cornucopia Productions, 2000). He is a professor in the Council of Humanities and Creative Writing Program at Princeton University.

LIBRARY OF CONGRESS CATALOGING-IN-PUBLICATION DATA

Komunyakaa, Yusef.
   Pleasure dome : new and collected poems / Yusef Komunyakaa.
      p. cm.
Includes index.
   ISBN 0–8195–6425–7 (alk. paper)
   1. Title
PS3561.O455 P58 2001
811'.54—dc21   00–010231